On Wild Hogs and Javelinas

On Wild Hogs and Javelinas:

History, Biology, Management, and Hunting

by

Richard B. Taylor

SAFARI PRESS

The trademark Safari Press ® is registered with the U.S. Patent and Trademark Office and with government trademark and patent offices in other countries.

Taylor, Richard B.

First edition

Safari Press

2017, Long Beach, California

ISBN 978-1-57157-467-1

Library of Congress Catalog Card Number: 2016934658

10 9 8 7 6 5 4 3 2 1

Printed in the United States of America

Readers wishing to see Safari Press's many fine books on big-game hunting, wingshooting, and sporting firearms should visit our Web site at www.safaripress.com.

For Lisa and Mallory,
Thank you for being part of my life!

Table of Contents

Foreword

No other animal has attracted more attention, good or bad, than feral swine. They can be found virtually everywhere, and their population continues to increase. DeSoto brought hogs with him on his Texas expedition in 1500 as a supplemental source of food. Like rabbits in Australia, the impact of the feral hogs' expansion is immeasurable, and much time and money are spent on controlling these oftentimes destructive animals. Sportsmen either love or hate hogs. Those who hate them see the animals as a detriment to the environment.

Hunters, however, relish the opportunity to pursue what some refer to as the poor man's grizzly. In essence, feral hogs are the ideal sporting animal as they are not only abundant but also affordable and edible, for wild pork prepared correctly is exceptionally tasty to even the most discretionary palate.

In this book Rick addresses the wild pig in a holistic manner from its unique history to its present-day occurrence throughout the United States. Throughout the '80s and '90s, both Rick and I witnessed firsthand the human-facilitated expansion of feral hogs throughout Texas. If there is one thing we would both agree upon, it is the fact that hogs are true survivors and here to stay.

Rick also addresses one of the iconic denizens of the semiarid regions of the Southwest—the javelina (collared peccary). What makes javelina in the U.S. even more intriguing is the fact that they occur only in Texas, Arizona, and New Mexico. The small, piglike collared peccary is particularly attractive to sportsmen interested in a memorable hunting experience in some of the most breathtakingly beautiful wild lands in existence.

For those interested in what makes these two fascinating species so important to our wild lands and at times our back yards, Rick's book will unquestionably become the reliquary for such information.

Bob Zaiglin, Certified Wildlife Biologist, Outdoor Writer, and Coordinator
   of Wildlife Management at Southwest Texas Junior College
Uvalde, Texas
June 2015

Acknowledgments

I owe many people gratitude for the results of this work. First and foremost I would like to thank my wife, Lisa, for all her patience and encouragement and for tolerating all the times I brought a wild hog home and used her kitchen to prepare it for the freezer.

Many thanks are also extended to Dr. Eric Hellgren and Mark Mapston for their help in my research as well as reviewing and editing the original manuscript of this book; to the late Mike Bradshaw, Texas Game Warden, for insight and encouragement; and Ludo Wurfbain, my publisher who believed in this project.

Special thanks go to Bob Zaiglin for writing the foreword, reviewing the manuscript, and letting me use of some of his great pictures.

My gratitude extends to Macy Ledbetter, Larry Weishuhn, Joe Herrera, Brad Porter, Alton Paris, John Miller, and the USDA/APHIS (Animal Plant Health Inspection Service) for the use of many of the pictures found in this book. I'd also like to thank *The Journal of the Texas Trophy Hunters* for allowing me to reprint previously published articles.

Special thanks go to Jim Hillje, John Huff, and all my "*compadres*" in the South Texas Wildlife District with whom I spent many steamy, hot, humid, cold, wet, tick-and-flea-infested nights in pursuit of wild hogs. Through it all, I could not have accomplished my goals in the field if it were not for the landowners who have enjoyed or suffered the influx of wild swine and have allowed me onto their private property to study or hunt these animals. I hope this book is a testament to everyone who has studied, hunted, watched, or been curious about the wild swine or javelina.

Introduction

There is an old saying in Texas that when the world ends, the only three things to survive will be cockroaches, coyotes, and fire ants. Well, I must add another creature that will also remain . . . the feral hog. The feral hog has adapted, encroached, and expanded its range throughout the United States and other countries. Since the last quarter of the twentieth century, the distribution and density of the feral hog have increased substantially throughout the southern United States and is presently found in more than forty states, including Hawaii. Once limited primarily to the southern states and California, the feral hog has made a dramatic northward expansion in its range since the mid-1980s.

It was generally assumed that climate, precipitation, and topography would keep the wild hog populations in check, but that has proved to be a false assumption. From the Gulf, Pacific, and Atlantic coasts and from the mountains of Tennessee and West Texas to the Canadian border, feral hogs have rooted, trampled, and grunted their way across the United States. In Texas, they are the second most numerous large mammal that can be hunted, second only to the white-tailed deer, which numbers around 3.5 to 4 million animals. There is not a reliable technique for determining the feral hog population, but by using other types of data and information, we can derive a best-guess assessment. This estimate places the feral hog population between 1.5 and 2 million animals in Texas alone!

In the wake of this expanding population comes destruction, competition, disease, economic losses, and numerous other problems. There is also another, less-discussed side of the story that includes hunting, sporting events, meat markets, recreational activities, and local economies. Many people consider the feral hog a nemesis while others consider it a bonus.

Where you stand on this subject is a matter of opinion. Through the pages of this book you will learn all aspects of this much-maligned creature. Some of this information has been previously published in other formats, such as scientific journals and popular articles in magazines, bulletins, or pamphlets. I've attempted to rewrite much of the scientific information to make it more user friendly, and I have added significantly to the nontechnical portions.

To fully understand and make a judgment, one must understand the biological aspects of the feral hog and its relationship to the environment and ecology. Where did this animal come from and how did it get to be so numerous? The history of the wild hog from the earliest Spanish explorers as they entered southern Florida almost five hundred years ago to the local landowner that just released a couple of tame hogs last week is discussed. The biology and ecology of the wild hog and why it has been able to expand its range and distribution is outlined. Terminology such as feral hog, wild hog, wild swine, wild pigs, European hog, and Eurasian or Russian boar will be defined; however, these terms will often be used interchangeably throughout this book.

With the increasing population has come a tremendous amount of environmental and agricultural destruction. What can be done about the damage and devastation frequently caused by free-ranging hogs? Can we control the wild hog or do we even want to? Is the species manageable and how can it be done? While successful management of the feral hog may be a pipe dream, perhaps the information on feral hog management may be enlightening or useful.

There is, however, another side to the story. Because many landowners are taking advantage of this resource, there are positive as well as negative aspects of wild hogs, and these are also addressed. As with all creatures in the wild, it seems everyone who has come in contact with the wild hog has a story to tell, and some of these stories or vignettes are related throughout this book.

The wild hog is an extremely wary and intelligent beast that challenges the skills of the most avid outdoorsman. Trapping techniques and hunting methods are discussed to bring the neophyte hunter successfully into the field so that he or she can literally "bring home the bacon." It is my hope that some of you expert hunters may even find a tidbit of helpful information here as well.

The feral hog provides excellent table fare that is as tasty as domestic pork yet doesn't have the extra fat generally found in market hogs. To thoroughly enjoy the taste of wild pork or javelina, the harvested hog meat must be properly prepared. I introduce the proper ways to prepare the hog and I supply recipes that I've personally used.

The javelina is found in only three states in the United States. While it is not related to the wild hog, its appearance and many of its characteristics are similar. No book on hogs would be complete without mentioning this Native American mammal.

The laws and regulations regarding feral hogs and javelinas from states that currently have populations of one or both species are found in the latter part of the book. I've also included addresses for the various wildlife agencies that harbor the javelina and/or substantial feral hog populations.

There are many misconceptions and beliefs regarding feral swine and javelina, so to separate fact from fiction, I present a question-and-answer format in Appendix I. Finally, I have included in the appendixes common terms used in hog management and hunting and a list of selected publications that you might find useful or enjoyable.

Volumes of technical research and scientific papers have been written on the feral hog and javelina. A recently completed annotated bibliography on wild pigs that was compiled by John J. Mayer and C. Barry Shedrow filled a whopping 248 pages! While there are a few books devoted to these two creatures, they are either too technical or they concentrate on hunting and give very little biological or management information. To date, there is not a complete publication on the javelina and feral hog that combines the biology, ecology, management, and hunting of these species. I have tried to include current research, biology, management considerations, proven trapping techniques for wild hogs, as well as hunting strategies for hogs and javelina. I've also attempted to show both sides of this controversial subject.

******

It seems hogs have been a part of my life for the last three decades. As a Future Farmers of America (FFA) student in high school, I raised my first show hog . . . a Yorkshire-Hampshire cross. I didn't exactly win the show, but I did become infatuated with the porcine beast. Another stock show or two later found me enrolled in the agriculture program at Texas A & I University (now Texas A&M University at Kingsville) in South Texas, and I officially became a javelina, the official mascot of the university.

Throughout college, I hunted at every opportunity for deer, hogs, and javelinas. After college, I pursued a profession as a wildlife biologist for Texas Parks and Wildlife Department (TPWD), where my obsession with porkers turned into several years of wild porcine research. Whether it was research, literature, or programs on wild hogs, most information to the public was funneled through my office. I still believe that I became TPWD's so-called "feral hog specialist" by default because nobody wanted anything to do with feral hogs.

Later, during my career as a state wildlife biologist, I was given the opportunity to become the principal investigator for javelina for the state of Texas. This position required me to monitor the status of javelinas, make recommendations, and investigate mortalities throughout the state.

It was at a local chamber of commerce event in Laredo, Texas, where I was giving a presentation on feral hogs that I met my soon-to-be Arkansas bride. Little did I know at the time that Lisa's dad, two nephews, and, indeed, her entire family were die-hard Arkansas Razorbacks. Soon thereafter, as a father of a 4H member, I was back to raising show hogs, hunting, and studying wild hogs and javelinas. Now, other than occasionally hunting hogs and still studying them, I'm relegated to the hog in my garage . . . a Harley-Davidson Heritage Softail!

******

I hope that through the pages of this book you may find the wild swine and javelina to be the special creatures that I find them to be. It's possible that I have left out information many experts will say is important, but in the end you will find that the main facets of the wild hog and javelina have been included. Although I have told numerous stories, I have purposely limited the number of actual hunting tales, which were chosen to illustrate just how challenging and exciting hunting hogs and javelinas can be.

The wild hog has become an integral part of United States fauna and, therefore, of the sporting industry. Their notoriety and popularity have increased with their burgeoning population. From hunting camps and coffee shops, to universities and boardrooms, these creatures have become a topic of heated debate. Ecologists, environmentalists, farmers, ranchers, researchers, and business people have joined in the conversation. Whether you consider them a game animal or pest, asset or liability, is clearly a matter of perspective.

The majority of this book deals with the wild hog and javelina in Texas because that's where I've conducted research, collected data, and observed and hunted them. I hope that individuals from across the United States and possibly other countries can find some value in the pages that follow. Ultimately, I tried to write it in an entertaining and enjoyable form for everyone to enjoy, and to this end, I hope I've come close. *Buena caza, mis amigos.*

History of Wild Hogs in North America

CHAPTER 1

Hogs are an Old World species originating from Europe, Asia, and northern Africa and are not indigenous to the New World. As the world was shifting and continents being formed, the swine family was left out of the Western Hemisphere or New World as it is called. Because of the extreme cold and ice, they were unable to cross the Bering land bridge between Alaska and Russia, the only possible entrance to the New World prior to separation.

The predecessors to the modern swine family date back prior to the ice age, approximately thirty-five to forty million years ago. Animal fossil remains in Europe indicated many swinelike variations disappeared during glaciations. Although the ice age drastically decimated the herds, they managed to survive between major glaciations. Their adaptability is still evident in the modern wild pigs that currently inhabit the United States.

With the disappearance of the Ice Age, wild hogs thrived during the Stone Age on the European and Asian continents of the Old World. In their book *Pigs from Cave to Cornbelt*, Towne and Wentworth claim bones found in caves indicate early man hunted and ate swine. Cro-Magnon humans pursued swine with crude weapons. Remains of the weapons and bones have been found mixed with ashes in caves. Cro-Magnon artwork picturing swine has been found in caves in France and northern Spain.

The domestication of hogs began somewhere between 7000–3000 B.C. with the coming of Neolithic man to Europe. Swine were always an important part of early civilization. In addition to food, they have been reported in mythology, superstitious rites, and religion. Since before Christ, man has loved, hated, revered, worshiped, and tabooed the hogs. As we enter into the twenty-first century, some beliefs still remain.

The first introduction of hogs into what is now part of the United States came around 750–1000 A.D. when Polynesian immigrants to Hawaii brought them; however, it was not until the early 1500s that hogs arrived onto the North American mainland. Christopher Columbus is credited with bringing the first hogs to the New World. He brought eight with him to the West Indies in 1493, and with subsequent releases over time, these animals thrived and their progeny expanded over several of the islands.

It was from these populations that early Spanish explorers extracted hogs for transport to the U.S. mainland. They provided a significant source of food and lard while reproducing quickly. While it was Hernàn Cortés who brought the first swine to the New World near Honduras around 1524, it was Hernando de Soto who is credited with bringing them to what is today modern-day Florida. These expeditions were the first well-documented swine importation into the United States mainland.

Hogs Arrive in Florida

Hernando de Soto, the first explorer to the United States mainland, obtained supplies and thirteen sows from Cuba in 1539. Upon landing in Florida, his expedition traveled more than 3,100 miles across the southern United States, journeying through Georgia, South Carolina, North Carolina, Tennessee, Alabama, Mississippi, Louisiana, and ultimately Arkansas, where he died. He took the swine with him as he traveled. Hogs may have been valued as an insurance policy against starvation. Some reports claimed the hogs shared the campsite with the Spaniards at night. Upon de Soto's death in 1542, he had seven hundred swine and three horses, all of which were sold at auction to his men and, possibly, some Indians. Due to several devastating Indian attacks, Towne and Wentworth noted that fourteen months prior to de Soto's death only one hundred hogs were reported, yet seven hundred were sold at his death, which is a fascinating example of their reproductive potential.

Some writers believe these hogs were the original source of the "razorbacks" that early pioneers found in the woods of Arkansas and eastern Texas. Evidence of free-ranging hogs in this region predates Anglo-American settlements by nearly one hundred years, and they occupied varying types of habitat wherever acorns were present.

The next importation of hogs into Florida came in 1565 when Pedro de Avilés brought four hundred individuals. These eventually fell into the hands of the Indians who let them roam in the woods. The Indians hunted the animals but did not attempt to domesticate them. Since hogs were originally brought to Florida, it's only natural that they still exist across the peninsular state. Feral swine can now be found in all sixty-seven Florida counties.

Eurasian boars added to the feral hog population of Florida. Eurasian boars are a free-ranging, natural species that have never been domesticated and occur in Europe and Asia. Eurasian boars from Tennessee were introduced into three localities of Florida and readily interbred with the feral hog population. Early colonists allowed their stock to range freely and were rounded up or harvested only when needed. These free-ranging hogs helped the feral population in Florida swell in numbers.

A late nineteenth-century mammal survey conducted by a Mr. Maynard noted the presence of feral hogs in certain ranges of the state but not in any great numbers. While feral swine can be found throughout much of the United States, the vast majority are found in Florida, California, and Texas. Therefore, feral hogs in Texas can be traced back to the original domestic breed imported in the 1500s.

The French and British brought additional pigs to the New World as the states were colonizing. In the American colonies such as Massachusetts, Connecticut (New Haven), and Rhode Island, hogs were also an important commodity. Many problems arose because of their free-ranging proclivities. The colonists could readily kill depredating wildlife that got into their gardens and fields without consequence, but since hogs were private property, killing them could incur a hefty fine. Early court records in the mid-1600s document many instances where hog problems were brought before the justice system, and it didn't stop there. Native Americans were also having problems with the colonists' hogs that destroyed their crops. This often caused serious anger, strife, and division between the two societies. Clearly, the swine were a mainstay for any settlers with intentions on colonizing the New World.

Expanding throughout the Southeast and Northward

While Texas was being settled and the hog population increasing,* other states were also being populated with swine. Dr. Gideon Lincecum, the famous frontier naturalist, also found hog problems in Mississippi after leaving Texas in 1835 just prior to the revolution. He recorded in his journal, "Our road passed through Port Gibson, Clinton, etc. When we got into the Choctow country, which was full of big hogs three or four years old, we had to be more careful at our camps. They were so troublesome that we decided to stop at the taverns along the remainder of the route, though the cost was four-fold greater."

Since Florida was the major staging point for early explorers, feral swine quickly became a part of their fauna. Soon the entire Gulf Coast had swine that quickly expanded into the mountains of Tennessee and Kentucky. Further inland, states such as South Carolina, Georgia, Arkansas, Mississippi, North Carolina, and Virginia can trace their feral swine roots from the late 1500s through the 1700s. As the southeastern United States was being explored and settled, swine were an important commodity for those settlers. Wherever explorers went in North America or colonization began, swine were usually taken along.

Much like East Texas, early settlers of the Appalachian Mountains allowed hogs to roam freely and many escaped to form a free-ranging population. That is what happened in North Carolina in the early part of the twentieth century. According to John Collins of the North Carolina Wildlife Resources Commission in his publication entitled "The Wild Boar in North Carolina," the Whiting Manufacturing Company of England bought a large tract in

*See chapter 2.

Graham County, North Carolina, in 1908. Within this tract was a mountain called Hooper Bald, a part of the Snowbird Mountains.

George G. Moore, an American advisor for the company, was allowed to establish a game reserve on Hooper Bald around 1909. In 1911, he built a split-rail fence nine rails high to enclose approximately five to six hundred acres. In April 1912, he received a shipment of fourteen European wild hogs from the Ural Mountains of Russia. The eleven sows and three boars were delivered by train and ox-drawn wagon to Hooper Bald where they were subsequently released, minus one sow that had died en route. Some of the hogs rooted out of the split-rail fence and escaped; however, the majority of hogs remained in the lot for eight to ten years and increased in numbers. By the early 1920s, there were approximately sixty to one hundred hogs in the enclosure. A hunt with dogs was conducted but only two hogs were killed. However, many escaped the lot during the hunt.

Those that escaped thrived in Graham County and spread into other counties, including counties in Tennessee and what is now the Great Smoky Mountains National Park. According to George Laycock, in his book *Alien Animals*, it was from these mountains of North Carolina, through their trapping and relocation, that the California population of European wild hogs got its start. More on the status of wild hogs in California is forthcoming.

Since the 1920s, the descendants of the escapees have been roaming the Great Smoky Mountains of Tennessee and North Carolina. Just as in other regions where feral hogs are known to roam, these European hogs readily interbred with any free-ranging swine in the area. Their offspring still inhabit the Great Smoky Mountains and the problems they have created continue into the twenty-first century.

The majority of wild hogs in North Carolina are located in the western counties—Graham, Cherokee, and Swain counties, with the greatest population in Graham County. Smaller populations are located in Clay and Macon counties. Two additional groups that were established through private stocking are located in Rutherford, Cleveland, and Burke counties, as well as Caldwell, Wilkes, and Watauga counties.

Arkansas was known for its razorbacks long before it was known for its Arkansas Razorbacks. The University of Arkansas at Fayetteville didn't choose the razorback as its mascot without a reason. These lean, mean hogs were known as razorbacks because of their high, hair-covered backbone.

Early settlers used the wild land and hills of Arkansas to grow their hogs, letting them forage throughout the forest for food. The settlers would trap the hogs in the fall in large pens and take them to market to sell or slaughter. This free-ranging practice continued into the twentieth century until the Great Depression forced many hardscrabble farmers to abandon their way of life. And so they left the country lifestyle and their semiwild hogs in favor of a more stable economic future in town.

Today, the only true razorbacks come from Fayetteville, but there are still feral hogs roaming the land of the "Natural State." According to officials, feral hogs are currently found in every county in Arkansas.

******

A group of Kansas scientists conducted a study in 1998 on the northward expansion of the range of wild hogs, and they found dramatic growth since 1988 of wild hogs from Oklahoma, Arkansas, and Tennessee into the central states of Colorado, Kansas, Indiana, and Ohio. They described this range expansion to be largely due to clandestine releases of wild hogs for the purpose of hunting.

In a recent news release, the Missouri Department of Conservation claims intense hunting pressure has helped reduce that state's increasing hog population. Statewide, the estimated population of wild swine in the Show-me state is estimated between one and three thousand animals and exists in twenty-six counties. In Missouri, most hunting opportunities are limited to public land at Fort Wood, in Mark Twain National Forest, on U.S. Army Corps of Engineers properties, and in Leonard White Ranch Conservation Area, located south of White Plains.

By 2014, the presence of feral swine in Pennsylvania, Idaho, New York, and Maine was being documented. As with most other areas, the initial populations were believed to originate from escapees or releases from shooting facilities. In Pennsylvania, most are located near the vicinity of hunting operations; however, some feral swine have been documented where no known hunting facilities are located.

On to California

While the hog population was expanding in the southeastern United States, Spanish explorers were arriving in California bringing domestic swine with them. As with any explorer to the New World, swine were an important source of meat and lard. California received its first introduction in 1769. Russian settlers reportedly brought the second introduction to Fort Ross in Sonoma County, and for the next hundred years European settlers continued bringing swine into that state.

A nice wild hog. (Photo courtesy of John Miller)

By 1834, domestic swine were found in twenty-one of the Spanish missions in California. According to Towne and Wentworth, by 1880 the domestic swine population in California exceeded 600,000 individuals. In several locations, commercial swine operators would release their swine to feed on the acorns during the fall and winter, and sometimes they would leave them to forage until market prices were better. During the California gold rush in the mid-1800s, hogs were an important part of the settlers' diet, for they provided a relatively cheap supply of food and lard.

The first introduction of European hogs or Russian boars to California occurred in 1925; these were imported from North Carolina. As with the Texas population, the California population soon spread, and by the 1940s sport hunters began to become interested in the wild boar. By the turn of the twenty-first century, the wild boar had become the number two big-game animal harvested in California, having surpassed all but black-tailed/mule deer in the 1980s. Feral swine now occupy fifty-six of fifty-eight counties in California, with the range and distribution continuing to increase through numerous introductions by man and natural dispersal.

The Texas Invasion

CHAPTER 2

Did you ever hear the story
Of that famous hog of mine?
She's a razorback and spotted
Black and white from hoof to spine;

With a snout made outa granite,
She can root just like a plow;
And the fence ain't been invented
That can turn that spotted sow.

From *That Spotted Sow and Other Texas Hill Country Ballads*
by Carlos Ashley

When Hernando de Soto died in Arkansas, Luis de Moscoso Alvarado took command of the expedition. Determined to return to Mexico overland, he traveled into Texas and possibly reached the Brazos River. Due to the fact his hogs had no food, de Moscoso's journey most likely ended when he reached the prairies of Texas's upper Cross-Timbers, west of present-day Fort Worth. This region lacked mast- or nut-producing trees, such as oaks and their acorns. This was most likely the reason Luis de Moscoso failed to travel farther west into the prairies, despite forcing the Indians to carry acorns and corn on their backs as hog feed. The Spaniards needed their traveling food supply, the swine, in order to advance into new territory.

Finding the route ahead exceedingly difficult and dangerous, he retraced his steps and traveled back to the Mississippi River where his men built boats. There, de Moscoso and his men slaughtered and butchered hogs, turning the meat into salted pork for their voyage. These hogs possibly came from herds he had in Texas. He received additional hogs from the Indians who had stolen them from him previously. After loading his hogs onto ships, he sailed southward down the Mississippi to the Gulf of Mexico, where he followed the Gulf Coast to Tampico, Mexico. Thus concluded the first incursion of hogs into Texas.

I've found no records reflecting the number of hogs brought into the state or how many may have been stolen by Indians or escaped to the wild. My opinion concurs with other writers that few free-ranging hogs resulted from this first introduction and they had little effect upon the present population of wild hogs in Texas.

Réne-Robert Cavelier, Sieur de La Salle, is thought to have established the first free-ranging hog population in Texas. Réne-Robert de La Salle may have succeeded in populating the state with hogs, but he failed in his attempt to colonize the Texas coast. Attempting to rediscover the mouth of the Mississippi River that he found in 1682, La Salle landed on the west side of the entrance to Matagorda Bay in February 1685. Bringing several hundred colonists, soldiers, and workers, he built a fort farther inland. From St. Domingo in the West Indies he brought supplies that included cattle, swine, and fowl, all of which reportedly multiplied and prospered.

After a few years, the living conditions at the fort became hopeless. Starvation, disease, and Indian attacks had taken their toll. In January 1687, La Salle went for help, leaving behind twenty people, seventy to seventy-five swine, and eighteen to twenty hens at the colony. La Salle never made it out of Texas before his own men killed him. The colonists remaining at the fort eventually succumbed to smallpox and Indian attacks.

When Spanish explorers located the lost fort a few years later, a Spanish priest named Damian Massanet reported finding many "dead pigs at the destroyed fort." It is not clear why the Karankawa Indians abandoned the fresh meat at the fort, for the records from the time make no mention of this.

There are, however, many conflicting statements among writers regarding the remnant hog population.

Mary Atkinson claimed in her book, *The Texas Indians*, that the Karankawas of the Gulf Coast "utilized Spanish livestock that went wild, including longhorns, mustangs, and razorbacks, a new and bountiful meat supply." According to W. W. Newcomb in *The Indians of Texas*, a Spaniard named Padre Fray Gasper Jose de Solis reported in 1767–68 that Karankawa Indians "live on horses, mules, deer, bison, bears, wild boars, rabbits, and hares," unlike the Plains Indians for whom fish, fowl, and particularly hogs were taboo for spiritual reasons.

Del Weniger's excellent second volume on the early explorers of Texas describes and discusses the animals these men found. He devoted several pages to the feral hog population, titling the section "The Dogs of the French," a term that goes back to the original French settlement of Robert La Salle. The Talon brothers who were with La Salle reported in 1698, "There will be presently a quantity of runaway pigs in all the country. The savages do not eat them, saying they are the dogs of the French." Whether any of the coastal Indians utilized the French hogs is unclear. A few of the original swine from La Salle's colony found haven in the thickets of the Gulf Coast; however, the odds of any progeny surviving to present day appears unlikely.

The Spanish began sending missionaries into Texas in the 1700s to establish missions, teach religion to the Indians, and lay claim to the territory. The Martin de Alarcón expedition of 1718–19 that founded the Mission San Antonio de Valero (Alamo) introduced swine along with other livestock into the countryside. Although some historians claim swine were part of the mission's livestock, records do not substantiate this claim and swine numbers were probably inconsequential. A 1745 census of San Antonio listed 2,000 cattle, 1,317 sheep, 304 goats, and 40 horses. Inventories of 13 operating missions in 1763 never mentioned swine. However, Fray Gaspar José de Solis who inspected the missions during the years of 1767–68 reported that in the woods from the Mission Bahia to San Antonio, "There are great numbers of cattle and horses, many animals such as deer, wolves, coyotes, rabbits, and now and then a lion, some wild cats, wild boar along the banks of the river. . . ." Carlos Castañeda reported in *Our Catholic Heritage* that an 1810 census of San Antonio listed 14 ranches in operation with a total of 85 hogs.

The Nacogdoches settlement of East Texas is one of the oldest in the state. While the missionaries did not raise hogs, evidently settlers in the area had some. In 1806 there were some settlements along the old San Antonio road near Nacogdoches. In 1819, on an excursion from the Sabine River to Nacogdoches, Mexican Col. Ignacio Perez and his troops observed "...good crops of cotton, corn, pumpkins, potatoes, and other vegetables and the troops fed on the many pigs and chickens they found." These early reports validate the importance of hogs and their existence in early Texas; however, the first significant populations of hogs that I believe helped establish a wild population originated with the colonists.

Stephen F. Austin received the first land grant in January 1821 with the first three hundred colonists arriving in November 1821. These colonists, often referred to as "the old 300," settled along the Brazos, Colorado, and Bernard Rivers near present-day Brenham, Navasota, and LaGrange. The Texas colonists were basically poor but self-reliant. The economy of the colonies was based on bartering products from farms and ranches. I can imagine trading home-sewn clothing for butter and eggs, an ox for a sow and her piglets, a ball of yarn for corn, or a rifle for a mare.

The farming colony's exports in Austin's words were "cotton, beef tallow, pork, lard, mules, etc." Swine was the most common livestock, although there was also cattle, oxen, and chickens. All livestock ran wild in the woods and foraged for themselves. Gathering the livestock often required enticing the animals with small amounts of corn or by using dogs or horses to shepherd them into the pen. Often wild hogs that couldn't be rounded up were hunted and shot by the settlers when they wanted fresh meat.

Noah Smithwick reiterated this in 1830 by stating, "Martin Varner (colonist) had a lot of wild hogs running in the bottom and when he wanted pork he went out and shot one." The diet of the colonists was largely salt pork, usually fried with corn bread, sweet potatoes, and molasses. With the exception of wild game, fresh meat was rare.

Nacogdoches had evolved into an important trading center between the colonists and Louisiana. According to Weniger, the 1834 census of Nacogdoches settlement recorded 60,000 hogs. Hogs were desirable because they had large litters, short gestation periods, matured quickly, and could survive and fatten on virtually all habitats. They were also inexpensive to raise.

Pork could be preserved by smoking and salting, whereas beef must be dried because it can spoil easily without adequate sun and drying time. Pork could be cured without refrigeration, and hogs provided grease and soap.

Most of the butchering and curing was done during the winter when conditions were cold enough to keep the meat from spoiling. Soap was made by mixing lye leached from hardwood ashes with grease. After heating and stirring, the mixture hardened in molds. The soap was used for everything from washing clothes, dishes, and people . . . and at times the mouths of little kids who may have let slip an unmentionable term.

By 1835, some 3,500 land titles had been issued to settlers through various *empresarios*. It wasn't long before these colonists were producing thousands of bales of cotton as well as teeming herds of cattle and hogs. When hostilities heated between the colonists and Mexico and Santa Anna began his march through Texas, many of the colonists feared for their lives and left so quickly they abandoned homes and livestock. This exodus is often referred to as the "runaway scrape" in Texas history.

Many of these abandoned and previously free-ranging hogs could not be recaptured, and in all likelihood these probably became the nucleus of our current feral hog population—with additional numbers intermittently dispersed due to Indian depredations on settlers over the next several decades. As a soldier in the Texas Revolution, Noah Smithwick stated that between Brenham and Bastrop and throughout the colony they ". . . found houses open, beds unmade, cribs full of corn, smoke houses full of bacon, chickens, cattle eating the grass and hogs fat and lazy wallowing in the mud all abandoned."

After fighting between Texas and Mexico ceased, settlement resumed in the original colonies and German immigrants began settling in central Texas. Around 1840, settlements such as New Braunfels, Kerrville, and

Fredericksburg began. Swine were the most common livestock. Although cattle were around in large numbers, there was not a market for the meat; cattle were raised principally for their hides. The prolific hogs were raised for their meat and lard, and were highly marketable during the period of rapid development in northeastern Texas between the years 1840–1860.

Settlers continued to import hogs into the Big Thicket region of East Texas. In 1838, a settler named Sherod Wright claimed he and his neighbors had hogs, "mainly for their own use. In summer hogs scattered over the uplands and in winter to the bottoms to forage on nuts." When Wright saddled up to ride, he'd put some corn in his saddlebags, paying a token to the process of domestication, but in spite of this "hogs eventually became nearly as wild as deer."

In 1841, two years after the government had moved to Austin, a political scandal over hogs erupted between the French chargé d'affaires and the Texas government. A French servant of the chargé killed the hogs of a local resident, a Mr. Bullock, after they had broken the chargé's fences, entered his home, chewed his linens, and destroyed some of his important papers. In turn, Mr. Bullock promptly beat up the servant. The chargé decried the action to the Texas government, and when it refused to take satisfactory action against Mr. Bullock, the French chargé d'affaires left town, never to return.

It wasn't only the French who thought wild Texas hogs could be unruly. Mary Austin Holley in 1836 wrote on the zoology of Texas: "The wild hog is frequently met with, and, although it has never been known to make a voluntary attack upon a man, yet when provoked, it is a very furious and formidable animal. These hogs are descended from the domestic swine, and have become wild by running at large in the woods." Mr. Weniger documented many reports by explorers and settlers in early Texas, and he states that Jose Enrique de la Peña describes pigs as big as a five- or six-month old calf. This account was from 1836 when de la Peña was camping at a creek about fourteen miles from Gonzales in south-central Texas. So, not only could pigs be disruptive but their size could also make them formidable.

William Bollaert, who traveled through Texas in 1843, stated in his journal that the "wild hog is the common hog run wild—hunted with dogs and shot—makes fine bacon." Mr. Weniger concluded that by the time of Texas's independence from Mexico the descendants of escaped domestic hogs originally brought into Texas had populated the southern and eastern parts of the wilderness. I believe that by the middle of the nineteenth century the range had expanded into the central and north-central expanses of Texas as well.

Wilhelm Steinert, a German traveling through Texas during 1849, reported in his memoirs "that hogs are increasing considerably in Texas and sometimes do much damage. They break through fences and destroy crops. In some parts of the country the people have tried to remedy this situation by putting a yoke on their necks, but this idea has not been successful." John Russell Bartlett with the U.S. and Mexican boundary commission in 1850 reported near Fredericksburg "A number of hogs were running about quite wild, of which a couple were killed, to add to our stock of fresh meat." These were animals that had been abandoned by settlers when they fled from hostile Indian depredations.

Free-ranging hogs in the woods. (Photo courtesy of Joe Herrera)

Frederick Olmsted traveled through Texas in 1854, and in his book *Journey Through Texas*, he stated that at his camp near Crockett on 1 January 1854, "... we were annoyed by hogs beyond all description. At almost every camp we were surrounded by them, but here they seemed perfectly frantic with hunger. They ran directly through the fire and even carried off a chicken that was dressed and pitted. While the horses were feeding, it required the constant attendance of two of us to keep them at bay, and even then they secured more than half the corn. Fanny [his horse] was so shocked and disturbed as to refuse all the food. For some minutes the fiercest of them would resist even a clubbing, eating and squealing on through the blows. These animals proved, indeed throughout Texas, a disgusting annoyance, though after procuring an excellent dog, a day or two after we were rid of the worst of it."

On his trip farther west near the head of the Guadalupe River in the Texas Hill Country, Kendall County, Olmsted claimed, "One of the greatest sources of profit is from droves of hogs which increase with remarkable rapidity and pick their living from the roots and nuts of river bottoms. The distribution of a few ears of corn at night brings them all every day to the crib." Throughout his travels, he reports bacon and pork was easier to obtain than beef.

In their book, *Land of Bears and Honey*, Joe Truett and Dan Lay tell a story about Mr. Ab Carter who was born in 1855 and raised in Liberty County in East Texas. Mr. Carter claimed his father's principal occupation at the time was keeping hogs and killing bears, and "... to a man with several hundred hogs running in the woods, bear killing was the most important part of the season's work."

In 1858 De Cordova reported the following to the New York Geographical Society:

> Peccary or Mexican hogs differed from the ordinary wild hog. Both are very ferocious and afford fine sport in the chase. Peccaries are seldom eaten, being very strong, but the latter is nearly equal to that of its civilized brother, whose flesh, although Father Moren has prohibited the use of it, is consumed in vast quantities in Texas due to the ease with which it can be preserved and transported.

In the upper and lower cross timbers and on the waters of the Yegua, immense droves of hogs can be raised and fattened without expense on the fine mast afforded by these regions of the country. There are at this time hundreds of persons who are doing well in this business with very little labor, and so great is [the] demand for the produce of this animal in our state, that it is impossible to have a super abundance, notwithstanding that the region of the country adapted to hog raising is so extensive. In addition to the amount raised in Texas, we import a large amount from New Orleans.

By 1860, the area within Stephen F. Austin's original colony contained an estimated 50,000 hogs. A citizen of Robertson County estimated probably 30,000 hogs in that county. Hogs continued to provide an essential source of food, lard, and soap for these early settlers. Bear in mind that with no fencing, the vast majority of these hogs ranged freely. Wild hog populations were kept localized and stable due to subsistence hunting by man as well as by diseases, parasites, and natural predators.

By the late 1800s, wild hogs were numerous throughout the big thicket of East Texas. Due to low numbers of wildlife such as deer, hogs actually provided more pounds of meat than game animals. Through the turn of the twentieth century, as settlement increased throughout Texas, the numbers of free-ranging hogs also increased. In the early 1900s Mr. Mearns noted that feral hogs were numerous in many parts of Texas along the Rio Grande.

The early 1900s were relatively prosperous for rural Texans until the 1920s and 1930s when economic hard times hit with devastating consequences. Unable to pay their mortgages and taxes, many rural residents were forced to leave their farms to seek employment in the cities. So as they packed their families and belongings and headed to the city, many left their livestock behind. The free-ranging hogs were especially vulnerable to abandonment.

To further demonstrate the dissemination of feral hogs in Texas around the turn of the century, J. Frank Dobie devoted a whole chapter to "Razorbacks" in his book *A Vaquero of the Brush Country, The Life and Times of John D. Young.* Mr. Young was a cowboy in southwestern Texas in the latter half of the nineteenth century, and he reminisced about the establishment of the Texas coastal meat packers. It was his contention that the meat packers created a demand for hogs. Because hogs were used as a method to dispose of the refuse created by the meat packers, Young said, "The hogs ran wild like the longhorns, and the woods were full of them." Evidently some men made a business out of capturing and selling the wild hogs. In those days, the best sport was to catch them in the open and attempt to rope them before they could reach cover.

The Russian Boar Arrives

Unlike the feral hog whose roots are traced to domestication, the Eurasian wild boar or Russian boar is a true wild hog that has never been domesticated. The Eurasian or European wild boars, that also include sows, can still be found in the forests of Europe and Asia. It is from these wild ancestors that domestication of swine actually began.

Few documented facts can be found concerning the history of European wild boars in Texas. The Denman releases along the central Texas coast are probably the first known importation in Texas. Between

A Eurasian boar in its natural Austrian habitat. (Photo courtesy of Larry Weishuhn)

1930 to 1933, Mr. Denman obtained approximately eleven European wild boars from the San Antonio Zoo and released them near Austwell in Aransas County. He released an additional ten to fifteen in 1939 on a different ranch located between Port O'Connor and Seadrift in Calhoun County. Once released, they readily bred and crossed with the local domestic or established feral hogs.

The next reported release of European hogs occurred in the early 1940s when a rancher in northwest Bexar County purchased several from a traveling zoo and subsequently released them into the wild. A fence-destroying flood allowed many of the animals to escape into the surrounding eastern Medina and southern Bandera counties. As with the Denman releases, these hogs also bred opportunistically with free-ranging domestic hogs or established feral hogs. Future releases of so-called European wild boars were most likely offspring between European and feral hogs, and not of a pure strain of European ancestry.

Into the Twenty-First Century

From the 1950s until present, hogs have been continually released through-out Texas in an effort to increase hunting opportunity and provide economic returns. Texas is approximately 97 percent privately owned and hunting leases provide a major economic incentive. Prior to 1992, domestic hogs or wild-trapped feral hogs could be purchased locally through livestock auctions or individuals and then released.

In 1992 the Texas Animal Health Commission enacted new regulations concerning the movement of wild-trapped swine in an effort to prevent the possible spread of disease. It would be impossible to estimate the numbers of hogs released by landowners and sportsmen prior to, and after the regulation was enacted. The hog is an unregulated animal in Texas and is not classified as a game animal. For this reason, very few statistics and harvest information are available.

Status and Distribution of Wild Hogs in North America

The history regarding the expansion of wild hogs throughout the United States provides a dramatic example of their ability to thrive and survive despite recent attempts to curtail this expansion. This history gives a timeline and general context of the distribution across the United States; however, to truly understand the magnitude, a more thorough discussion is required.

In 1991 John Mayer and I. Lehr Brisbin published an excellent book on the history, comparative morphology, and current status of wild pigs in the United States. While most of the book focuses on the results of highly technical research, there is an excellent chapter on the history of the introduction of feral swine in each state. I've included updated information on the various states that have burgeoning populations of feral swine, and the regulations regarding them can be found in chapter 12.

Texas Parks and Wildlife Department (TPWD) first attempted to monitor and document the European wild boar in a 1945 publication on exotic game when it reported on the Denman release along the Texas coast. In this publication, the author clearly stated that European wild boars were breeding with domestic or feral hogs. The next report on exotics by TPWD came in 1964 when biologist Al Jackson surveyed the number of European boars in the central Texas region and on the central Texas coast. Based on the survey, he estimated there were 400 individuals in Calhoun County, 175 in Bexar County, and "heavy concentrations" in Medina County. He also reported wild boars had crossed with feral swine in many areas so that pure stock was limited and hard to distinguish from crosses. In 1967, the TPWD estimated there were 10,000 European boars interspersed with feral hogs in the Edwards Plateau south to the Rio Grande Plains and in eastern Texas. Feral hog and crossbreds were obviously included in this estimate

The first attempt to determine the status of feral hogs in Texas came in 1979 when questionnaires were sent out to TPWD biologists across the state to determine their distribution, utilization, and management implications. At that time no attempt was made to determine or estimate the population. In 1992, by utilizing available data from previous TPWD exotic-game surveys as well as the 1979 report, private surveys, and interviews, the state established the distribution of feral hogs in Texas.

At that time, the feral hog was distributed throughout most of Texas with the exception of the western panhandle and the northern Trans-Pecos region. By 2000, they had begun infiltrating the Chihuahuan desert area of Big Bend National Park, which raised concerns regarding the potential effects posed on this fragile ecosystem. Feral hog densities fluctuate from extremely dense populations in East, Southeast, and South Texas to low in far West Texas. Feral hogs are found in all habitat types from dense forest, swamps,

Wild hog zone sign.

chaparral brush, and oak-woodland. In Texas, feral hogs occupy most of the white-tailed deer range and prefer the drainages and bottomland habitats but thrive as well in upland ranges where there is adequate food and cover. As the northward and westward expansion increases, climate does not appear to be a limiting factor; however, diverse food availability is important.

The feral hog is an extremely wary and secretive creature whose adaptability and nocturnal habits have made it a difficult animal to determine a census accurately. Density estimates for the feral hog in Texas are purely speculative and based on an array of factors. The table below illustrates the increase in feral hog density in southern Texas that were determined while conducting fixed-wing aerial surveys of white-tailed deer.

Deer range and densities correlated with hog distribution, previous research studies, feral-hog habitat, biological estimations based on interviews, and actual census results were all incorporated to estimate the feral hog population in Texas to be between 1.5 and 2 million animals. In 2011, the Texas AgriLife Extension Service conducted a comprehensive review of various research studies in order to develop a population model that would determine the feral hog density in Texas. The developers estimated the average hog density in Texas ranged from 1.3–2.5 hogs/square mile, and based on this model,

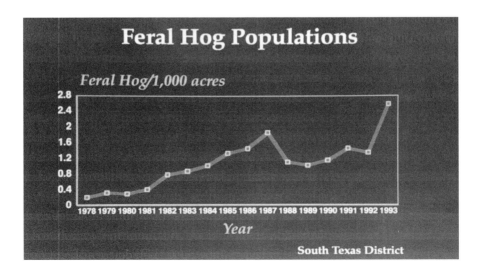

they estimated the feral hog population in Texas to be between 1.8 and 3.4 million hogs, the average being 2.6 million. They also found feral hogs inhabit 79 percent of the land mass in Texas. The study further indicated an annual population growth of 18–21 percent annually. Although it's difficult to test the accuracy of the model in terms of actual density, it illustrates population growth and the importance of population control.

Whatever the actual feral-hog density is, Texas has the distinction of harboring the greatest number of hogs in the United States. While accurate estimates are virtually impossible, it seems that Texas represents about 50 percent of the estimated 4–5 million hogs in the United States.

Many other states also have attempted to quantify the numbers of feral hogs. Many techniques including track counts, aerial surveys, root indices, mark and recapture, camera surveys, and computer-based modeling, to name a few, have been tried, but still no reliable technique has been found. The California Department of Fish and Game has not conducted any population studies but surveys a percent of hunters to determine harvest estimates.

In 1998, Gipson and coauthors completed a study on the range expansion of wild hogs across the central United States that established wild hogs were present in twenty-four states. In this study, they found a dramatic northward expansion in the range of wild hogs since 1988. Since 1998, another twenty states and Canada can be added to the list.

The Southeastern Cooperative Wildlife Disease Study (SCWDS) of the College of Veterinary Medicine at the University of Georgia began monitoring and producing maps on feral hog distribution in 1982. These maps were subsequently revised and updated in 1988, and in 2004 they clearly show a dramatic increase in the expansion of the feral hogs' range. For example, in 1982 only 475 counties in 17 states reported feral hogs, whereas in 2004, 1,014 counties in 28 states reported wild swine. In 2007, research conducted by Mississippi State concluded that feral-hog distribution had increased to 38 states.

The SCWDS implemented the National Feral Swine Mapping System (NFSMS) in 2008 as an interactive, web-based program to collect and help track the distribution of feral hogs throughout the United States. Using this

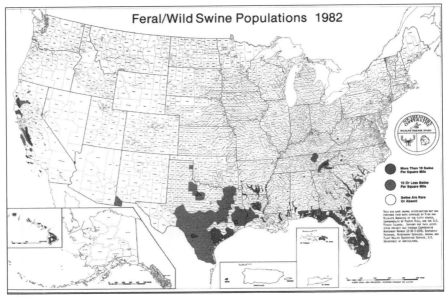

Wild swine populations 1982.

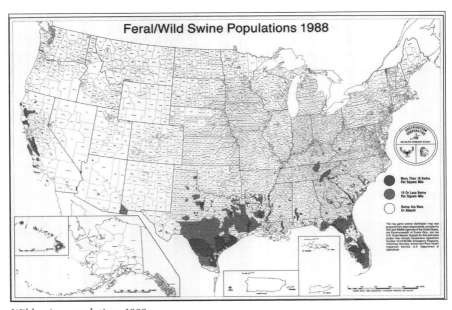

Wild swine populations 1988.

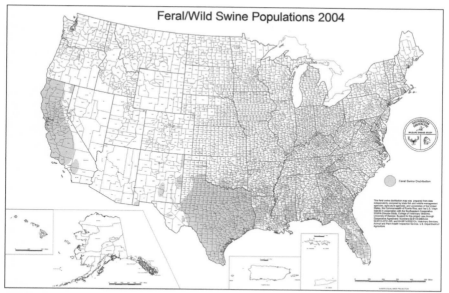

Wild swine populations 2004.

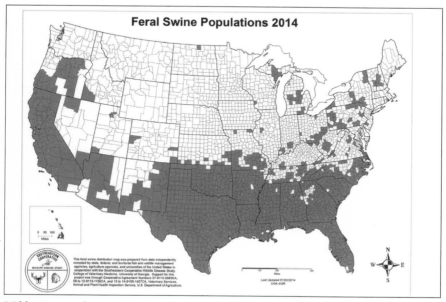

Wild swine populations 2014.

system, SCWDS reported that the feral swine distribution had dropped to 36 states due to the eradication of swine in Nebraska; however, by 2015, distribution had again risen and feral hogs were now to be found in 40 states. The distribution of U. S. swine fluctuates due to individual states with low populations continuing to eradicate them before they get out of control. Unfortunately, when one population is eradicated, another one appears. Currently, the estimated swine population in the United States is between four and five million animals.

Population Explosion

The reasons for the increase in numbers and expansion of the range of the feral hog in Texas and throughout the United States are numerous. Constant introductions throughout Texas and other states coupled with the high reproductive rate of swine and limited hunting pressure are probably the most significant factors. The continuing intentional releases of domestic swine by sportsmen and ranchers for hunting have augmented the population throughout the last several decades. Furthermore, many landowners and sportsmen maintain feeding areas throughout the year to bait wildlife—a primary technique used by many Texas hunters to harvest game—and feral hogs are capitalizing on this practice, responding in droves for easy meals.

Feral hogs are also benefiting from improved agricultural and land-use practices. These include farmland that has reverted to rangeland, better land management, and improved livestock grazing practices by landowners. These improvements have resulted in more food and water, better cover, and generally better habitat—all of which can sustain a burgeoning hog population. As farming becomes more productive and efficient, hogs utilize these crops. Improved animal husbandry, disease eradication and vaccinations, and increased predator control have further benefited wild hog populations. Water conservation and water supplies from stock tanks, lakes, and irrigation have benefited wild hogs.

Historically, diseases were believed to have kept the wild hog population in check. The eradication of the screwworm has benefited the wild hog in much the same way it assisted in the increase of white-tailed deer populations. As commercial swine operators improved their operations and animal husbandry progressed, vaccinations curtailed most diseases among domestic breeds. This, in turn, meant that diseases could no longer be transmitted to a wild population. Ironically now, commercial swine operators are fearful of diseases that the wild hogs can transmit to their commercial operation. In 1978, hog cholera, a deadly disease to hogs, was eradicated in domestic swine; it is subsequently not found in wild swine.

Other than man, feral hogs have very few natural predators once they have reached two months of age. Large predators such as mountain lions and coyotes are still being pressured by human control measures, so they have very limited natural impact on feral swine. Even if these large predators were not controlled, it is unlikely they would be able to keep wild swine numbers in check. In summation, just about everything that historically kept the wild swine population in check—natural mortality, diseases, parasites, predators, and subsistence hunting—has been corrected or altered!

Hogs have been around for centuries but have increased substantially in the last few decades. It is obvious that they are an integral part of Texas, Florida, California and many other states' fauna. In terms of a huntable ungulate with huntable numbers, they are currently number two behind the white-tailed deer in Texas and Florida. They are extremely wary and secretive, and very adaptive to local conditions. They are in the United States to stay.

Wild hogs have become so numerous and dangerous in some parts of Texas that in Knox County the local Texas Department of Transportation installed signs along the roadway stating, "Watch for Wild Hogs." In South Texas where hogs are much more troublesome, the locals have already learned to watch for them.

The Biology of a Wild Hog

CHAPTER 4

Born and bred on Cedar Mountain,
She is wilder than a deer;
And she's known by reputation
To the ranch hands far and near.

Though a sow of mine had raised 'er,
On that mountain she was free;
And I always kinda doubted
That she really b'longed to me

She didn't claim no owner—
Save the God who put 'er there—
And for mortal man's relations
She just simply didn't care.

From *That Spotted Sow and Other Texas Hill Country Ballads*
by Carlos Ashley

Feral hogs *(Sus scrofa)* are also called European hogs, Eurasian or Russian boars, razorbacks, piney woods rooters, woods hogs, corn rustlers, and a host of less descriptive names. They are an Old World species that belong to the family Suidae and are the same species as our domestic swine breeds. There are approximately twenty-three generally recognized subspecies

A typical feral hog. (Photo courtesy of Bob Zaiglin)

of wild hogs in the world; however, some differences of opinion do occur among professionals. Long before the continents separated, and for whatever reason, the Old World hog found itself landlocked on the Asian continent unable to cross the Bering land bridge from Russia to Alaska. It would take tens of millions of years before the hog would find its way to the New World or Western Hemisphere. Human introduction by early explorers ultimately brought them to the United States.

Feral hogs include domestic hogs gone wild, true European wild hogs or Russian boars, and varying degrees of hybrid crosses between the two. The javelina, on the other hand, is a native of Texas, the United States, and the Western Hemisphere. In South Texas, feral hogs are frequently confused with the javelina *(Pecari tajacu)* or collared peccary, but they have no direct relationship.

The feral hog's day begins and ends with its continual quest for food. Breeding and brood-rearing may temporarily interrupt it, but the continual search for food maintains priority throughout the day or night. Feral hogs are opportunistic feeders and rely heavily on vegetation. During the warm months the search commences at dusk and ends at daylight, with hogs resting throughout the day. During cooler periods, hogs are more active throughout daylight hours.

Geographic location and climatic conditions do not appear to be a hindrance in the range expansion of feral hogs. Climate and land use can affect nutritional levels and food availability, thus limiting range expansion and density of populations. While conditions may limit forage availability, feral hogs exhibit the inherent ability to respond and adapt to changes.

Feral hogs represent a challenge to resource managers, and further investigations are continually being conducted to determine what long-term effects feral hogs have on indigenous species. Feral hogs compete with native wildlife for preferred foods, yet the extent of competition remains unknown. To understand whether to manage or control the wild hog, people must understand its basic life history and factors such as diseases, parasites, physical abnormalities, and mortality.

Appearance

The wild hog is similar in appearance to the domestic hog with several notable exceptions. The wild hog has longer bristles and a straighter tail. The most recognizable physical features of a wild hog include a long snout, lean hams, and a sloped back. Smaller hams notwithstanding, the long snout and large shoulders developed because of rooting and survival activities. Domestic hogs are selectively bred for their hams and meat, while wild hogs breed for survival. As time progresses, domestic traits are eventually replaced by characteristics that enhance survival. In appearance, one can clearly observe the domestication process reversed.

Striped and solid-colored juvenile wild hogs. (Photo courtesy of Brad Porter)

Wild hog offspring are usually horizontally striped tan and brown in color until this camouflage pattern fades away into a more permanent color. Many early researchers believed that this coloration of the young was indicative of true European lineage, but that theory has been debunked. Another common misconception is the belief that pure Russian boars have split-end hair shafts. Most wild hogs have split-end hairs while domestic hogs usually exhibit single-end hair tips, but this is not an absolute. In a wild hog population, the light coloration of the split tips against the darker color of the remaining hair gives the hog a grizzled coloration. Wild hog hair, believed to aid in insulation, is usually coarser and denser.

Color

The color, shape, and size of feral hogs varies among individuals. The dominant color phases are black or grizzled, although brown, red, and even white colorations sometimes accented with spots and stripes are common.

Color variations of wild hogs. (Photo courtesy of Bob Zaiglin)

Grizzled is described as dark gray or black with light hair tips. European hogs and feral hogs that have been in the wild for generations tend to exhibit this coloration.

To illustrate a few color variations in feral hogs, I have seen black hogs with a single broad, white stripe; spotted hogs; solid white hogs; red hogs; and hogs in all shades of brown including light tan, and all of these could be confused with domestic breeds found in pens. I recall conducting helicopter surveys of white-tailed deer on one ranch in South Texas with a landowner whose children were raising show hogs, and we would jovially compare the wild hogs we observed to the domestic ones his children were raising in their pens.

Size

An average size of a mature male feral hog in South Texas will weigh around 150–175 pounds. Average sizes may vary amongst different populations and geographic regions, and individuals may grow to several hundred pounds. Unless pregnant, females are generally smaller. In general, the larger hogs are likely recently released into the wild or are castrated males. Just about every hunter that has ever stalked a wild hog has heard stories of super hogs weighing 500 to 600-plus pounds. Occasionally, a wild hog may attain this size; however, chances are highly probable that it is not far removed or bred from its domestic origins.

I knew a man in South Texas who purposely tried to grow a wild hog as big as he could. He fed it unlimited feed and the pig never weighed more than about 900 pounds. When I saw the hog, it could barely walk because it was so heavy. In the fall of 1999, a wild hog weighing 1,087 pounds was purportedly killed in southwest Texas. While not disclaiming it as fiction, modern photography and/or inaccurate scales can do wonders.

One of the largest hogs I have seen harvested in southwestern Texas weighed about 465 pounds! From snout to rump it was nine feet long with hoofs measuring over 3½ inches across. It was killed by a couple of well-respected government trappers and weighed at the local wool and mohair warehouse.

Another super-size wild hog was killed on a plantation around Alapaha, Georgia. This monster, nicknamed "Hogzilla," was supposedly 12 feet long, weighed 1,000 pounds, and sported 9-inch tusks! The hunters buried the carcass after photographing it before it was weighed, thus proof or an independent source could not verify its size. However, as the picture traveled through cyberspace via the Internet, it stirred such a ruckus locally and frenzied discussions nationally that National Geographic sent an expert to Georgia to locate it. With the help of the hunting guide who shot the hog, National Geographic was able to locate the remains. It was determined that the actual length was about 7½ feet long with an estimated weight of 800 pounds. DNA testing also determined that it was a mix between domestic and wild hog.

Not to be outdone, an Alabama boy supposedly shot a 1,051-pound monster with a pistol in the spring of 2007. Fittingly nicknamed "Monster Pig", the story made the national media circuit for several days. Investigative journalists found many discrepancies in the story thus authenticity of this hog is also questionable. If indeed, a hog of this magnitude is ever found and substantiated, it will be noteworthy.

A huge hog . . . an authentic photo? Probably, but beware of hoaxes or staged photos.

Teeth

Hogs have 44 teeth with an upper to lower dental formula on each side of the jaw of 3/3 Incisors, 1/1 canine, 4/4 premolars and 3/3 molars. Permanent teeth are usually complete by the time the hog reaches 20 to 22 months. Canines grow continually, and up to 75 percent of the tooth is embedded in the jaw. It is the canines that establish a hog's trophy status and the amount of danger it poses.

Among serious hog hunters, the canine teeth are called many things including tusks, tushes, cutters, blades, witters, grinders, and ivory. These four continuously growing tusks are constantly sharpening themselves on each other. The top ones (witters or grinders) tend to curl outward whereas the bottom ones curl up and out. The top teeth are the primary sharpeners or whetstones for the bottom. When the mouth is closed or during jaw action on each respective side, the upper and lower canines are always touching each other and sharpening themselves. It is this sharpness that can pose serious danger to humans and other hogs.

Habitat Preference

Feral hogs can be found in virtually all habitats throughout the United States. They generally prefer drainages, creeks, and bottomlands. They are found in mountainous regions as well as swamps. In South Carolina, feral hogs are found in river bottoms and associated bottomlands, shifting to upland pine forests in late winter and summer. This is very similar to the areas of East Texas. In Louisiana, Georgia, and Florida, hogs can be found in swamps and marshes.

Major factors involved in habitat shifts are food, water, climate, and available cover. Climate is important to the feral hog and it directly affects its choice of habitat. Hogs prefer damp or cooler environments during hot

Good bottomland feral hog habitat.

temperatures, and habitats are chosen for protection from the extremes of cold or hot weather. As with all members of the hog family such as the domestic breeds, feral hogs lack the ability to sweat; therefore, they must utilize their physical characteristics and adapt their behavior to keep cool. Hogs often travel outside their normal home range in search of better life-sustaining requirements for survival.

Home Range and Activity Patterns

Home range and territory will vary given the geographic region, the season, and the availability of food, for hogs frequently travel great distances to reach a desired food source. Research indicates that a home range can vary from 1,000 acres to over 23,000 acres. Although the latter is extreme, the actual home range is closer to the former. Overall, the home range of a feral hog is generally from 1 to 20 square miles or more, but is usually less than 5 square miles.

In one home range study conducted in Florida's subtropical environment, researchers found female home ranges typically to be smaller than that of males. Daily home ranges are usually smaller than seasonal or annual ones. Generally, spring or summer home ranges are smaller than the winter ranges, again due mainly to the availability of food. Feral hogs will travel great distances even outside their range to a good food source. Wild hogs often use the same trails between feeding, nesting, or watering grounds. At times they will mark trees where they rubbed mud from wallows or even scar them with their tusks.

On an international level, daily and seasonal activity patterns vary due to factors such as climate extremes and hunting pressure. For example, research in Italy indicates that activity patterns for wild hogs are malleable and adaptable; in Australia wild hogs are primarily nocturnal.

South Carolina wild hogs shift their activity patterns from nocturnal during summer to diurnal during autumn, winter, and spring. In Texas and Tennessee wild hogs are primarily crepuscular. Research in South Texas using global-positioning-system (GPS) tracking collars suggest that from January to March wild hogs increase their activity during warmer periods; however, during summer the data indicate that temperature has no influence. Males generally travel greater distances than females, although females raising young may display greater overall activity.

Social Structure

Females, called **sows**, usually live in family groups, or **sounders**, consisting of one or more females and their offspring. Males or **boars**, on the other hand, tend to live a rather solitary life, becoming social only to breed. Breeding occurs throughout the year, with peaks in the spring and summer.

Boars may even attempt to collect a harem of females. Courtship includes pushing the female in circles with his body and snout and frequently rubbing the sow's vulva. During this ritual, the boar may be urinating frequently and vocalizing with quick grunting sounds.

During peak breeding season or when a female is in estrus, males will fight fiercely for females. The fights may be head to head, shoulder to shoulder, head to tail, or pushing and slashing with their tusks. The tough shoulder hide, called a **shield**, on the outside of a boar is thick scar tissue resulting from continual fighting among males. The shield is located on the outer sides and may extend from the base of the neck halfway down the side of a boar. The shield does not develop on a male unless the boar receives wounds and scars from fighting. For this reason, the females seldom have it.

A sample of 721 males from an introduced population in South Carolina indicated that shields began to develop as early as 9–12 months of age and increased to be found in all adults, 36 months of age and older. The thickness varied seasonally but was greatest during the breeding season, corroborating the shield's function as a protective barrier during male-to-male aggressive encounters.

A castrated male is called a **barrow** or "bar" in the hog-hunting circles. Often, when a male is captured in a trap, bayed, or cornered by dogs, many hunters will castrate it on the spot in the hope that the animal will produce

A sounder of hogs.

longer tusks. Although, in my experience, I've seen many cut hogs that never produced these hopeful results.

The social unit organization of a feral-hog population in the southeastern United States can generally be divided into three primary categories: Mixed adult/immature individuals comprise the largest commonly observed group, followed by immature groups, and then various groups of adults. Adult males are frequently most observed as solitary individuals. Based on field experience in Texas, I believe this social unit organization is characteristic in this area also, and probably throughout their entire range. Habitat types and increased hunting pressure may impact the various group structures.

Senses

Wild swine have an exceptional sense of smell. Their olfactory powers are so great that I have seen them root holes as deep as three feet in South Texas in an effort to dig up the roots or tubers of desired plants. They are constantly sticking their noses into the air in an attempt to get a whiff of whatever may be around, be it food or danger. In France, their domestic counterparts have been trained to search for truffles, an edible, underground, fleshy fungus (mushroom family) much desired for gourmet cuisine.

When not making excessive noises while eating, a hog's hearing is very well developed. Unlike many domestic breeds, the feral hog's ears are erect, enabling them to channel sounds better. Their eyes, on the other hand, are small and their vision is poor. As with most mammals, hogs cannot distinguish vibrant colors but rather various shades of white, black, and gray.

I believe wild hogs also possess the infamous sixth sense—the ability to sense danger. On numerous occasions, I have seen wild hogs run off for no apparent reason. I have been the only person in a pasture, well concealed with the wind and sun in my favor, and not moving a visible muscle, yet they have bolted for safety. It's as if they knew I was there and what my intentions were.

Communication

Hogs communicate with each other in a number of ways: vocalizations, behavior, and smell. There are several sounds that hogs use to communicate. Hogs are fairly noisy as they feed, continually emitting a grunting sound. This low, guttural sound allows other hogs to know their location. For the hunter, hearing this sound can prepare him for a successful stalk.

Another vocalization is the alarm sound that is characterized by a loud expulsion of air sounding somewhat like a *"whuff."* This usually takes place when a hog has been unsuspectingly startled or scared. This single syllable *"whuff"* or grunt is generally the last sound you hear as the hog rushes off.

Hogs also signal distress. This squeal occurs when the hog is scared or in pain. It can be heard when handling live hogs, when a hog is first struck by a hunter's bullet, or if a hog is wounded.

During breeding activities, male and female hogs may emit distinctive jaw-popping sounds. When cornered or trapped, hogs often pop their jaws, and this is a usual precursor to an attack. On numerous occasions, I've had trapped hogs pop their teeth prior to a charge.

Hogs have a dominance hierarchy and use visual signs as a warning. The initial warning is a fierce stare that intimidates younger or subordinate animals to back down. Laid-back ears and stiff, raised hair is another warning sign for a subordinate pig to back off. The final visual sign of warning is the stiff-legged sidle walk or broadside push, which, if not hindered, will result in fighting. Fighting usually occurs between two males over a female. The nuzzle is a movement in which the hogs push others frequently such as a sow making the piglets move in a way momma wants them to go.

The olfactory sense is important for breeding, feeding, or territorial purposes. When breeding, few animals smell as odoriferous as a big boar. This robust smell is used for attracting females and to warn off other boars. The sow in estrus emits a smell of her own to attract a boar. Boars defecate and urinate to establish territory and warn other hogs not to intrude.

Reproduction

Research in Texas has found feral hogs capable of breeding year-round, with peak breeding periods occurring in the summer and fall. We studied reproduction of feral pigs in two regions of southern Texas including the Gulf Coast prairies and western South Texas plains. The pregnancy rates of adults older than 21 months of age ranged from 78 percent in winter in the Gulf Coast prairie to 6 percent in summer in the western area.

The majority of feral hogs will produce only one litter per year although they are capable of producing two. A small percent of sows may have a second litter when nutritious forage is available year-round, or if litters are lost soon after birth. In South Texas, the long growing season, high nutritional value of the vegetation, and quantity of various mast-producing plants contribute to this success. Second litters are more apt to occur in mature adults because of larger body mass and, in turn, more nutrient reserves.

Litter sizes may range from 4 to 12 with an average of 5 to 6 piglets. In our study, the average litter size for feral hogs throughout their range is

5.7. Feral hogs have larger litter sizes than the Eurasian wild boar, which average about 4.8 piglets per litter. The litter sizes in adults were greater than those of 12–21 months.

We found that feral hogs in South Texas had similar characteristics to feral hogs in other parts of its range. Seasonality of reproduction of feral pigs in South Texas also was consistent with reproduction in other native or introduced populations. Factors attributed to driving reproduction in feral hogs include nutrition and photoperiod. In South Texas the quality of forage during the breeding periods was high. Pigs are also very promiscuous and may mate with multiple individuals. Using genetic information from wild pregnant sows in South Texas, one study found 33 percent of the litters were sired by at least two boars.

In our study, we believed that high temperatures play a role in the seasonality of breeding. Peak breeding coincides with peaks in precipitation and moderate temperatures for the region. While sexual maturity is attained at 9 months, under good nutritional conditions, females may breed at 6 months. Female feral hogs are polyestrous and are in heat for a 48-hour period on a 21-day estrus cycle.

Gestation for hogs is approximately 115 days or as the old saying goes: "three months, three weeks, and three days." Although feral hogs seldom will have more than one litter per year, they are capable of breeding at 6 months, so at the end of the first year a female may be a grandmother! However you describe it, feral hogs are extremely prolific. In South Texas, season peaks of birth were observed in early spring and early summer. The sex ratio of fetuses in South Texas was slightly male-biased but did not differ from 50:50.

A hypothetical population model with a single adult female having an average litter of 6 young with an even sex ratio that includes 3 males and 3 females could have a final year population of 25, assuming no mortality. If you carry that out over several years with no mortality, the population can increase exponentially! So even considering the natural mortality of feral hogs, one female that produces only one litter can increase the population appreciably.

Wild hogs will build nests in which to farrow their young. This characteristic is common with most mammalian species. For the wild hog, the birthing place is generally a small depression in the ground lined with grass, leaves, and twigs. The sow will also try to find a protection under brush or in a thicket. When the time for parturition nears, she will enter the nest and lie down on her side to give birth. Within minutes of birth, the young will reach their mother's teats and establish nipple order. This they will defend against the other littermates. Within a few days the young will be up and following their mother; they will already have begun to forage and eat solid foods, but milk is still the primary source of nutrients for the piglets. Young hogs or **shoats**, are weaned around 7–8 weeks.

The majority of wild pigs are born with horizontal red, light tan / brown, and yellow stripes similar to the geometric marks on watermelon. This is nature's way of camouflaging the youngsters. When they are about 8–12 weeks old, the striped pattern gradually turns into a solid, grizzled, or dark coloration. Many of the early researchers believed that the striped young were a distinguishing characteristic of the Russian boar. This has proved to be incorrect because many feral pigs also exhibit the striped pattern.

Food Habits

The diets of feral hogs have been researched extensively throughout the United States, including in California, Texas, Florida, and Tennessee. While much of the foraging activities of feral hogs are known, the long-term effects of foraging on native flora and fauna are relatively unknown and could possibly be the most detrimental.

As part of a team of biologists for Texas Parks and Wildlife Department, we investigated the food habits and seasonal food components in the diets of feral hogs in the semiarid environment of South Texas. We also examined the relationship of food habits to habitat and climate, as well as the possible impact feral-hog foraging had on game and nongame species. We compared our results with other food habit studies conducted throughout the United States to determine potential differences. I feel that by knowing the annual and seasonal diets of feral hogs as well as climatic relationships, it's possible for managers to make better decisions.

The results of our surveys showed that the diet of feral hogs in the Rio Grande plains of South Texas was composed chiefly of plant materials. When available, feral hogs selected forbs from among herbaceous forages. Oaks are not abundant in western South Texas, so acorns are replaced by various acacia beans (e.g. guajillo, blackbrush), mesquite, and corn.

Animal matter constituted only a small percent of the feral hog's diet in South Texas. This compares with the majority of other studies conducted throughout the United States. In South Carolina, animal matter included centipedes, earthworms, grubs, crabs, and mussels, whereas in Tennessee, primary animal matter included earthworms; centipedes; millipedes; and beetle, moth, butterfly, and fly larvae (maggots). (Because I believe it's important to understand how biological information is obtained, this study is discussed in detail in Appendix II.)

Mortality

Other than humans, feral hogs have very few natural predators, and this lack of natural enemies contributes greatly to their success. Mountain lions, bears, and wolves may take a few but not enough to significantly affect the population. There are many places where appreciable numbers of large predators coexist with multitudes of feral hogs. A prime example can be found in the Nueces River drainage of South Texas. This area sustains one of the densest populations of feral hogs in the state along with a relatively heavy concentration of mountain lions.

The young are especially susceptible to predation from smaller predators such as bobcats, coyotes, foxes, alligators, and feral dogs. Disease is another cause of mortality in wild hogs, especially among the young. Young pigs also die from starvation, parasites, or suffocation, which can occur when a sow rolls over a young one in the nest. Many studies indicate that dental problems also play a role in mortality.

Although hogs have been documented as reaching ten years or more of age, this is not the norm. Of all the feral hogs that we collected in our South Texas study, only one in 300 reached 72 months (6 years) of age. As a whole, the life expectancy of feral hogs is 4–5 years.

Diseases and Parasites

Feral hogs carry diseases, which is one of the main reasons to be concerned about an increasing feral hog population. According to health officials, as many as twenty-eight diseases have been identified as being carried by feral swine. In certain geographic locales, a significant percentage of the feral swine are infected with diseases, which can have a negative economic impact

This mountain lion was caught when it came back to the feral piglets that it had killed the previous night.

on farmers raising domestic pigs nearby. The diseases that cause the most concern among landowners, livestock operators, and animal health officials are pseudorabies and swine brucellosis.

Pseudorabies is not a form of rabies as we know it. Commonly referred to as "mad itch," this herpes virus weakens pigs, causes young sows to abort, and also kills young piglets. The virus attacks the nervous system and produces intense itching—hence the name mad itch; this stage is followed by paralysis and death. Young pigs are the most susceptible to the disease. Symptoms include lack of coordination, staggering, muscle tremors, and convulsions. Death occurs within twelve hours after symptoms appear.

In older or growing hogs, the disease is less severe. Symptoms in adults include fever, sneezing, coughing, nasal discharge, trembling, convulsions, and abortion. It is transmitted primarily through breeding (via sexual contact) but is also believed to be transmitted through respiratory secretions of the infected animal. Some scientists and epidemiologists claim that domestic swine producers in Florida are nine times more likely to have pseudorabies in their herds if feral swine are nearby.

Pseudorabies is not transmittable to humans but can be a fatal infection to other farm animals such as cattle, sheep, goats, dogs, and cats. Yet it is the potentially deadly effect on commercial-swine operations that causes the most concerns. Wildlife, including raccoons, possums, skunks, foxes, and small rodents may also be fatally infected.

Swine brucellosis is caused by the bacterium *Brucella suis* and is a disease that can cause abortion, low conception rates, stillborn or weak pigs, infertility in boars, and other reproductive problems. It is transmitted through reproductive discharges such as afterbirth from sows or semen from boars. Infected swine are carriers for life and must be destroyed because there are no effective treatments. While it generally will not kill the hogs, the drop in reproductive rates will decrease profit for commercial operations.

Although rare, it can be transmitted to other animals including humans. In humans, it is known as undulant or Malta fever and can be treated with antibiotics. Flulike symptoms include recurring fever, chills, sweating, weakness, headaches, muscle and joint pains, loss of appetite, and weight loss.

Hog cholera is caused by a virus and is a rapidly progressing sickness that was once the most economically devastating disease in domestic swine in the United States. It was eradicated from the United States in 1978; however, there is concern that feral hogs can possibly reintroduce this disease to domestic swine.

Feral swine represent a real danger, disease-wise, to domestic swine. In addition to the diseases already mentioned, it is possible for feral swine to harbor or be carriers of diseases such as foot and mouth disease and African swine fever that are not currently present in the United States. Other diseases that hogs may carry include leptospirosis, tuberculosis, scours, swine dysentery, swine influenza, and plague. All of the above-mentioned diseases may detrimentally affect domestic herds and cause severe economic problems for individual hog producers within the pork industry.

Eradications Programs

Nationwide pseudorabies and swine brucellosis eradication campaigns were initiated to stop these diseases from spreading. In 1989, a National Pseudorabies Eradication Program began, and the Swine Brucellosis Eradication program has been in place for over thirty years. The primary purpose of these two programs is to eliminate these diseases from domestic herds through a state-by-state, three-stage program. Stage three is the top level where no more than one brucellosis-infected herd is found over a two-year period. Although feral swine pose a threat to these programs, scientists believe these diseases can be eradicated in domestic swine herds.

Precautions for Individuals

The United States Department of Agriculture, Animal and Plant Inspection Service, has established guidelines to minimize the potential threat of these diseases to domestic animal operations. These include the following precautions: blood tests of all breeding stock and all new stock; maintenance of an exclusion fence from wild swine; avoidance of butchering wild swine on the farm or feeding offal (guts) to domestic swine; and, above all, never introducing wild swine into the herd or the environs.

Hunters and landowners should take precautions when handling wild swine. They should avoid direct contact with blood or reproductive organs by using disposable or rubber gloves when cleaning the animals. Burn or bury the used gloves with the remains of the wild hog, followed by thoroughly washing your hands with soap and water. It's important to note that these diseases do not affect the meat and it can still be eaten. All pork should be thoroughly cooked.

Parasites

Feral hogs can have numerous types of internal and external parasites. The variety and severity depends on many factors including location, season, and climate. Excessive infection rates of internal parasites may contribute to mortality. While under certain conditions, external parasites may impact certain individual hogs, they seem, overall, to have little effect on mortality or on the general population.

Internal Parasites

The **roundworm**, or ascarid, is a large intestinal nematode and one of the most prevalent internal parasites. Intestinal roundworms are common in wild swine but reportedly have minimal impact on wild populations. The life cycle begins in the intestines where adults produce eggs that are passed through the feces. The eggs are then eaten by swine, where the larvae hatch in the intestines and burrow through the intestinal wall and travel through the blood stream. They work their way through the liver and eventually to the trachea where they are coughed up and swallowed; they then mature in the intestines, where the cycles begins again.

Roundworms are usually pink to yellowish in color and may be as long as one foot. The majority of damage from roundworms occurs in the lungs but severe scarring in the liver may also occur. The major effect is on young pigs less than five months of age and symptoms may include diarrhea, coughing, poor health and appearance, and weight loss. A heavy infestation may even cause death.

Trichinosis is an internal nematode parasite that is highly infectious to man and is generally associated with consumption of improperly cooked pork. The parasite begins its life cycle in the intestinal tract before migrating into and encysting in the muscle tissue where it may survive for several years. In the arid region of South Texas, our studies revealed an infection rate to be nonexistent; however, in wetter and more humid zones, the infection rate is higher. Trichinosis is uncommon in wild swine, with one of the only documented regions of infected wild swine occurring in Florida. A study of slaughterhouses indicated that most infected domestic hogs were fed garbage. While trichinosis is transmittable to humans, proper care and thorough cooking of pork eliminates or kills the cysts.

Lungworms are fairly common in wild swine. As the name suggests, lungworms are internal nematode parasites found in the lungs and air passages. Lungworms are whitish in color and usually from 1½ to 2 inches in length. Lungworm eggs are deposited on the ground and then eaten by earthworms; the earthworms are then eaten by hogs, which subsequently become infected. The worms then begin their life's journey from the intestines and stomach. Affected lungs may appear perforated with hemorrhages. Animals with heavy infestation may show signs of respiratory problems and even pneumonia.

Kidney worms are nematodes found in the kidneys and surrounding tissue, and occasionally in the abdomen or throat. Scarring can be found in the tissue where the larva has migrated. Kidney worms may cause mortality and increased infection from other internal parasites. I know of no known health implication; however, hunters should shy away from eating scarred pork kidneys.

Stomach Worms

Wild swine are host to three species of stomach nematodes, and in cases of heavy infestation these hogs may appear weak and sickly. The life

South Texas wildlife district with hogs collected for research. Author is on top of pile. (Photo courtesy of Joe Herrera)

cycle of stomach worms begins in the stomach where eggs are produced and passed in the feces. Dung beetles eat the eggs and swine become infected by consuming infected beetles; thus, the cycle repeats itself. Hunters may find stomach worms when cleaning the wild swine, but they are not thought to be transmitted to humans. Other internal parasites may include thorny-headed worms, whipworms, and liver flukes.

External Parasites

Feral hogs may harbor several types of external parasites. The most common include fleas, ticks, lice, and mites. Geographic regions of high humidity or constant moisture increase the infestation rate of external parasites in feral hogs.

Hog Lice

Hog lice are commonplace on wild swine and can usually be seen behind the ears, around the belly, in the underside folds of skin between the shoulders and chest, and between the back legs. While generally not problematic, heavily infected swine may show signs of irritation caused by intense scratching of itchy body parts. This activity may even decrease the animals' natural disease resistance. Because lice are bloodsuckers, young pigs may develop anemia.

Fleas and Ticks

Fleas and ticks are fairly common on wild swine. Perhaps eighteen species of ticks have been found on white-tailed deer in North America. Most likely, there are probably that many tick species found on wild swine. The brown dog tick and the lone star tick are a couple of the more common species found.

Fleas are also common on hogs especially in the wetter and more humid areas of the eastern and southeastern belts near the Gulf Coast. In South Texas, we often find hogs free of external parasites in the drier upland farms and ranches. However, even in a dry year we were attacked unmercifully by fleas and ticks along river bottoms and drainages when collecting specimens. On one memorable hog-collecting trip in the Nueces River bottoms of South Texas, they almost drove us crazy; it took us several days to decontaminate ourselves of the little beggars.

Mange Mites

There are two types of mange found on wild swine: sarcoptic mange and demodectic mange. Sarcoptic mange is the most prevalent kind of mange, and in this type the mite burrows under the skin and causes irritation and thickening of the skin. Heavy infestation causes extreme itching and discomfort through the continual rubbing and scratching of infested body parts. In severe cases, the entire body surface may lose hair and become covered in thick scaly skin. In severe cases, appetite may be reduced and overall health and weight may be depressed. Demodectic mange is more common in white-tailed deer than in swine; it is usually less severe than sarcoptic mange because the mites do not penetrate so deeply into the skin.

Hog Abnormalities

Feral hogs can have deformities just like most animals in nature. While I've never seen an albino hog, I'm confident that somewhere one has been born. It is highly unlikely that it would survive the tough natural world since it would be vulnerable to predation, sunburn, disease, and other factors. Abnormalities that are found in hogs, however uncommon, are worth mentioning and include the mule-footed hog and neck wattles on hogs.

Mule-Footed Hogs

Mule-footed hogs occur when the cloven hoofs grow together to form a single hoof. According to one man in East Texas, mule-footed hogs seem rather common in the vicinities around Athens, Palestine, Van, and Lindale. He claimed that when trapped they were more aggressive and stronger than the normal feral hogs.

There is an actual domestic swine line of mule-footed hogs. Fans of this breed have formed a breeder's organization called the National Mulefoot Hog Association. The American mulefoot is the only documented population found with a breed standard and a long history of agricultural use. This breed is unique to the United States and is significantly rare. According to the Oklahoma State University the most distinctive feature of the American mulefoot hog is the solid hoof that resembles that of a mule. Pigs with solid hoofs have attracted the interest of many writers over the centuries, including Aristotle and Darwin.

The origin of the American mulefoot breed is not clear, but it has a well-documented history over the last century. F. D. Coburn in his classic 1916 book, *Swine in America,* notes that the mulefoot hog was found in Arkansas, Missouri, Iowa, Indiana, across the southwest, and in some parts of Mexico. (In southern Missouri and northern Arkansas, mulefoots were sometimes called "Ozark pigs.")

The report went on to say that, "A remnant population of the American mulefoot has been owned by R. M. Holliday of Louisiana, Missouri, for nearly forty years. He remembers from boyhood that his family and others raised these hogs by putting them on islands in the Missouri and Mississippi Rivers to forage during the summer and then rounding them up in the fall for slaughter. This practice was terminated by the Army Corps of Engineers in the 1950s." Could the mule-footed hogs we find in the woods actually be the descendants of its own breed or just a genetic abnormality?

Neck Wattles

Neck wattles are skinlike flaps hanging from the throat near the base of the lower jaw. These harmless projections usually hang in pairs and are covered by normal skin. According to one swine science book, it is a trait caused by a simple dominant gene. Furthermore, approximately 75 percent of the offspring of two hogs with wattles will also have wattles. I personally have never seen neck wattles on a wild hog; however, I have heard reports that they exist in feral hogs, which is why I am including them in this section.

Other abnormalities include anatomical defects, most of which are associated with inherited recessive genes. Some inherited defects may be lethal such as hind-leg paralysis, cleft palate, skeletal and other physical defects, and hydrocephalus (fluids in or around the brain), while others may not be lethal. Diseases, malnutrition, or other environmental factors, which aren't fatal, may also produce abnormalities. I have heard a report from the Trinity River bottoms in East Texas of a six-footed hog. This big boar evidently has an extra set of legs protruding from the front knees.

The Bad, the Good, and the Ugly

CHAPTER 5

So we organized against 'er—
Got the best of dogs and men;
But we never got good started
Puttin' that hog in a pen.

Now we really went a-huntin'
When we tried to catch Ole Spot;
We left the ranch at daylight
And her trail was always hot.

She might be pickin' acorns
On the banks of Sandy Creek,
Or in somebody's turnips
Cultivatin', so to speak.

From *That Spotted Sow and Other Texas Hill Country Ballads*
by Carlos Ashley

While working for Texas Parks and Wildlife in the late 1990s, I had just completed a late night spotlight deer survey and was headed back home for much needed rest. With only a few hundred miles on my new government pickup, the interior of the truck still had that new vehicle smell. Headed south out of the south-central Texas town of Utopia, my mind was preoccupied with the day's activities when out of the grassy bar

A road killed feral hog.

ditch erupted a darting herd of big dark forms. That's right, my truck was the bowling ball and the wild hogs were the pins. As they shot out of the ditch, I knew I couldn't swerve, so I white-knuckled the steering wheel and plowed through the herd. I could see a vehicle behind me and I watched him also swerve.

I pulled off onto the roadside when the other vehicle stopped beside me. After assuring the occupant that everything was OK, I turned around to check the carnage. In the middle of the road were four dead wild hogs. With one headlight, I made my way home only to get the repair bill of several hundred dollars. This is just one example where wild hogs are becoming more and more of a driving hazard throughout their range. Most are dark in color, and unlike deer, their eyes don't reflect easily in the headlights to warn approaching traffic. With their low center of gravity, a crash becomes like hitting a boulder.

As the feral hog population has burgeoned throughout the United States, damage such as that done to my vehicle has become more commonplace. This proliferation of feral hogs has come about because of better livestock and wildlife management through improved agricultural practices, range and habitat management, water development, and supplemental feeding. Better domestic animal husbandry such as vaccinations and the eradication of certain swine diseases have also indirectly benefited wild hogs. Besides man, feral hogs have few natural large predators after they reach about two months of age. Before that coyotes, bobcats, mountain lions, and a few other large predators prey on the young porkers.

In 1991, Texas hosted a feral hog symposium entitled "Feral Swine: A Compendium for Resource Managers." This event attracted approximately three hundred people who were concerned with the effect the prolific feral hog population is having on the environment. Similar symposia have been presented in Florida, California, and several other states, also attracting similar crowds. These symposia have drawn people from all over the United States and as well as from other countries. Scientists, ecologists, landowners, and sportsmen all have a stake in this issue, and all have opinions as to what strategy to pursue.

Since 2008, International Wild Pig Conferences have been held biennially in different states to address all aspects of feral hogs. These include state-by-state updates, research projects, diseases, and control methods to name a few topics. The common theme is the increase and expansion of the feral hog population and the unanimous concern regarding its management and control. Much research has been conducted and volumes have been written on the wild hog, its biology, and the environmental effects of an increasing feral population.

Although untold numbers of people have discussed and debated the negative attributes to this exotic invader, many people admire it. In fact, in many instances, the feral hog has created a cottage industry. From hunting and meat markets, to taxidermists and local economies, the feral hog is creating its own economic niche. So call it what you may—good, bad, or ugly—how you view it is clearly in the eye of the beholder.

A statewide attitude survey was conducted in Texas in 1993 to assess distribution, problems, and the commercial potential of feral hogs. The results indicated the majority of respondents had mixed feelings towards the feral hog depending upon their economic involvement. The majority of negative concerns came from those who had suffered damage to farm crops. Another finding showed that there were only limited commercial hunting opportunities available for hunting feral hogs for profit, so the potential in that area was underutilized.

Due to the increase in wild hogs at Big Bend National Park in the Trans-Pecos region of Texas, the National Park Service initiated an attitude survey in 2003 regarding wild hogs in this region. Conducting an attitudinal survey among neighboring landowners and other stakeholders is a prerequisite before the park can take any management actions. This initial regional study was subsequently expanded to determine the consequences of feral hog invasions in several ecoregions of Texas, excluding the high plains in the western panhandle.

Overall, respondents felt that feral hogs came from their neighbor's property and were an agricultural pest. They cited rooting, wallowing, and crop damage as the principal problems. Management implications from this study included the need for ongoing and increased educational programs on feral hogs, how landowners can make better use of feral hogs on their property, and the impact of this study on public policy and the decision-making process.

A secondary questionnaire tested the landowner's or land manager's knowledge of feral hogs, which was handed out at landowner workshops. Surprisingly, the average score was 11.5 out of 26 questions, thus revealing a lack of understanding about feral hog biology and their impact on other animals.

Similar studies have been conducted in Florida, California, and Illinois. In 1982, a study on the economic importance of feral swine in Florida concluded ". . . feral hogs represent a valuable recreational resource and are an integral part of the social fabric of many Florida counties."

The Bad

There is one consolation for all who destroy wild hogs—they are working for the public good.

Sir Samuel W. Baker, *Wild Beasts & Their Ways* (1890)

Agricultural Damage, Rooting, Wallows, and Water

Because of its severe impact on biological diversity, feral hogs are one of only fourteen mammals on the International Union for Conservation of Nature (IUCN) list of "100 of the World's Worst Invasive Alien Species." Although actual damage is hard to quantify, commonly repeated estimates of wild swine damage in the United States is $800 million per year. Crop damage estimates range from $1.8 in northern Florida to $57 million in Georgia. Reported agricultural damage, including crop damage, rooting, and wallowing caused by feral hogs in Texas exceeds several million dollars annually.

The Wildlife Services branch of the United States Department of Agriculture spend several thousand dollars each year for feral-hog control in Texas alone. Wildlife Services documented 4,700 cases of reported damage in 1998 compared to only 66 reports in 1983, an example that demonstrates the significant increase in damage caused by feral hogs in Texas. Although the extent of agricultural and urban damage is fairly well documented, the damage caused by feral hogs extends beyond these boundaries. In 2005 the Texas Legislature appropriated $500,000 to the Texas Department of Agriculture to launch research efforts to address the state's feral-hog problem.

They have been called a small bulldozer in low gear pulling a root plow with unlimited fuel, or a continuously refueling bulldozer. The feeding habits of feral hogs cause the most problems and concern among landowners. These hogs cherish such farm crops as corn, milo, rice, wheat, watermelons, peanuts, and hayfields, wreaking havoc and causing millions of dollars in damage. In Texas, feral hogs are one of the top three animals for causing agricultural damage and the number two predator—behind coyotes—in the depredation of sheep and goats in the hill country of central Texas.

Feral hog damage to corn crop. (Photo courtesy of USDA/APHIS)

In its search for food, wild hogs root with their snouts and forefeet to dig up the soil. These excavations may be several inches to a few feet in depth and may extend many feet in all directions. Soil type, location, and food availability determine the size and depth of these holes. In soft ground, a heavy, mature hog can plow short trenches deep enough to bury a basketball. Because the primary reason for rooting is to search for a meal of roots, tubers, invertebrates, and amphibians (in wet areas), food type also plays a key role in the dimensions of these excavations.

I discovered the danger these rooted holes represent to humans many years ago while working at the Chaparral Wildlife Management Area, located between San Antonio and Laredo. We were conducting white-tailed deer research that entailed spotlighting at night with two observers in a seat located above the cab of the pickup. Upon turning a corner of a grassy, overgrown *sendero* (a cleared lane that can sometimes serve as a ranch road), the front left wheel of the truck suddenly and without warning dropped out of sight into a depression. The sudden stop almost catapulted us over the top. Fortunately, there was a rail that prevented what could have been a long night at the hospital. The cause of this accident was a rooted hog hole that was at least two feet deep. It took another truck to pull us out of this predicament!

Wallows are indentions found in wet, muddy areas where the hog has rooted or rolled around to keep itself cool. Wallows can be in wet seeps, livestock tanks, collections of water around windmills, or muddy creeks. Hogs roll around in the muck to fight the heat and coat themselves with mud, thus protecting themselves from biting insects. Wallows are easy to distinguish from rootings because wallows have a bowl-like appearance in the mud; these frequently shows hair marks where the hog was lying.

In addition to eating crops, trampling and rooting while feeding in farmland causes collateral damage. Their rooting and wallowing activities can scar and damage native rangelands, destroy habitat, destabilize tank dams, spoil pooled water and watering areas, and generally damage or destroy agriculturally related entities such as livestock and wildlife feeders.

In the Great Smoky Mountains of Tennessee and North Carolina, researchers found movement activities were associated with temperature and elevation. Rooting and wallowing occurred at higher elevations in the warmer months and at the lower elevations in the cooler months. As food availability increased or decreased due to temperature or seasonal changes, foraging activity was altered. The wild hog's ability to adapt to various elevations allowed it to cause damage to all areas it inhabited.

An additional problem is competition between feral hogs and livestock for food. Food-habit studies as well as historical references prove that hogs are primarily herbivorous and will eat and root on rangeland that could be used by domestic livestock. The rooting activity may further negatively affect forage production. The extent of damage is dependent on many factors such as geographic location, soil type, grazing pressure, and environmental conditions. Damage caused by feral hogs to fencing can be expensive: cost of replacing the fences, an increase in predation, and the potential loss of livestock.

Look how deep wild hogs rooted here in the Chaparral Wildlife Management Area.

Feral hogs compete with native wildlife for preferred foods such as mast and forbs. The extent of the impact feral hogs may have on native wildlife populations—in terms of competition for food, predation, and displacement—is unknown. In South Texas, for example, the native javelina is declining while the feral hog population continues to increase. It is unknown if there is a direct causal relationship.

There is also concern about the transmission of diseases, specifically swine brucellosis and pseudorabies, to domestic livestock and native wildlife. In Texas, these diseases have been documented in wild swine; however, the extent of the transmission of diseases from wild hogs to wildlife is unknown. Most large commercial swine operations have extensive protection procedures and clean facilities. The smaller farms and mom-and-pop-type producers run the greatest risk of having their domestic hogs infected with diseases. Many of these operations have poor facilities that include deteriorated or nonexistent fences, and these enable wild swine to come in contact with domestic ones.

Feral hogs are not just a United States problem, but also an international problem. In Australia, a publication of the Bureau of Resource Sciences entitled *Managing Vertebrate Pests: Feral Pigs* suggests feral-pig damage to agricultural production is possibly near 100 million dollars annually. Australian damage includes predation on newborn lambs, damage to grain crops, reduced yields of sugarcane, fruit, and vegetable crops, as well as damage to fences and water sources. New Zealand and many European countries have also documented extensive damage by feral hogs to agricultural commodities.

In *Wild Beasts & Their Ways*, published in 1890, Sir Samuel W. Baker states, "It is almost incredible, in certain countries where pigs are numerous, to witness the total destruction of crops committed by these animals. I have seen fields completely turned up as though by some agricultural

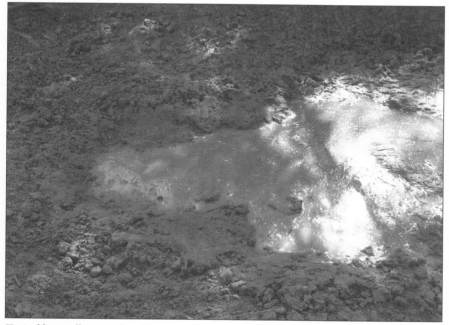

Typical hog wallow on edge of livestock tank.

implement, and actually nothing left; the industry of the cultivator being entirely wasted. Hundreds of wild pigs have been digging during the night in a newly sown field, in search of the grain, which would appear too insignificant for their notice.

"Among sugar-plantations they commit terrible havoc, as they bite the canes to obtain the juice. The wounded portion bleeds and ferments, rotting the cane, and damaging the quality of the sugar. In fact, wild pigs may be classed as only second to rats as destroyers of general produce." This was reported over a century ago!

Impacts to Water, Soil, and Vegetation

Feral hogs can pose significant damage to watering places, especially to environs hosting rare, sensitive, or fragile vegetation. Their rooting and wallowing activities can pollute or spoil water, destabilize tank dams, increase soil erosion, and increase turbidity or mudding; this, in turn, could affect fish and other aquatic life. Mentioned earlier, the wild hog in Big Bend National Park has begun encroaching into this desert environment. If hogs survive and establish themselves around the natural springs, water sources could be ruined and the fragile creatures that depend on this limited resource could be lost.

I have seen hogs tear up and destroy water troughs, pipelines, and water guzzlers (wildlife water catchments). Landowners may need to take protective measures to prevent destruction of watering areas or facilities, thus increasing the economic burden caused by the hogs.

While rooting by feral hogs has a direct impact on soil properties, researchers disagree on what those effects are. Litter decomposition is the primary means by which nutrients enter soil. Some researchers believe that rooting by wild pigs may enhance decomposition rates, thus increasing the nutrient cycling process. Rooting may also accelerate plant decomposition, alter nutrient cycling, and increase leaching of certain minerals. The extent and the effects are dependent on location, soil type, topography, and many other factors. There is secondary impact wild hogs may have on soil properties as well: Tree health and vigor may decline because the nutrients are drained too fast.

Typical rooting by wild hogs.

Native vegetation may be damaged and plant successional changes reduced through extensive rooting. Rooting may disrupt vegetational communities and their successional patterns, thus altering ground or forest-floor habitat. It also may impede plant reproduction if seedlings are consumed too vigorously. Species diversity and amount or volume of vegetation also may become restricted. One researcher noted a substantial increase in vegetative cover when hogs were excluded from a given area. There is also the possibility that undesirable nonnative grasses and forbs will increase as native species are rooted or eaten.

Feral hogs can also damage forests by uprooting seedlings in pine forests. Another researcher documented hogs rooted over 8,300 two-year old longleaf pine seedlings per acre at rates estimated from 200–400 seedlings per day. Under the right conditions, the rate could be increased substantially. In one day a single hog could remove an acre of planted pines.

In Louisiana, extensive damage was documented in fresh, intermediate, brackish, and salt-water-marsh habitats with damage estimated at approximately 227.5 acres out of 141,640 acres observed. As feral hog populations encroach in these marsh habitats, damage could increase significantly seriously, negatively impacting these unique and sensitive ecosystems.

Then there are the accidental or indirect impacts such was reported by the *Crosbyton Review* published on 29 February 29, 1912: "A very destructive fire occurred during the month of June 1879. The fire originated on the Z-L Ranch in Crosby County (Texas), where there was considerable shinnery [dense growth vegetation]. Hundreds of wild hogs ranged this dwarf oak country, prolific and hardy upon the acorns that grew there. Hank Smith, the first settler in the South Plains region, described this fire and the hogs.

"One day a cowboy decided he would set fire to the shinneries and run the hogs out. He did it all right, but is to be hoped that no one else will ever try to drive wild hogs out of shinnery country with fire. The fire got away and started on a wild rampage in a northeasterly direction. No one has ever learned for certain which way the hogs went.

"The fire swept thousands of square miles to the south and southwest, north and northeast of Mount Blanco. [The fire ravaged] all through the country at that time, especially along the streams, where hundreds of magnificent groves of fine timber, particularly cottonwood and hackberry. This fire killed the timber and in effect literally wiped it out."

So no matter how angry you get toward the wild hogs and the damage they cause, let the above story be a lesson that things can get worse.

Negative Impacts on Wildlife

According to some studies, feral hogs may compete with several species of wildlife for specific seasonal food. Because hogs are efficient foragers, they may reduce the availability of food for other wildlife. In our South Texas study we reviewed food preferences of various game and nongame wildlife to determine potential effects feral hogs may have on them.

White-tailed deer (*Odocoileus virginianus*) and javelina or collared peccary (*Pecari tajacu*) are the most numerous and economically important game species found in South Texas. Competition between native wild-life and hogs for food and space is a concern among land managers and sportsmen. One researcher stated that competition between hogs and deer differed on a seasonal and yearly basis and was based on abundance and diversity of foods.

White-tailed deer are primarily browsers, but forbs, mast, and cactus are extremely important food items in South Texas. Javelina feed on prickly pear pads and fruit, forbs, hard and soft mast, and some browse. The high consumption of herbaceous plants and mast by deer and hogs indicates seasonal competition. Hogs, deer, and javelina have dietary overlap and compete for preferred foods such as acorns, mesquite beans, prickly pear fruit, and acacia beans.

Competition for food is most critical in the late winter when vegetation availability and diet quality is low but diet overlap is high. Late-winter defoliation of browse plants and droughty conditions increase competition between deer and hogs for other available foods in South Texas. The degree of competition is unknown and assumed to be directly related to range conditions, vegetation diversity, forage availability, and animal density.

Woody browse constitutes only a small amount of the hog's diet; therefore, there is very little competition with deer and javelina for browse. Grass, a major component of a hog's diet, was only a minor component of the diets of deer and javelina. When food becomes limited, feral hogs are capable of shifting their diets to a wide selection of other available foods and with no apparent consequences. In South Texas, corn is an important feed for deer and javelina in late winter. Competition for supplemental feed, especially corn, at wildlife feeders may be intense at times.

Seed-eating birds such as turkey, quail, and mourning doves generally pick seeds from the ground, and hogs will consume seed-producing plants and seed heads. Although some competition may exist for the seed heads, it is unlikely that feral hogs by themselves would cause a depletion of that type of food source. They may even benefit seed-eating birds by knocking the seeds off a plant, thus producing more plants and subsequently increasing the

Feral hogs and wild turkeys are competitors!

availability of that particular food source. In addition to eating seeds, turkeys eat green vegetation throughout the year supplemented by insects when available. Feral hogs compete directly with turkey for seasonal foods such as fruit, nuts, and seeds. However, the extent and effects of hog competition with game birds is unknown.

As a predator, feral hogs do not appear to pose a significant threat to wildlife in the Rio Grande Plains. Animal matter constitutes a minor part of the diet; however, it is unknown whether the animal matter was scavenged or preyed upon. Our South Texas food habit study reinforced similar conclusions found in East Texas concerning the insignificance of predation on deer by feral hogs. Another food-habit study conducted in South Carolina reinforces the insignificance of predation on ground nesting birds, or any serious predatory effect on other populations of vertebrates.

Although some researchers have documented the destruction of simulated ground (dummy) nests by feral hogs, our study found no evidence of predation on ground-nesting birds in South Texas. Reptiles appear to be the most susceptible species to feral hog predation in the Rio Grande Plains. In East Texas, lizards were found in the diet of feral hogs, and similarly, in the coastal prairies of South Texas, reptiles and amphibians were commonly found in feral hog diets, with snakes the only vertebrates found in all seasons. Cold temperatures may conceivably increase vulnerability of reptiles and amphibians by decreasing their activity as hog activity increases.

The food preferences and destructive impact on the habitat by wild hogs have many scientists concerned about the effect they may have on sensitive wildlife and plant species. One special Texas concern involves the endangered Houston toad. This species is found only in southeastern Texas, in the pine,

Feral hogs in cattle feed trough. (Photo courtesy of Bob Zaiglin)

oak woodland, or savannah habitats and in low lying, wet, shady areas. In these ideal hangouts, feral hogs destroy toad habitat by rooting, wallowing, and even preying upon toads.

In Texas, where baiting for wildlife is an accepted practice to entice game, feral hogs can be the dominant creatures waiting for the feeder to disperse feed. Not surprisingly, many hunters and sportsmen put thirty-four-inch-high pens around their feeders. The deer are able to jump over where the hogs are not.

The same is also true about wildlife watering facilities: modified livestock waterers, stock tanks, or quail waterers. Because feral swine find water irresistible, I have seen a tremendous amount of damage to these facilities in my visits with landowners and in other travels. When feasible, protecting the wet places with a hog-proof fence can save repair costs and heartache.

Urban Damage

The damages that feral hogs commit are not limited to the agriculture community. Take for instance, the numerous golf courses across the United States. Ask the golf course maintenance personnel if these miniature rotor-rooters are only problems for the farmer and rancher! Many urban golf courses throughout the United States have reported damage from hogs rooting up huge chunks of turf.

Suburban neighborhoods, such as the exclusive retirement community of Oakmont in Sonoma, California, have been invaded. Damage to the fairways, lush lawns, and flower gardens are documented. Unfortunately, there's not much that can be done regarding this matter other than erecting a hog-proof fence around the course. Even then, there are no guarantees it would take care of the problems. Hogs have a tendency to go under or through any type of obstacle put in their way, especially if there's something they desire on the other side.

The same scene has played out in Texas, where Austin neighborhoods such as Jester Estates and Lost Creek have reported problems. Municipal courses on the outskirts of San Antonio such as Cedar Creek and Mission del Lago are stuffed with the hog's favorite food—grub worms. The damage

Damage from rooting hogs on a San Antonio golf course.

to the courses has cost the city of San Antonio thousands of dollars a year in labor to repair.

I have been told that a single golf course green can cost from $15,000 to $30,000! The director of golf for the city of San Antonio Parks and Recreation Department requested my assistance because of destruction caused by feral hogs at these two courses. I discovered firsthand the dilemma feral hogs pose to the urban dweller.

Unfortunately, city and county governments face tremendous challenges when attempting to correct the problems caused by feral hogs. Hog-proofing a golf course with fencing is often impractical and you can bet hunting within the city limits or on city property will be challenged by animal-rights activists. The use of snares could capture nontarget species such as domestic dogs, and using hog dogs to chase hogs into backyards and across busy thoroughfares is not an option. Although trapping is an alternative, the cost involved in continuous monitoring is outrageously expensive. Furthermore, even if the hogs were trapped, relocation and release into the wild is prohibited by law. And worst of all, euthanizing the trapped hogs can be politically sensitive and generate a firestorm of protests.

Bearing in mind all the above, my recommendations included a mixture or techniques including selective fencing of immigration corridors, increased and continuous trapping efforts, and donating the pork to local charities. Only time will tell whether these recommendations will prove successful. But as I explained in my report, limited efforts will result in only limited results.

The Fort Worth Nature Center is a 3,621-acre refuge believed to be the largest city-owned refuge in the nation. It includes forest, prairie, and Trinity River bottomland habitat; the entire center is located within the city limits. This refuge provides some of the best wild hog habitat in northern Texas. The nature center's hog-management program has been hailed as a national model for controlling nuisance wildlife effectively and humanely. The growing hog problem became serious around 2000 and through extensive negotiations with various stake-holders including environmental and animal-rights groups, an approach was developed. Trapping was conducted at night, checked at daylight, and the animals humanely euthanized before the refuge opened to the public. The limited time that hogs spent in the trap reduced stress on the animals and the quick dispatching of the animal averaged about four minutes per trap. According to Rob Denkhaus, the natural resource manager for the center, the environmental damage at the refuge has decreased significantly, proof that the hog control program is working.

The Good

Many people believe the feral hog has many redeeming qualities. Does the feral hog promote forage growth and water penetration in the landscape, thus improving habitat for some wildlife species? Economic returns may be increased through hunting lease values, hunting rights, or by providing an additional hunting species. Hunters in many states such as Texas, California, Florida, and

Tennessee consider the feral hog an important sporting commodity. Feral hogs provide an excellent off-season hunting opportunity. They are challenging to hunt, they are extremely intelligent and wary creatures, and they provide very good table fare. Local economies, taxidermists, meat-packing facilities, and many other entities profit from this species.

Ecological Benefits

Although damage inflicted by feral hogs is well documented and extensive in places, they also have some potential ecological and definite economic benefits. Ecologically, hog rooting opens and disturbs soil, thus allowing not only water to penetrate but also promoting the production of forbs. On well-managed ranges, foraging and rooting activities by feral hogs may actually benefit game and nongame birds. Some researchers claim these activities stimulate vegetation regrowth and slow the development of woody plants, thus increasing grass and forb seed sources and availability. Their foraging activities also may thin ground vegetation allowing more accessibility to seed-eating birds.

Litter decomposition is the primary means by which nutrients enter soils. Some researchers believe that wild pig rooting may enhance decomposition rates, thus increasing the nutrient cycling process. An increase in nitrate concentrations as well as gaseous carbon dioxide in the soil air due to the increased decomposition has been noted. A European study indicated that boar rooting behavior actually enhanced the growth of pine trees.

Festivals, Competitions, and Local Economies

Hog hunters bring many economic benefits into the local economy, especially during the off-season. The local economies benefit through purchases at grocery stores, sporting goods stores, feed stores, restaurants, and motels. This doesn't include the money paid to the landowner, guides, meat locker, or taxidermist, who indirectly continues to spread this income into the economy.

Basing my estimates on average costs in 2015, a hog hunter staying in a motel two nights would spend approximately $250 during his stay, including meals, groceries, gas, and supplies. If 1,000 hunters came through a town over the course of a year, they would bring in approximately $250,000 to the local economy. While the economic benefits vary with each ecological region or municipality, hog hunting can benefit a community. Non-hunting activities such as tourism, sightseeing, shopping, and positive publicity may provide additional economic benefits. The local chamber of commerce or tourism director can increase the economic benefits by providing these nonhunting activities so hunters will bring their families to enjoy the local attractions.

One of the first festivals designed to promote the wild swine was the Wild Hog Cook-Off, which is located in Cotulla about halfway between San Antonio and Laredo just off Interstate 35. This festival had been running annually for several decades. As the name implies, it is where outdoor chefs from all over Texas compete in a cook-off to claim the title of best wild hog barbecue. Wild hog meat is extremely tasty, and there is nowhere in the United States where the taste is more enjoyed or revered than in Cotulla, Texas. In addition to the cook-off, events include a ranch rodeo, carnival, and numerous booths and exhibits.

Sabinal, Texas, is the self-proclaimed "wild boar capital of the world" and is home to the world championship wild hog-catching contest. This competition involves humans catching wild hogs by hand and putting them in burlap sacks before racing to the finish line, and there are numerous divisions: peewees, runts, light, medium, and heavyweights.

Wild hogs are trapped on area ranches and hauled to a holding facility near the fairgrounds. The competitive divisions determine the sizes of the hogs used. Out first are the peewees, youngsters less than five years old, followed by the runt division of kids aged five to nine, then the light, medium, and heavyweights. As with the Cotulla festival, this festival features many other events include a chuck wagon cook-off, food, games, crafts, and a dance.

When my son, Shane, was eight, he won a trophy in the runt division. Several years later, my daughter, Mallory, and a friend beat out several boys' teams to win a belt buckle. The Lions Club sponsors the Sabinal wild hog catching and the proceeds benefit many charities: eye-screening for local and regional children, sponsoring handicapped children to a special summer

Wild hog catching in Sabinal, Texas.

camp, and so on. So you might say as an added benefit, wild hogs are used to benefit many charities.

The north-central Texas town of Paducah claims to be the "Wild Hog Capital of Texas" while in North Texas, the town of Crowell promotes itself as "The Wild Hog Capital of the Old West." It is obvious that wild hogs have infiltrated the very heart of the public and are being touted for the benefit of the local populace. Similar festivals occur outside Texas: the Ocmulgee Wild Hog festival in Abbeville, Georgia; the Hog Wild Barbeque Cook Off and Family Festival in Brookhaven, Mississippi; and the Go Wild Hog Festival in Temple, Oklahoma. There are probably many other towns across the United States to have found a use for the much-maligned wild hog.

Hog-dog trials and contests are becoming more and more common throughout the southeastern United States. Many people may ask what exactly is a hog dog and what does it do? Just as there are dog shows for breed competition and field trials for bird dogs, the hog dog trials are where wild hogs are trapped on local ranches and brought to the trials. The arena is typically about thirty feet in size with the dogs and handlers located on one end when the hog released at the opposite end. The handlers release the dogs, and the dogs try to stop the hog. The handler then must go to the bayed hog and either throw the hog down or remove the dog. It is as much a test of the owner's ability as it is the dog's.

There are two main types of hog dogs: the bay dog and the catch dog. The bay dog finds the hog and then chases it until it is stopped and cornered. The catch dog then takes the whatever opportunity there is to bite and latch onto whatever part of the hog that presents itself—until the hunter arrives to dispatch the animal. In a contest, these dogs are put to a test to demonstrate their abilities. Many of the legal contests are leaving out the catch dogs due to animal cruelty concerns that both hogs and dogs get hurt.

The contest may have several competitive divisions including one-dog baying, two-dog baying, and puppy baying. A wild hog is placed in an arena with the objective of seeing how long it takes the dog or dogs to stop the pig from running. Once the pig is stopped and faces the dog, the timed event is complete.

The two-dog baying contest represents a team and demonstrates how well two dogs can work together. If the dog catches, latches onto, or bites the hog, it can be disqualified. One of the funniest and most enjoyable competitions is the puppy contest. Here, young dogs are placed in an arena with juvenile wild hogs. This is puppy-training time as well as contest time. In what could be seen as reversal of roles, I've seen little pigs chase the dogs around and bay the puppies. On another occasion I watched the two enemies square off nose to nose, sniffing each other like long lost friends. Similar to watching good bird dogs, guard dogs, or seeing-eye dogs work, watching trained hounds at hog dog trials can be a very enjoyable spectator contest.

Hunting, Leasing, and Meat Markets

Economically, feral hogs have the potential for rewards through many avenues, the first of which is hunting. Feral hog hunting provides economic returns for landowners through leasing and/or package hunting. On privately owned land in Texas, lease values may be increased if wild hogs are present. The cost of a private ranch hunting lease ranges from $5 to $15-plus per acre or $1,000–$5,000 per gun per season. On many Texas ranches, wildlife is as valuable as or more valuable than livestock. Wildlife is an extremely important commodity for the landowner.

For wild-hog package hunts, prices range from $150 to $1,500 depending on the type of hunt. Trophy boar hunts with dogs, horses, meals, and lodging may even exceed this figure. Off-season hunts can bring $75–$125 per day minimum for the landowner or outfitter. Again, the prices increase with the amenities. Archery hunts, pistol hunts, and muzzle-loading hunts are also options. Landowners, outfitters, guides, locker plants, and taxidermists all have an economic stake in feral hogs.

A hog-hunting outfitter and friend of mine named Maurice Chambers is frequently asked to speak on the value of feral hogs. His speeches and his

Trophy buckle for hog dog competition. (Photo courtesy of John Miller)

Mounted heads of trophy hogs.

answers to audience questions are something to behold. At a feral-hog meeting in Fort Worth one year, Maurice gave some figures that made everyone take note. He mentioned a bow hunting website that in one year had 881,038 hits by hunters seeking a place to hunt hogs. He also mentioned a couple of outfitters who bring in 200–300 hog hunters per year at an average of $300 dollars each. To sum it up, Maurice plainly states, "It's like having $100 bills running around in your pasture . . . and they're already there and they're free. All we have to do is market 'um and take the money."

Although the numbers of hogs mounted is hard to estimate, the average cost of a shoulder-mounted wild hog is about $400. If a taxidermist takes in ten a year to mount and there are a hundred taxidermists in Texas, conservatively, taxidermy also is a profitable endeavor.

While many hunters process their own wild hogs, many others take them to the local meat processor. As a biologist, I was required to collect biological data from harvested white-tailed deer, and through the course of a hunting season, I'll observe several hundred hogs at various locker plants. In addition to meat processing, most of the hunters want sausage to be made with some of the meat. The average cost to process a wild hog generally exceeds $100. To many processing facilities, processing several hundred wild hogs can be very profitable. If you multiply each single facility by the number of lockers processing wild hogs in Texas, it would clearly be a million-dollar industry in itself.

Wherever hunters gather or congregate, they bring tremendous revenue to the local economy. In Uvalde County of southwestern Texas, hunters bring in an estimated seventeen million dollars to the local economy. What chamber of commerce would not be grateful to this economic influx? In Uvalde, and others areas around the state, the local chamber of commerce and businesses salute the hunters with a wild-game dinner. And no wild game dinner would be complete unless the wild boar was represented! Through the years I have been to numerous wild-game dinners held in every imaginable place from camp houses to Hiltons, and without fail at every affair, the wild hog has been a part of the menu.

A Paducah, Texas, meat processor.

Prepared correctly, the meat of a wild hog is better tasting than store-bought domestic pork, it is leaner, and it reportedly has less cholesterol. Europeans and many upscale restaurants believe these features warrant the premium price it costs at the dinner table. If you've never tasted a wild hog, you're in for a treat.

The value of the meat has recently opened up a whole new venue for wild hog. It is being sold domestically and exported to foreign countries where it is highly prized. Although trapping hogs to sell may be labor intensive, many people are profiting from this new market. In Texas and Florida it has become a million-dollar business. A recent review of prices found on specialty-meat websites indicated wild-boar-meat prices ranged from $8.00 per pound for bacon to $20.00 per pound for short loin. On another site, 1¼-pound wild boar tenderloin was priced at $49.99 and a 10-rib rack weighing approximately 3½ pounds was listed at $119.00!

A 1999 newspaper article claimed there were three processing facilities in Texas that were licensed to process feral hog meat. The meat packers sell to distributors who ship to a few specialized U.S. restaurants and to the European Union. Meat from wild boars is consumed in Germany, France, and Belgium. Although Australia is the largest supplier to the European market, it is estimated that approximately 250,000 to 300,000 pounds of live feral hogs are processed weekly in the United States. USDA regulations regarding the testing, handling, and processing of wild hogs in the U.S. stifle this potential market. In Texas, from 2004 to 2009, a total of approximately 461,000 wild pigs were processed at locations requiring a federal permit. If the average weight per pig was 100 pounds and sold at 20 to 60 cents per pound, the revenue would be $11.5 to $27.6 million. These are no small sums!

In 1999, I received a letter from a man in Normangee, Texas, located northwest of College Station, claiming he had been purchasing wild hogs from hunters/trappers for seven years. In that year alone, he reportedly had shipped over 7,000 hogs to market for slaughter! With a price ranging from 25 to 60 cents a pound, and an average weight of 100 pounds, this gentleman possibly grossed $175,000 dollars on the low end (25 cents). Depending on what he paid the hunters and trappers, it was probably still worth the effort.

Feral hogs going to market for sale and slaughter. (Photo courtesy of Texas Animal Health Commission)

And Finally, Bartering

Attempts at eradicating a hog population have been unsuccessful and are virtually impossible. Controlling a population requires continuous effort and is expensive. Hunting, trapping, and fencing are the most common methods to control feral hogs.

Operating a ranching enterprise can be an expensive occupation without having destructive wild hogs exacerbating the problem. Bartering for services while controlling the hogs may be beneficial to the landowner. These services can include road repairs, lodging updates or improvements, wildlife feeders, water improvement, plumbing, general contracting, horseshoeing, or even opera tickets. There are many skilled professionals that have services to offer in exchange for the right to hunt a wild hog. Landowners should tap this resource and utilize their services. In bartering, everyone wins! The landowner gets needed repairs, work accomplished, and a reduced hog population while the hunter has a place to go and spend time outdoors while pursuing a challenging quarry. Another option for landowners may be in entering partnerships with reputable trappers and outfitters.

Remember, the same effort and energy used to combat an expanding wild hog population can be redirected to benefit the landowner. Implementing a feral-hog-management program may require extra effort and time, but it helps lower or keep the population stable, yields economic returns, and provides recreational opportunities for sportsmen.

The Ugly

What is ugly? To a small child, a cat is cute, but to a mouse, it may be the ugliest thing in the world. To the mountain lion or coyote, a litter of piglets is indeed a beautiful sight. However, to ground-nesting animals, the wild hog is one of the ugliest creatures on earth. To a mother, regardless of a child's physical attributes or the trouble he or she may cause, he or she is still beautiful to her. Now I'm not comparing wild hogs to humans but rather pointing out that a person's opinion and perspectives may be different.

The Webster dictionary defines ugly as very unattractive in appearance, disagreeable, morally offensive, objectionable, or likely to cause inconvenience or discomfort. The feral hog may indeed be an ugly and offensive animal to individuals who are suffering economically, aesthetically, or in any way. But to many individuals such as some landowners, hunters, meat processors, and others, it may be an attractive commodity.

Boar Stories

CHAPTER 6

She preferred the solemn silence
Of her Cedar Mountain home,
And most of all she wanted us
To let 'er plum alone.

Ever Fall I'd try to mark 'er,
But she'd get away agin;
And I reckon that my cussin',
Though artistic, was a sin.

Well, I sold my brand in '30—
Moved ever' hog and cow:
Rounded-up . . . yeah . . . all but one head,
All but that blamed spotted sow.

From *That Spotted Sow and Other Texas Hill Country Ballads*
by Carlos Ashley

It seems that everyone who has ever hunted or been around wild hogs has a story to tell. These stories in themselves could fill volumes and go back for generations. Carlos Ashley's poem was originally published in 1941, and I have used various stanzas to open my chapters. No publication could be complete without the sage comments of one of the Southwest's most famous storytellers, J. Frank Dobie. Dobie was a dedicated and outstanding researcher who made a career of chasing stories; let's just say he went to great lengths to get a story. As the following anecdotes show, he succeeded.

In his book, *A Vaquero of the Brush Country* on the reminiscences of John Young written in 1929, Dobie dedicates a whole chapter to the razorbacks. In it, he recounts an 1848 hog hunt in East Texas written by Captain Flack in *A Hunter's Experiences in the Southern States of America*. It seems that an old East Texas hunter named Green decided to head to California in search of gold, but before he left he decided to sell his land and cattle as well as 200–300 half-wild hogs in the bayous and swamps. He wanted to butcher them and sell them as pickled pork and use the money for his trip. After enlisting the assistance of half-a-dozen hunters, they went into the reedbeds and started a fire to run the hogs out. As the hogs came running out, they were subsequently shot.

Dobie explained that many early hog owners would drive the hogs to the coast to fatten them on a diet of fish and meat-packer refuse. In the upper reaches of southwest Texas, range hogs could be fattened on the flesh of cattle that had been killed for their hides. Sometimes, he claimed, cattle were killed for the hogs without much attention to the hides. According to Dobie, a Col. Ike Pryor of San Antonio bought about 1,000 cows in Mason County around 1873. He was going to drive the cattle up the trail from Texas, but there were about 500 calves with the cows. Since he didn't want the calves, he killed them and fed the veal to the hogs because he said there were "great numbers in the country."

One fable has it that Paul Bunyan laid his famous pipeline through Arkansas by driving a herd of razorbacks ahead of him to root the ditch he needed to lay. Although the Bunyan story is only a myth, in the Big Thicket region of East Texas, the hog is credited with discovering oil near Saratoga. According to Francis E. Abernethy, in his book *Tales from the Big Thicket*," one of the earliest families to the area claimed that their hogs kept coming in covered in oil-caked mud. The hog owners found the location of the mud hole, and as the story goes, this is where the first gushers from the famous

Saratoga oil field were discovered. I'll bet the owners of that property quit cussing their hogs!

Hog Drives

Although cattle drives have been ingrained in the Texas mystique, hog drives were also very common during the nineteenth century. Settlers would gather together and spend several days roping and catching their free-ranging hogs and then putting them in pens. Using horses and dogs, the hogs could be driven just like the much more popular cattle. They were generally difficult to get started on the trail but once they were pressed beyond their familiar territory, they were fairly easy to push. According to Dobie, in 1827 the gatekeeper of the Cumberland, Kentucky, river turnpike certified over 105,000 hogs had been driven through the gate on their way to the south Atlantic states.

In the 1860s and 1870s, tens of thousands of hogs were driven from as far away as one hundred miles to the pork-packing industry in Alexandria, Missouri. Some of these drives had more than a thousand hogs and were as long as a mile. As the hogs escaped or were lost on the trail, they became feral, and it is possibly from this group that many wild hog populations were derived. During a hog drive, the hogs lived on whatever they could root up and forage on along the way. Drovers would eat hogs along the way and trade them for whatever other supplies they needed as they passed farms along the way.

John Young reminisced about the importance of the razorback in the cowboy's diet. He remembers when the acorn crop in southwest Texas failed and the hogs were plentiful but were "too poor to kill." At that time, the Midwest had a big crop of corn and the demand for hogs was brisk, so he and a group of men decided to capture some free-ranging hogs and drive them to a railroad shipping point about 100 miles away to either ship or sell.

After working for about a month roping and hauling hogs to a large pen, they finally had about 650 hogs captured and ready to go. The pen was in an open prairie and when the pen was opened to begin the drive, the hogs stampeded, scattering in every direction. He said they lost 200 hogs before they got out of sight of the pen, but once on their way and away from familiar territory, the hogs were somewhat easier to move. Although hogs are good swimmers, they lost an additional 50 as they crossed the San Antonio River and later while attempting to cross the Guadalupe River. They finally arrived at the shipping station and were able to sell the razorbacks for $6.50 a head. They were relieved to be rid of them!

Judge Mayes of Llano, Texas, recounted another hog drive that took place in 1882. A stranger by the name of Brown came to the Mayes house and requested to stay in exchange for work. He left for Round Rock one day and returned two weeks later reporting that he'd found a market for hogs there. So the neighbors all joined together and gathered between 300 and 400 hogs, each weighing about 300–400 pounds, some "so wild that they had to knock the teeth out, having lost most of their dogs gathering them." There were about ten men and five or six wagons and they made about four to five miles a day.

He claimed the hogs were trail broke after the first day and then would drive well. It took about two months to drive and return from the 100-mile trip, letting them fatten up for a few days before selling them for 2¼ cents a pound.

Hog roundups continued in East Texas into the 1940s according to Mary W. Clarke in the May 1947 issue of *Cattleman* magazine. Her story is about a latter-day hog roundup in the Trinity and San Jacinto River bottoms of Liberty County in East Texas. Her article is interesting because even in 1947 there was unfenced land bordering private property that was still available for hogs to forage. It was obvious that the use of horses, dogs, corrals, hog marking, and other techniques had not changed in more than a century! Although free-ranging hogs with marks are still classified as private livestock, East Texas was probably the last stronghold of this free-ranging endeavor. Today, very few free-ranging marked hogs can be found, therefore making the current population fair game for any hunter.

Stories from the Field

One evening while I was heading for a ranch to conduct a spotlight deer survey with coworkers Rodney and Jim, a group of about twenty hogs crossed in front of the truck. Among the group were about eight to ten piglets about

It's easier to drive hogs with a helicopter than with horses. (Photo courtesy of Macy Ledbetter)

the size of a beer can. Without hesitation, we bailed out of the pickup and commenced the chase, scattering pigs everywhere. I've always been the first to warn people about the dangers of female hogs with young, yet here we were, three grown men chasing wild hog babies in the deep South Texas brush. If you've ever seen a greased pig race, you can imagine the scene as the piglets squealed and oinked while careering through cacti, ducking and dodging.

In under a minute we had scattered the group and the older hogs had bolted from the grounds. Rodney scooped up a little one, and I was still in pursuit.

As I was about to pounce on my little piglet, Rodney hollered, "Rick, watch out!" Here came Mamma. Fortunately, she decided not to challenge the "big beast" chasing her young.

As the piglet crossed the road with Jim and me in hot pursuit, Jim crashed into a small mesquite tree, which turned the shoat's course. I dove or rather fell headfirst onto the youngster, managing to grab it.

Now, with two piglets in hand, what would we do with them? Well, after congratulating ourselves about our athletic abilities, we took a few pictures and let them go to grow up and continue to populate South Texas. Grown men chasing wild pigs in the brush? Without a doubt, a wild hog chase will bring out the strangest aspects of human nature or at the least, the kid in a brush-country biologist.

Many people can relate a thrilling experience they've had with the wild hog but not all stories are exciting. One such memorable story occurred while collecting wild hogs on a South Texas ranch for a diet and reproduction study I was involved in. It occurred in the summer of 1990 when temperatures easily reach 100 degrees and the nights are not much cooler. We'd been hunting all day without much success and decided to hunt into the night using spotlights. Right about dark a thunderstorm rolled through that lasted only about 15–30 minutes—just enough time to get things wet but not enough to stop the planned evening hunt. About 10 P.M., we loaded the trucks and headed into the field, spotlights glaring at all the stock tanks and potential feeding areas we could find. Around midnight, we'd managed to harvest about ten hogs. Bringing them to the lab (a barn with barely enough light to operate), we began the necropsy.

With the temperature hovering about 80 degrees, the humidity having reached the saturation point, and not a breath of air to be found, the fleas

Picture of author holding piglets he had just caught.

and ticks began looking for a new home. The Nueces riverbottom of South Texas seems to have the greatest population and the hungriest fleas and ticks in Texas. The home they found was a group of tired, sweaty, hungry field biologists up to their armpits in hog entrails. Our hands covered with the foul smell from the internal organs and accompanying fluids, it was impossible to scratch, flick, or knock off the invasive little buggers. They really enjoyed the facial area, particularly the ears, neck, and hair! Finding the parasites' tickling feet impossible to endure, I'd use the cleanest of my dirty fingers to pick them off . . . each time transferring some of the bloody stuff on my hands to my head.

After about two hours of this misery, we completed the task and raced for the shower. The camp house where we were staying was an old trailer house located about five miles through brushland from the headquarters and barn, currently occupied by one of the ranch hands. Unfortunately, the ranch hand had sloshed down a few too many beers and couldn't hear our banging and pleas. Finally, after about fifteen minutes (or was it an hour?), we were able to rouse him from his slumber. Bear in mind we're still fighting the ticks and fleas. We drew straws to decide who would get the shower first, and of course, yours truly was last. The sad part of the story is there was only one towel. By my turn, it was soaked and dirty, but at four in the morning, it was still the best shower I think I've ever had!

When I present educational programs on wild hogs in Texas, the most frequent question I am asked is whether a wild hog has ever hurt me. Although I've been charged, knocked down, and harassed by the creature, I've never been seriously injured. The worst scene that I have encountered was more of an indirect attack by a young wild boar. It was the summer of 1998 and we were conducting mountain lion research in South Texas. We were using Aldrich-type foot snares to catch these lions; however, we would find hogs in some of the snares nearly every day. I believe the number of hogs we captured with snares over a five-year study easily reached into the hundreds. The young ones we would release while the older, meaner ones we would dispatch to get out of the snare. A snared wild hog is not a friendly creature.

One day my wife, Lisa, and I were checking the snares for lions, and upon finding a hog in one of the snares, we got out of the Jeep to remove it. Unfortunately, there was just enough slack cable attached to the snare that it charged us and chased Lisa back into the Jeep, where she refused to leave until I had killed the hog.

Another morning I had snared a young male and decided to release it. He was less than a year old, weighed approximately seventy-five pounds, and had relatively short canines, but he was a tenacious little rascal. As I attempted to lasso him with my rope, he charged! Backing up, I jerked the slack out of the rope, tripped over a prickly pear cactus, and dislocated my little finger; fortunately, I was out of range of the angry pig. When I

Lisa Taylor with snared hog that forced her back into the Jeep.

got back on my feet, picked the cactus spines out of my backside, and tried to straighten my finger, he was still trying to get me. Well, by now I was angry and promptly returned to my truck, retrieved my .22 magnum, and promptly removed him from my snare. And to this very day, I am reminded of that little cuss when I drink a glass of wine, my little finger protruding outward like an English lady at a tea party.

Vignettes

Through the years, I have experienced my share of hog-related incidents, and I have heard or read some great stories of people-porcine encounters. Some are undoubtedly fact and some for sure are exaggerated. One of the most interesting stories I've ever heard of involved a man outside the South Texas town of Pawnee. According to the *Beeville Bee-Picayune*, seventy-nine-year-old Willie Heinen was surprised one dark evening in October 1993 by nearly a dozen feral hogs coming toward him from around the corner of his house. Seeking the safety of his vehicle, he was unable to open the truck door, before they attacked.

The hogs knocked Mr. Heinen off his feet and "commenced to eating on me" he said. He claims he didn't do anything to provoke them, but they simply appeared and came after him.

"They were hungry," Heinen explained. "Those things are always hungry."

He claims one large boar was at his head apparently trying to rip his throat, but fortunately he was able to hit the hog's face with his right hand. At that point the boar and the rest of the pack ceased the attack and ran off. He was treated at the hospital for numerous wounds on his right hand, left leg, and face. After six months he still had not regained full use of his right hand.

In 1998, a sheriff's deputy was patrolling in the Texas Hill Country about 11:30 at night when he came upon a pickup truck parked on the side of the road. The vehicle was still running so he called out to see if anyone would reply. The lawman heard a faint response of "Help!" from about fifty yards in the brush.

There he found a full-grown man perched in a tree. The man refused to climb down. As the deputy approached the individual he heard a noise near the tree. Pointing his flashlight at the sound, he saw a group of wild hogs coming at him. The next thing he remembers is ending up on the top of his patrol car with a shredded shirt. Eventually, he claims the hogs dispersed and he and the tree man left in a hurry. The name of the officer and the man in the tree was not disclosed in the report.

Although unprovoked attacks are infrequent and rare, wounded or cornered hog attacks occur more frequently. Experienced hog hunters or dog hunters all have riveting stories to tell. Mark McDonald, former outdoor writer for the *San Antonio Express News,* wrote a story of a man who came to South Texas from California to take a big boar with a bow. From his bed at Wilford Hall Medical Center in San Antonio, the guy told his story to Mark.

A pack of dogs had a highly energized, nasty boar bayed in a whitebrush thicket on a ranch somewhere south of San Antonio. Mr. California goes in after the hog armed only with a bow and arrow. When the hog made a break for it, the beast charged through and under the hunter, knocking the man off his feet.

"I could feel a surge of power taking my legs out from under me," the hunter said. "I went sailing in the air. Next thing I knew, I was on my back, looking up at the stars and the hog was all over my legs and up to my knees. I could feel jaws grinding my leg bones. I thought to myself, *South Texas is a helluva place to come and die.*"

After the piece was reported in the *San Antonio Express News*, Mark had a couple of phone messages from the "outfitter," whose name escaped him. This guy claimed that the injured hunter had been hell bent on going it alone. "The hunter wouldn't let me back him up with a pistol," claimed the outfitter.

Hmmmmm . . . Mark quizzed a couple dog handlers later and the story they told was the outfitter had been drinking that night and had hung his client out to dry. This tale happened in 1994 or '95. Details of such stories often get hazy in the heat of the moment, in bravado, and in machismo, but this incident was real enough to one California bow hunter.

The danger a hog poses may even be accidental as described by Newton Hyde in his book *Love, Live to Hunt the Hog.* He writes:

This guy was hunting alone and shot down two big bars (barrows). And evidently when he was sticking them, one of the hogs kicked his hand. The knife cut the main artery in one of his legs. When his folks found him the following day he was lying dead, about forty or fifty feet from the hogs. He had bled to death and fast.

While hunting or approaching a downed animal can be dangerous, accidents, as this incident shows, can be just as deadly.

Mr. Hyde, who claims to have hunted hogs for more than fifty years, said there were only two times he'd ever been scared while hog hunting. This story is about one of those times: Hyde was hunting with his hog dog named Old Rover when the dog bayed a hog in a washout.

He could see Old Rover in a hole that was about four feet deep and covered with vines, but he couldn't see the hog. He was leaning over the hole to find the hog when the bank caved in and he fell on top of the hog! Immediately he started kicking and scrambling to try to get out of the hole. When he finally got out, he saw that Old Rover had caught a big black boar. He swears it was Old Rover that saved him from serious injury.

He turned around and jumped back on the hog, putting a rope around its head, tying it up against a root. At that point Mr. Hyde marked the hog (notched its ear) and let it go. When it came out of the hole, it charged him, and again Old Rover grabbed the hog. When Hyde was about a hundred yards away, he called the dog off.

Personally, I would have called it a day and gone home once I was safely out of that hole the first time!

Wild Hog Management

CHAPTER 7

The term "hog management" may be misleading because in actuality the wild hog is very difficult to manage. It will eat, breed, and travel whenever and wherever it feels like it. Webster defines the term management as "the act or art of managing: control, direction." However, there are means and methods of control as well as a possible direction to help the landowner, sportsman, or ecologist. In that sense, perhaps progress can be achieved. California was the first state to attempt to manage the wild hog by designating it a game animal, selling hog stamps, and limiting harvest. California realized there was economic potential to wild hog hunting and not just detrimental effects.

The wild hog is an extremely prolific and adaptable creature that is nearly impossible to eradicate and difficult to even control. Hunting, trapping, and fencing are the most common methods to control feral hogs. Controlling a population requires continuous effort and may be expensive. Attempts at eradicating a hog population have been unsuccessful and are virtually impossible.

What is feral hog management, and why would we want to manage a species that is perceived to be so destructible and menacing? To put it simply . . . if you can't beat 'em, join 'em. Economics is a motivating factor with most management decisions. Money spent attempting to eradicate or control a hog population can be diverted into a moneymaking, hog-controlling project. Landowners should consider using hunters and sportsmen to control their hog population while reaping the benefits of hog control and added income. It's a win-win situation, in which sportsmen receive hunting opportunities and landowners receive income while controlling their hog population.

Hog management can be broken down into six basic categories: information and education, prevention, eradication, control, sustained yield, or a combination of these categories.

Management Techniques

Information and Education

Feral-hog management begins and ends with information and education. Before any other action can begin, it is imperative that an individual understands the biology, behavior, and repercussions of a burgeoning wild hog population. It has never ceased to amaze me how many people there are who subscribe to incorrect or misleading information. It seems that the majority of people including landowners, hunters, conservationists, and animal rights activists have limited knowledge of the impact feral hogs have on the environment.

To illustrate this point, we conducted a study in Texas in 2003 to determine the consequences of feral-hog invasions in several ecoregions in Texas. Through questionnaires, we examined the observations, experiences, and actions of landowners and managers concerning feral hogs on their property. There were a total of 775 survey participants that included mailed questionnaire respondents and those in pesticide-applicator workshops. The majority of the respondents were landowners (92 percent).

When we asked the respondents to complete a 26-point quiz, we found the average score to be 11.5. This average score indicated that the respondents could correctly respond to <50 percent of the 26 questions. Five statements revealed a particular lack of understanding of feral-hog biology in terms of the impact the animals have on other wildlife, what feral hogs eat, and how many offspring they can have per litter. Based on the respondents' knowledge of feral hogs, the study concluded that information and education should be expanded. This could include informational brochures, seminars, and workshops.

Biological knowledge as well as the laws and regulations regarding feral hogs will help manage the species. The ultimate application of our results is the impact they had on the public policy and decision-making process. By providing briefings to state policy-makers, the outreach effort associated with the project has resulted in early efforts to provide financial resources for dealing with feral-hog issues.

There have been numerous other studies throughout the United States similar to this study that mirror our results. Clearly, the first step to managing the feral hog is expanding information and education to all people. There are many ways for individuals to obtain this information, starting with your local game department, Extension Service, or USDA Natural Resource Conservation Service. In addition to personal communication,

Information and education are essential in managing wild hog populations.

94

these agencies have pertinent literature such as pamphlets or brochures available. There are numerous publications listed in the back of this book that should also be of assistance.

Anyone interested in the management of feral hogs might also want to consider attending a symposium. California, Florida, and Texas—to name a few—have all hosted feral-hog symposiums. Many other programs can be found at the local or regional levels.

Probably the easiest and fastest way to obtain information is through the Internet. By typing the words feral hog, wild pig, wild boar, or any similar term into the search engine will return countless results. In Texas, the Wildlife and Fisheries Extension Unit has incorporated Internet-based tools such as videos, websites, social media, blogs, and IPad/IPhone applications with their literature and seminars. Web-based information is a vital tool to assist the public in obtaining information on the feral hog and its management.

Prevention

The best way to control a population is not to let it get started. I've known landowners and hunters who believed that having a few hogs or even releasing a few into the pasture for some occasional pork couldn't possibly get out of hand. Well, within a short period of time, liberators had regretted their actions, but, by then it was too late. A population had become established!

If you do not have hogs presently on the property, and if your habitat is good, you will most likely have them sooner rather than later. When that time arrives and you've seen hogs or located their sign, you should begin your control program immediately. Do not hesitate to begin an intensive trapping and hunting program. The longer you postpone initiating the program, the harder it will be to control the population.

The best way to avert wild hogs on any plot of ground is: **DO NOT RELEASE THEM!** This may sound overly simplistic, but to this day, un-educated or uncaring individuals continue to haul hogs into formerly uninhabited grounds and release them. Intentional releases by landown-ers and sportsmen are the cause of the majority of range expansions in the United States; consequently, preventing this action will go a long way in reducing the hog-population explosion and the subsequent problems they cause. Despite the urge to increase hunting opportunities, economic gains, or other perceived benefits, **DO NOT RELEASE** hogs into areas where there is not a population. It is also important to contact the neighboring ranchers and discuss the matter so that they or their hunters don't release them, either.

I worked with one landowner in south-central Texas who wanted feral hogs on his game ranch. I explained to Bill that he would regret it but if he was determined to host hogs, release castrated males only. "I'm not going to castrate anything," he said in not so simple terms.

He released the hogs, and within five years they had overpopulated the ranch. As a result, game animals suffered, habitat and agricultural damage was rampant, and his feed costs became astronomical. Bill admitted to me that I had been correct, and as far as I know, he is still fighting to control the hog population on his property.

Exclusion

Another way to prevent the influx of hogs is by exclusion; this can be done by establishing a hog-proof fence. Fencing may prove to be expensive and temporary because if hogs want to cross to the other side of the fence for any reason, even the best fence can't keep them out.

Exclusion is the first line of defense against an encroaching hog population. In addition to hog-proof fencing, there are several other methods of exclusion: habitat modifications, change in agricultural practices, animal husbandry practices, and crop and livestock changes. These exclusionary options may be useful in certain circumstances, but all may be cost prohibitive. For practical applications, each individual situation and corresponding option must be individually analyzed. Remember, everything that land managers do to improve and aid their livestock ultimately benefits the wild hog. Water improvement, habitat improvement, supplemental feeding, food plots, and eradication of diseases unintentionally enhance the wild-hog population.

Changing agricultural practices also may curtail the onslaught. Replacing a hog's desirable food with one it dislikes will slow the ingress into an area. If you recall, the hog's activity is centered on its quest for food. Take the food away and the hogs will diminish. For example, if a farmer raises corn or vegetables, he might want to consider growing a crop such as cotton. If hogs cause problems for sheep or goat ranchers, an option might be to switch to cattle in selected pastures. I realize the above scenarios regarding a farmer's or rancher's livelihood is simplistic and most likely cannot be changed for economic or personal reasons. But it does illustrate what can be done to prevent hogs from becoming established. Unfortunately, there are very few landowners willing to change their practices to keep hogs out.

Ranch improvement projects such as brush control, establishing watering areas in remote parts of the ranch, and planting food plots on the ranch to enhance and distribute livestock and wildlife management helps spread the hog population. Water and feeding spots can be fenced to keep out hogs but will also keep out domestic livestock.

Hog-Proof Fencing

Exclusion is generally accomplished through fencing in an attempt to minimize feral-hog damage. In some deer-hunting operations, fences around feeders have been used with success because a deer can jump over them whereas hogs cannot. In Texas, the most common and effective type of fencing around small areas such as feeders are heavy-duty thirty-four-inch hog panels. Young white-tailed deer fawns may have trouble jumping over the hog panels so cutting out the upper first section of paneling in a few of the panels allows greater access for fawns. On large acreage, fencing is impractical, but net-wire fencing can deter hogs and when used with other methods, can be fairly effective.

For effectively restricting feral-hog movement, the design and proper installment of hog-proof fencing is critical. As a rule, no fence is completely hog proof. It seems no matter what design or technique is used, hogs will eventually find their way inside it. Designs that have had success include heavy gauge net wire, mesh wire, and electric fencing.

Net-wire fencing can be rolled wire or cattle panels with openings that shouldn't exceed four inches, thus preventing the hog from getting its nose

An example of a hog-proof fence around a deer feeder.

too far in so as to spread the mesh. Burying the net wire six to twelve inches also improves the success. Because the wild hog has a slender long snout and is so strong, it can easily force its way through the strongest fence. Some people have even used chain-link fencing with a portion buried beneath the ground. This eliminates or lessens the hog's ability to root through the fence, but chain link is expensive and hard to install. Combinations of a net-wire fence with an electric wire placed six to twelve inches above the ground approximately twelve inches away from the base of the fence is optimal.

An electric hog-proof fence also may be constructed consisting of a heavy gauge, net wire fence with two electric outriggers. To be effective, a minimum of 8,000 volts should be available. The outrigger wires should be pulsed with suitable grounds placed no farther apart than every quarter of a mile. The recommended post placement should be at least ten feet apart. Depending on the terrain, this type of fence can be expensive.

In South Texas research trials, a two-strand polywire electric fence reduced daily feral-hog intrusion by 50 percent and excluded 75 percent to bait stations. The use of a two-strand electric fence is relatively inexpensive compared to other fencing. In addition to a physical barrier, electric fencing poses a psychological barrier. For optimum results, dab a peanut butter and cooking oil mixture or other sweet lick-type food on the wire prior to initial use at frequent intervals (every 3–6 feet). This ensures the initial contact by the hog's tongue as it licks or bites the bait results in a very memorable shock to the nose or tongue! This is especially recommended when using the multicolored one-inch-wide electric polytape or polywire.

Electric fence manufacturers working with researchers are constantly experimenting with various types and designs to come up with an economically efficient wild-hog barrier. It is important to note also, that nontarget animals such as white-tailed deer may also be deterred.

While the electric fence may sound like the ultimate hog-exclusion fence, I am reminded of a story I once heard. A man had planted a food plot with some luscious legumes (peanuts or peas, I don't remember) and had placed

A wild hog jumping out of trap.

an electric fence around it to keep out hogs. The fence functioned perfectly until the crop matured and became enticing to the hogs. The story as related to me was the hogs would start running and begin squealing way before they reached the fence. They fully expected the electrical jolt, having been shocked before, but the desire for food was much greater than the stinging blue spark they received as they went through the barrier.

Topography, terrain, soil types, and possibilities of washouts during heavy rains have a bearing on the feasibility of hog-proof fencing. Fencing is extremely difficult to construct across rocky, mountainous, hilly, or rough terrain. Fence maintenance is also a major consideration when implementing a hog fence. The fence must be maintained continuously for it to work. Fencing in combination with other control techniques is the most effective hog detriment and control option. Ultimately, the best control method can be found within a fenced area with snares along the perimeter and traps and hunters in the pasture.

Eradication

"Yea, right!" When people talk about eradicating an established feral-hog population, I simply say: "expensive, impractical, and probably impossible." Eradicating a population requires unlimited funds, full-time commitment, and no place for the population to immigrate. Eradication is not successful if surrounding properties act as a reservoir for immigration.

One of the most extensive attempts at eradicating a feral-hog population took place at Hawaii Volcanoes National Park. In this national park, wild-pig populations had destroyed or altered natural habitat and processes; this destruction conflicted with a legislative mandate to protect and manage native ecosystems. From 1930 to 1971 the National Park Service eliminated approximately 7,000 pigs. From 1971 to 1980 a public hunting program resulted in the harvest of over 4,000 wild pigs.

According to reports, eradication was not achieved due to a number of factors: insufficient or lack of sustained efforts, inadequate monitoring, and immigration from surrounding lands. So from 1980 to 1988, a pig-proof fence was constructed around the entire park. After the fence was constructed, systematic hunting, trapping, and snaring was initiated to eradicate the hogs. This resulted in an additional 175 pigs taken from three of nine management units during the first six months and cost more than 1.5 million dollars! And we must remember annual costs including materials and labor to maintain the fence, which only had an estimated life span of five to fifteen years.

A successful eradication program occurred in 2005 on the 62,000-acre Santa Cruz Island, California, over a fourteen-month period at a cost nearing 4 million dollars. Using a professional predator control company, victory was achieved through a combination of methods including aerial gunning, trapping, and ground hunting with dogs and Judas pigs. The long-term success of this program can be attributed to its island status with no adjoining properties for hogs to emigrate from. If the nearest feral hogs roam anywhere

An attempt at hog eradication. (Photo courtesy of Macy Ledbetter)

within a couple hours' drive of a pasture devoid of such creatures, it is not a question of "if" but a matter of "when" they will extend their range and populate the land. With time, money, and effort a landowner can possibly eradicate a hog population if it has not become firmly established. Where they've established a foothold, the best that landowner can hope for is control.

Hog Control Methods

Hog control is the primary method for dealing with an expanding hog population. Since it's too late for prevention, exclusion is not an alternative, and eradication is virtually impossible, controlling the population is the only option. Control must be continuous to keep the damage minimal and the population in check. Remember the more intense the control effort is, the better the results will be. There are numerous ways and methods to control a feral-hog population.

Hunting and Trapping

Hunting and trapping are the most widely used methods to control a wild-hog population. Although hunting and trapping techniques will be addressed in later chapters, attempting to control a wild-hog population requires a different attitude and mind-set. Hunting and trapping wild hogs in an attempt to control a population is serious business whereas doing it for sport, recreation, or food is enjoyable.

To control hogs through hunting and trapping requires hard work and persistence. It can be very labor intensive and expensive. Optimally, hunting and trapping should be used in conjunction with each other. Recreational, sport, or public hunting will have very limited effect and will be relatively unsuccessful. Such was the case on Fort Riley, a military installation in the northeastern flint hills of Kansas.

After documenting an influx of wild pigs in the fall of 1993, biologists from the Fort Riley Natural Resources Division and the Kansas Cooperative Fish and Wildlife Research Unit assessed the situation and attempted to eradicate the population. In the first season approximately one hundred people hunted for pigs; hunters shot only four hogs. Hunters killed no pigs in the second season although that was their target.

A successful day of hog shooting. (Photo courtesy of Macy Ledbetter)

Public hunting of hogs on Wildlife Management Areas in Texas produces similar results. The mere presence of large numbers of hunters within an area may change the hogs' behavior, even pushing them out temporarily . . . only for them to return when the woods become quiet again. While providing outstanding hunting opportunities, the ability to use public hunters to control a thriving feral-hog population is hopelessly inadequate.

Hunting with dogs should be used when possible because hogs do not like dogs. The use of dogs will generally cause hogs to leave their domain; however, once the pressure stops, the hogs will return. Incidental or intermittent hunting or trapping may psychologically benefit the landowner or sportsman but will have no long-term effect on the population.

Shooting

As most sportsmen can attest, there is a difference between hunting and shooting. Shooting can include hunting, or in the context of control it can comprise any means and methods to decrease the population. As opposed to a well-planned hunt, shooting is approached with a different attitude from the disciplined, recreational sport hunter. Generally, shooting will have a very limited effect on the overall population unless it is intensively conducted over an extended period of time. Many landowners require their deer hunters to shoot every hog they see even if the hunter already has a full freezer; thus, most shooting of feral hogs is incidental to other types of sport hunting.

Fortunately, there are always needy people or organizations to whom the meat can be donated. In Texas, I'd estimate thousands of pounds of wild pork are given away to the needy. Depending on the individual state, game and fish laws and regulations generally require a hunting license for shooting or hunting. In Texas, feral hogs can be hunted year-round, with no seasons or bag limits; they can even be hunted at night. When hunting at night, it is best to use a red lens over the spotlight in feeding areas or areas of known hog activity. Always contact your local game warden if you intend to hunt at night unless you have a clear-cut understanding how he will handle rifle-toting spotlighters late at night on land where deer are known to roam.

Outlaws with ideas of bagging venison, not pork, regularly operate under the guise of legitimate hog hunters.

Aerial Shooting

One of the most effective techniques in controlling a feral-hog population is aerial gunning from helicopters. This technique has been used successfully in the South Texas brush country and in West Texas; it can be used any place where tree-canopy cover is thin and low growing. It is a selective technique where individual animals or selected land can be treated, but it requires an experienced pilot and gunner. It is a legal method in Texas; however, permits and licenses are required. Once the flight begins, you can cover thousands of acres in a day with this technique. And hanging out the door of a dipping, turning helicopter

Start harvesting from the last hog and move forward.

Aerial shooting. (Photo courtesy of Macy Ledbetter)

provides challenges slightly more difficult to shooting clay pigeons while riding a carnival Tilt-a-whirl.

Historically, a 12-gauge shotgun with 3-inch magnum shells loaded with buckshot was the primary weapon of choice. Although it's still a very good option, the semiautomatic, AR-type rifle has become the preferred choice. This rifle topped with a laser sight and red-dot scope is highly effective and deadly. When the pilot locates a hog or sounder of hogs, he pursues them from a distance until they are running in a line. That is the point when the shooter should begin harvesting the pigs—beginning with the last one and working toward the leader. Using this method will often allow the entire group to be dispatched.

This method is extremely effective where vegetation cover is low and topography is relatively flat or rolling. Experienced pilots can work the more rugged terrain; however, the overstory must still be low and thin. More information on aerial hunting can be found in the hunting section of this book.

In one morning a helicopter with an experienced gunner was able to harvest 48 hogs while conducting research in South Texas. Harvesting up to 100 hogs per day in heavily infested areas is not uncommon. I've even heard as many as 250 being killed in a single day! The cost of aerial hunting varies, but in South Texas, a 2-seat helicopter generally costs about 300–400 dollars per hour. And of course, larger machines will cost more and are not any more effective.

The benefits include immediate satisfaction, cessation of damages, and reduction of hogs and other predators, if desired. Aside from rough terrain and extensive overstory, other limiting factors include weather, cost, and inherent risks of low-altitude flying. Federal and state laws must be obeyed and necessary permits are required for the helicopter company. Check the laws before implementing an aerial reduction program.

High-Tech Techniques

There are other methods used for hunting hogs, specifically at night. Since in most states hogs are considered a nuisance, many high-tech techniques are

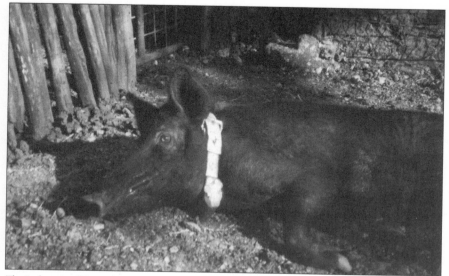

The Judas pig. (Photo courtesy of USDA Wildlife Service)

being tried. Thermal imaging cameras, much like the military use, can be used in hog hunting. The images appear in black and white so the warmer-body hogs are readily visible and easily distinguishable from other active-night-animal species. Through a specialized scope, or night vision scope, thermal imaging uses the hog's body heat against cooler night temperatures to illuminate the scope. Night-vision binoculars can also be used to find the hogs; these are followed-up with a spotlight to harvest the hog. The more expensive the camera or scope, the better the clarity; therefore, it can be a very expensive tool.

Motion sensor cameras can be used to detect the presence of hogs. By reviewing the film, the hunter can easily decide whether or not it's worth hunting in a certain area. The cameras are date and time sensitive, so documenting these data can improve success as well as time efficiency. I know some hunters who also use laser sights to hunt hogs when a scoped or open sight is difficult to use. This is especially useful when hunting hogs at night with the use of dogs. These hunters claim you can easily see the red aim point at night.

Radio telemetry is another technique land managers and hunters are using successfully. For this technique a pig is trapped, fitted with a radio collar (or a dog transmitting collar), and released. The collar will probably need to be modified, possibly with a horse harness because regular collars have a tendency to slip off. At this point, the hog will return to its sounder where it unknowingly gives up its relatives. When using a radio telemetry receiver to track and locate the sounder for harvesting, be careful to not kill the collared pig. Within a few days, it should find more pigs to associate with, thus allowing the process to continue.

This Judas pig, as it's called, has been used for many years by the USDA Wildlife Services when conducting aerial gunning operations in South and southwestern Texas. With radio collars becoming more obtainable and less expensive, this method is finding its way into the civilian hog-control arsenal.

There are also products on the market that will actually light up an area if a sensor is tripped. These hog lights are used around feeders with the hunter stationed nearby. When the hogs arrive after dark and trigger the light, *wham*, the hunter takes the shot. I've seen many of these lights stationed near the hunters' camp. This allows the hunter to enjoy the camp camaraderie, and if a hog shows up, all the hunters can view it and take appropriate action. It is very important that you check with your local game agency to make sure these techniques are legal.

Finally, the use of remote-controlled aircraft or drones are showing potential. A Louisiana company places a thermal imaging camera on a drone then flies it over areas where hogs are known to roam in the hopes of spotting the heat-induced, hog-shaped glow on the camera. Once spotted, the operator radios the ground crew who goes to the area with a night-vision scope to complete the mission by dispatching the hogs. While the use of drones in hog control is in its infancy, it may indeed become a valuable resource in the future. Originally very expensive, all of these high-tech-type tools are becoming more affordable and easier to obtain.

Trapping

There are many types of traps for hogs. These include box traps, corral traps, drop nets, and snares. Information on trapping techniques, trap design, and baits are found in the next chapter.

Scaring or Frightening

The use of loud noises or frightening devices may provide temporary relief from an onslaught of hogs. Some people have tried techniques such as propane canons, loud music, or lights. However, feral hogs, like the adaptable white-tailed deer and coyote, will eventually become accustomed to the noises and return to their previous habits. To date, I have not heard of an effective long-term frightening device.

Chemical Repellents

There are many commercially available, wildlife repellents on the market today; however, I have not found any of them effective. Commonly used home-remedy repellents include mothballs, cayenne pepper, and ammonia-soaked rags have been used with limited success . . . generally on a temporary basis until the hogs decide the repellents are edible! As we've stressed throughout this book, feral hogs have excellent olfactory senses. They can smell anything and everything! Unfortunately, they tend to like the foulest-smelling items. Using items such as mothballs, human hair, and other such things will not keep hogs away—it might even attract them.

Birth Control or Sterilization

Although birth control sounds like the ultimate solution for managing a wild-hog population, there is not a viable product on the market that can be effectively used as a birth control for wild hogs. There are several promising products currently being researched by the USDA and the Animal Plant Health Inspection Service (APHIS) Veterinary Branch for the expressed purpose of controlling wild hogs. While sterilization and castration may be available to domestic hog producers, it is not practical on free-ranging wild hogs.

Immuno-contraceptive vaccines have been studied in domestic and farm animals as a nonsurgical castrating agent. According to Killian, et al. (2003), vaccines are being researched that target several aspects of reproductive physiology in male and female feral swine. Preliminary results indicated that a single shot vaccine was highly effective in reducing fertility of females during a thirty-six-week study. It also negatively impacted testis weight and serum testosterone in males.

There are several issues regarding any such application to wild hogs, including the duration of infertility, the reversibility of the effects, and the development of an oral- or nasal-based conduit that is applicable in field use. The person who invents such a process and the way to administer it to wild hogs will surely be as famous as Thomas Edison. It would be that revolutionary.

Toxicants

To put it simply, toxicants are poisons that are used for predator control. There are a few countries that utilize effective toxicants for the control of feral hogs, but they are not available in the United States. Poisons such as Warfarin, an anticoagulant used in rat poison, and compound 1080 in a product called PIGOUT have been used successfully in Australia to control pigs. However, there are currently too many restrictions on the use of poisons in the United States, not to mention the political and sociological implications that they bring. However, a toxicant has been developed and approved in Australia that is currently being investigated in the United States. The use of toxins appears to be the best option currently being investigated for eradicating or controlling feral hogs. Research has

Hogs attempting to get bait from HogHopper.

determined that poisoning is eleven times cheaper than shooting and eighty times cheaper than trapping.

The use of poisons to control any wildlife species is a very controversial subject with concerns that must be addressed. Factors include humaneness, effects on nontarget species, secondary hazards for humans, effectiveness, antidotes, toxicity, cheap deliverability, and so on. Australia is the pioneer in this endeavor and has three types of poison baits that are successfully being used to control hog populations. In all probability, two will never be used in the United States; however, there is a strong possibility that the third one may eventually become available.

Australian researcher Dr. Steven Lapidge has discovered the Achilles heel of the hog, and this chemical is the same ingredient that we use in preserving meat . . . sodium nitrite. The chemical had to be safe for humans, highly toxic to pigs, bait-deliverable, humane, and relatively inexpensive. His research concluded that sodium nitrite, a preservative already available, is highly toxic to hogs in certain forms. Sodium nitrite restricts the oxygen in the blood to the brain, and this causes a state of unconsciousness in which the hog falls asleep and dies without any noticeable pain and suffering. Environmental and humane groups in Australia concur to its usage, and in some areas of Australia this chemical was over 80 percent effective in controlling localized populations.

As an independent researcher, I was fortunate to be involved with some of these early trials. We used specially designed feeders called the Hog Hopper, which is similar to domestic pig feeders. With a Hog Hopper, the pig must raise a hinged door with its snout to get to the bait. Trail cameras were used to document usage. Another specially designed bait-delivery system being investigated is called the Boar-Operated-System or BOS, which consists of an upside-down cone on a feeding plate centered on a metal pole. Again, the objective of the device is for the hog to lift the cone with its snout to get to the bait. Nontarget wildlife such as raccoons and black bears seem to be the major hurtle to this system.

While many obstacles exist for sodium nitrite to become commercially available, it currently is the best toxicant for hogs. Trials are continuing in several states, and toxic trials should begin in the near future. By 2011 in cooperation with USDA, (APHIS), Texas Parks and Wildlife Department, and other agencies, the Australians sent nontoxic samples to the United States to begin delivery trials and to start the process of getting it registered here. As of this publication, the trials are ongoing. Most scientists, including myself, are quick to point out that even an effective toxin will only be another tool in the arsenal to control feral hogs, so hunters should not be alarmed. There will always be hogs to hunt!

Managing Populations for Profit

The term "sustained yield" means utilizing and maximizing the available hog resources as an economic benefit on a continuing basis. Since wild hog populations will continue to occupy desirable habitat, the key of sustained-yield management is harvesting individual hogs for profit. Instead of indiscriminately killing every hog you see, a sustained-yield harvest will maximize the value of the hog.

Consider harvesting strategies that will maximize economic gains while reducing the population. For example, if a large tusker boar can bring you $500, don't indiscriminately harvest him but rather save him for a hunter or to use as a bartering tool for ranch improvements. Such harvest strategies may include limiting the harvest of older boars, concentrating on older sows and pigs, or even castrating young males so they survive but not reproduce.

Another example of sustained yield is using bow hunters to harvest your wild hogs. While labor intensive to the landowner or outfitter, the limited success of a bow hunter allows more hogs to survive, thus increasing revenue without over-harvesting the hog resource.

Biological data collected by the Florida Fish and Wildlife Conservation Commission suggests that late summer and early fall is the best time to harvest hogs in South Florida on a sustained-yield basis. By reducing the population at this time, competition for available food, principally acorns, would also be reduced. Additionally, there are generally fewer nursing sows and usually surplus numbers of subadults in the population for harvest. Biologically speaking, this is the best time for harvesting; however, I have yet to see a population negatively affected through year-round hunting. In Texas, spring hunting on Wildlife Management Areas has had very little impact on overall population numbers.

Implementing a Feral-Hog Management Plan

I recommended implementing a feral-hog management plan within the overall ranch-management program. It may mean incorporating the feral hog into the livestock, farming, or ranching enterprise. This could include requiring leasees to harvest hogs, offering feral-hog package hunts, marketing the meat, bartering for ranch improvements, and entering into partnerships with reputable trappers and outfitters.

Intensive feral-hog management programs may include trophy-boar management, **harvest strategies**, supplemental feeding, habitat improvement, watering sites, agricultural modifications, improved sex ratios, and even genetic improvement. Harvest strategies include limiting the harvest of young boars to let them mature, increasing the harvest of sows to improve the sex ratio, and even trapping and castrating males prior to release. The theory of castrating males brings with it the hope of increasing the body size and length of the canines to produce a greater trophy.

Some innovative hog aficionados have even begun to improve their wild-hog herd through **genetic selection and breeding**. In this case, herd boars with desirable genetic traits such as body size, coloration, and exceptional tusks are trapped or bought and subsequently bred with good sows. The offspring are then released into the pasture to improve the genetics of the free-ranging herd or for future hunting. Individuals wanting to become involved in a captive wild-hog breeding program should contact their respective wildlife agency regarding the legality of such actions.

Supplemental feeding may include allowing access to wildlife feeders or food plots instead of fencing them out. It may even include a protein-pellet diet accessible for hogs. Increasing the amount of water may also benefit the hog population, and simply allowing troughs to overflow will create wet areas

SCWDS Feral Swine Aging Chart

(The term erupting refers to teeth that are not completely in.)

<2 Months -- Incisors 1 And 3 Present But No. 2 Incisors Not Erupted

2 Months -- No. 2 Incisors Erupting

2 - 8 Months -- All Incisors Present

8 Months -- Permanent Canine Erupting

8 - 14 Months -- Permanent Canine Fully Erupted But Second Molar Not Erupted

14 Months -- Second Molar Erupting

14 - 24 Months -- Second Molar Fully Erupted But Third Molar Not Erupting

24 Months -- Third Molar Erupting

24+ Months -- Third Molar Fully Erupted

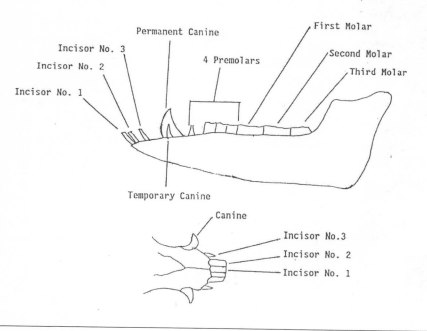

Aging chart of feral swine.

for them. Agricultural modifications may include replacing a five-strand barbed-wire fence with a heavy net-wire fence to retain the hogs. I know one landowner who built a one-way gate into his pasture from a farmer's field and then baited heavily from the farm into his pasture. The hogs would come into his pasture through the one-way gate but couldn't retreat back to the farmland. The landowner was able to market the hogs through hunting, and the farmer had less damage to his crops.

Good management of any game species incorporates **data collection and record keeping**. As a wildlife biologist and consummate data collector, I can assure you of the importance of collecting information. Data collection includes **survey data**, sex, weights, ages, and body condition. Although collecting hog-herd density numbers is difficult, recording hog numbers during big-game surveys and collecting incidental observations can be used to determine harvest strategies. The use of trail cameras to survey white-tailed deer over bait or at feeders is an acceptable census technique that can be used to assist in monitoring hog populations. I've looked at thousands of trail-camera pictures of hogs throughout the years and believe it to be one of the best methods available.

The **Passive Tracking Index (PTI)** has been used successfully to monitor feral hogs. This involves the placement of tracking plots or dragged roads throughout an area where hogs occur or are known to travel. Hog sign such as tracks and scat are recorded for a set time, then erased and rechecked after another couple days. This technique is relatively inexpensive to implement and can provide location, density estimates, management target areas, efficiency of removal, and reinvasion data on hogs in a given area.

Incidental observations including numbers, sizes, and locations should be recorded throughout the year. Documenting litter sizes can be used to establish future harvest quotas. For example, if a drought persists and you notice small litter sizes, you may not want to book as many hunters. Similarly, your harvest quotas and subsequent hunt bookings may need to be adjusted based on mature hogs that you've documented. By recording this information, you may also be able to pinpoint the best places to hunt or direct your strategies.

Determining the age of white-tailed deer through tooth wear and replacement is a very common technique used by wildlife professionals and land managers throughout the United States. While many people aren't concerned with determining the age of the feral hog, it can be accomplished in much the same way. Aging feral hogs by their teeth is basically the same as aging domestic hogs through tooth wear and replacement.

Other information such as weights, fetal development, lactation, etc., can be used to determine peak breeding dates and subsequently the best hunting seasons. By knowing peak breeding dates on your land or hunting lease, you can determine if harvesting prior to this time or after the young are born is desired. Data collection may be crucial to your land management as well as to your economic goals and objectives.

Implementing a feral-hog management program may require extra effort and time, but it helps lower or keep the population stable, provides economic returns, and affords recreational opportunities for sportsmen. Remember, the same effort and energy used to combat an expanding wild-hog population can be redirected to benefit the landowner.

The Future

Although biological information on feral hogs is plentiful, more research is needed to determine the lasting, long-term effects of feral hogs on our indigenous wildlife and native plants accurately. A viable and accurate census method is needed to determine population levels. In Texas and some other states, there is no clear jurisdiction regarding feral swine. From agricultural agencies and health departments to game departments, it seems they all have input but very little control. To deal with feral swine more effectively, perhaps their classification should be clarified and jurisdiction placed under a single regulatory agency.

There should also be more effort in developing environmental and ethical solutions to control the expanding wild-hog population. These efforts should include repellents and toxicants. Information and education is the most important facet available to combat feral hogs, and the dissemination of both should continue. Brochures, newspapers, magazines, radio, television, workshops, and symposiums are some examples of an information and education campaign.

Much of our current campaign efforts are geared toward the transmission and the eradication of disease in wild hogs. But, are there any negative consequences of eradicating diseases of feral swine? With no natural predators and very little natural mortality, will the population of wild hogs increase at a higher rate than current levels? Can the ecosystem, habitat, other agricultural commodities, producers, and landowners afford more wild hogs?

The feral hog is a problem in many countries throughout the world. It arrived in the United States over five hundred years ago and has firmly established itself in over two-thirds of the United States. As it continues to expand its range, distribution, and numbers, it will become mandatory to implement more stringent guidelines and strategies to deal with it. In the meantime, people must learn to live with this exotic invader.

Hog Trapping

CHAPTER 8

Now the more I tried to catch 'er,
And the more I give it thought,
I begin to get the notion
She's opposed to bein' caught.

I couldn't help admire that sow,
When all was done and said;
For, to tell the truth about 'er,
She was really thoroughbred.

She had character and courage
And the heart to do the right;
And when it came to fightin',
Now she shore as hell could fight.

From *That Spotted Sow and Other Texas Hill Country Ballads*

by Carlos Ashley

Trapping wild hogs is almost as exciting as hunting them and is a sport in itself. Throughout history, trapping hogs was a necessary and very popular technique for capturing and controlling these creatures. It is not new in Texas. John Young reminisced to J. Frank Dobie in his book *Vaqueros of the Brush Country* that settlers sometimes made traps to catch hogs. The trap was nothing but a picket pen with a door swung from the top that opened inward when pushed against. It fell shut as soon as force against is released and would not open outward. They used corn for bait and because many of the hogs were used to pushing through fences around cornfields; consequently, the trap relied on the hog's natural instinct to work. Once one hog entered, the others would follow, "frantic to join the feast." Young claimed settlers along the coast would occasionally seine fish to feed their hogs.

Additionally, trapping is not only challenging but also a great way to obtain meat for the freezer. Feral hogs are extremely wary and can offer a very serious challenge to landowners, managers, or sportsmen, especially in the spring when food is readily available. Live traps are also an easy way to dispose of hogs since they can be loaded on a trailer conveniently and then taken to the butcher or market. Trapping is most successful during the cooler months but with ingenuity can be successfully done throughout the year. During the hotter months, it is very important to check traps early in the morning or the chances of hogs dying in the heat-stressed afternoon increase greatly. Traps should be left unset during daylight hours during the summer months.

Research investigations regarding control techniques conducted in the Great Smoky Mountains National Park of Tennessee indicated capture success was greatest during the spring months as well as in August, November, and December. Lack of hog activity was a limiting factor regarding the overall success of the trapping program. Specific sites and specific nights had consistently higher degrees of hog activity. Pre-baiting the trap site promoted hog activity and ultimate success because hogs exhibited a reluctance to enter traps on their initial exposure to bait. Minor activities may be the result of a single solitary boar and not indicative of a feeding area. Thus, trapping success may be limited. This study was conducted in the early 1970s and gives insight on how long hog reduction has been attempted. Much more has been learned about trapping hogs in the last forty years, as the information in this chapter demonstrates.

Basic Trap Information

Traps can be of permanent or portable design. When trapping hogs, non-target animals can be released and trapped hogs can be immediately disposed of, slaughtered, sent to market, or relocated. Check the state law to determine if a wild hog can be released. In Texas, it is illegal to capture and move wild hogs without first testing them for swine brucellosis and pseudorabies and quarantining them for thirty days. Most game departments and ecologists, including myself, strongly urge against the practice of hog translocation due to the negative repercussions that feral hogs bring to the environment.

Once an area of hog activity has been located, I recommend placing the trap in a shady location. This prevents the loss of a trapped hog that can become overheated, exposed to the elements, and die. A thorough discussion on hog sign and what to look for can be found in chapter 10. Although there are many trap designs available, I prefer a trap that will allow multiple entries. The key to these traps is in the door design.

Habitat conditions, climate, and season may also play a role in trapping success. Since vegetation is a major part of the hog's diet, lush habitat conditions may impact trapping success. Hogs are not as likely to be enticed by bait if they aren't hungry. Conversely, cooler temperatures and poor habitat may increase success. Research in South Texas concluded that extremely hot temperatures in July and August decreased trapping success.

Trap Designs

Box Traps

The most common type of trap is the box trap. The size of the trap is generally 4 x 4 x 8 feet in size, although I have seen every size imaginable. Most traps are constructed with galvanized 4-inch-square cattle panels. The different types of doors include the drop door, root or lift door, and spring or swing gate. The swing gate may be in a saloon door configuration, with half doors hinged on either side opening in the middle.

Although not preferred, many people still use the old favorite drop door. The drop door is released when an inside trigger mechanism wired to the gate is moved. It is held above the opening by a trigger mechanism and a wire is strung from the trigger to a trip within the trap; it is frequently tied to a feed trough or bucket. Sometimes it is strung across the bottom near the bait. When the hog enters the trap, it trips the wire, causing the door to be released. The door drops, capturing all hogs that have entered.

The problem with this type of door is twofold: Any hogs on the outside of the trap are missed, and you've just trained the missed hogs to stay away from the trap! A benefit of this type of door is that very few hogs can lift the door with their snouts, so captured hogs stay put. The drop-gate trap also will catch multiple pigs, depending on how many entered before one of them tripped the latch. Larger traps, round traps or corral type can effectively use these gates.

The two-trap door designs preferred in Texas include the root door and the spring door. These doors allow multiple entries because they close behind

Round box trap. (Photo courtesy of Brad Porter)

Box trap with spring door.

the entering hog to prevent escape but allow other hogs to continue entering. It is not uncommon to catch ten or more hogs in the same trap. Hogs on the outside will see the trapped hogs eating the bait and will attempt to join the others. They won't know they're trapped until the feed within the trap is gone, and by then it's too late.

The root door should be about 18–24 inches tall by 18 inches wide and hinged at the top; it should be slanted into the trap at a 30-degree angle. The spring door is generally 36 inches tall by 18 inches wide, hinged on the side. Any heavy-duty spring such as a trampoline or screen door spring can be used to retrieve the door to the side of the trap. Don't use a spring that's too strong or it may prevent the entry of smaller pigs. This door should be placed on the corner of the trap with the side of the trap acting as the stop. Also, it is important that the doorway entrance is cleaned of grass and debris so that it doesn't prohibit the door from closing snugly. Any gap left in the gate that a hog can get its nose in will enable the hog to escape.

Hog traps should be securely anchored to the ground or constructed with bottoms. Larger hogs can be extremely strong and easily lift the trap if they can get their noses under an edge. Some trappers don't like to use a trap bottom because the floor looks unnatural, thus alerting the hog to a potential danger. While a hog may avoid a trap with a bottom, the majority of professional trappers I have dealt with prefer their traps to have bottoms.

I trapped a couple hogs once in a bottomless trap, and as I approached the trapped hogs, they literally started running with the trap! They managed to get their nose in the squares and were able to lift the trap slightly off the ground then push it forward as I approached. They weren't able to go far, but it demonstrates the importance of having a bottom and securing the trap to the ground.

Roofs or partial roofs also may be required to prevent the hogs from jumping or climbing over the top. Constructing a round box trap that is 6 to 8 feet in diameter may curtail some from escaping over the top. A round trap can be rolled on its side into the bed of a standard-size pickup and easily rolled off when reaching your destination. Square traps allow hogs to congregate in the corners, and I've seen hogs climb on the backs of others and escape. Many hog trappers put brush or cut limbs on top of the trap to make it appear more natural. This brush covering also provides shade once a hog has been trapped, thus preventing possible overheating and death, especially in warmer climates.

Corral Traps

Round or corral traps are used to catch numerous hogs. These traps are usually much larger than box traps and are generally made with livestock paneling in a circular pattern and with a radius of 12 to 20 feet. A door is placed somewhere along the seams where the panels are connected. Frequently, doors or entryways are made by overlapping the panels at the seams and using T-posts to make a tension-type gate.

There are heart-shaped corral traps with the entryway at the center of the heart. I've also seen many drop gates used on these traps with a trip wire strung from the gate to a feed bucket or trough on the far side of the trap.

Corral trap with drop door.

Corral traps are very efficient for trapping large groups of hogs. Another benefit of the corral trap is that it can be mobile and light enough for a single individual to move it and set it up. Many individuals have even put loading chutes on one side so the trapped hogs can be loaded into a trailer to be hauled to market or another location. The Judas pig with plenty of food and water is good bait for these type traps. Whatever type of trap you use, prebaiting is essential for success.

Prebaiting

Prebaiting an area at least one to two weeks prior to trapping will increase your odds of success. I've heard many people complaining about unsuccessful attempts at trapping hogs. They put their trap out, throw bait in it, set it, and maybe catch one hog, if any. If they're lucky enough to catch one hog, chances are they just scared the remaining hogs away from the area.

125

Prebaiting an area will help to get the hogs to return to the area where the trap is to be set. Wire the trap door open and bait inside the trap, leaving a small trail of bait through the door to the outside of the trap to lure the hog inside. It helps to leave the bait outside the trap to get the hogs comfortable with feeding in and around the trap. Leave the trap door wired open for several days so the hogs will get used to entering the trap for the bait, and be liberal with the bait.

Setting up a remote sensor trail camera at the bait site can also give you important information. In addition to documenting hog presence, trail cameras can document sounder size and herd composition; it can also indicate the date and time hogs appeared. I would recommend leaving the camera set during trapping operations to determine how many hogs may not have been captured.

Corral trap with funnel door.

Liberally prebait and bait the trap.

Setting the Trap

After it is apparent that hogs have been entering the trap, generously bait the inside of the trap while ceasing to bait the outside of the trap. Since a multiple entry door, such as a root door or spring door, is dependent on the hogs pushing it open, it is important to prop the door open initially by placing a wedge between the trap door and the side or the trap door and the base. This opening alleviates any reluctance for the hog to enter. When the hog enters, its back or body causes the wedge to drop down or away, and the tension of the gate then closes the door.

For drop doors, tie a piece of rope or light wire to the trigger mechanism, stringing the rope loosely through the top of the cage, and let the remainder of the rope hang down into the cage. Tie a bucket or small trough of bait to this end of the rope/wire, thus completing the trap. As the hog enters the trap and starts feeding out of the bucket, the attached rope or trip wire will pull the triggering mechanism from the trap door, causing the door to drop.

As the hog enters the trap and starts feeding out of the bucket or trough, the attached rope or trip wire will pull the prop between the trap door, causing the door to close. With a multiple-entry-type gate, a trapped hog may entice additional hogs to enter by pushing through the closed spring or root door.

Baits

The most common type of bait is whole corn or milo, and many people use variations of these. Some sour it in water or soak it in diesel. If this doesn't work, try pouring something sweet over the corn, such as molasses, syrup, honey, vanilla extract, even strawberry flavoring or powdered raspberry Jell-O! I've heard of many types of attractants and even tried a flavored air freshener for the car, which I was told would work. It worked all right as long as the hogs could find the bait. Did the freshener increase the success or speed of them finding the trap? I doubt it.

Hog trappers have successfully used food scraps like breads, pastries, fruits, and vegetables from their local restaurants and grocery stores as bait. Other successful baits include livestock feed, fish, and carrion. Fish and fish parts have been used successfully but may be hard to find. Ground horse hoofs, with garlic and sugar, honey or molasses have also been used.

Animal matter such as fresh highway road kills, dead rabbits, or even guts may also work. Some people have even left a dead hog in the trap to act as bait. Many people believe that if you leave a dead hog in the trap, others will be hesitant or scared away and not come to it. This is not totally true. If you open the hog and display the entrails, other hogs may be enticed to enter. Different times of years play a role in what will attract wild hogs. When fresh green vegetation is available, the use of rotting meat may be beneficial. Hogs are like people in that they like a little diversity in their diet. Remember that hogs are very intelligent and you must outwit them.

I've had very good luck using animal entrails or road kills. I remember one mid-November day on the second weekend of deer hunting season. Late summer rainfall brought exceptional amounts of vegetation and a heavy acorn crop that was keeping wildlife in the woods. In Texas, baiting for white-tailed deer is a common practice, but because the conditions of the habitat were excellent, very few animals were coming to the wildlife feeders.

A few deer hunters were hoping for a wild hog and had set traps baited with corn. Not many were successful. One lucky deer hunter did harvest a white-tailed doe and the ranch manager threw the guts into the trap. The following morning, three wild hogs were in the trap and ultimately in the hunter's freezer. I wish I could take the credit for this bait, but using meat is a common practice among the USDA Wildlife Services trappers in South and Central Texas. In conclusion, always remember to try something else if certain baits aren't working. It may even behoove you to move your trap to a different location.

There are many commercial hog attractants available today on the market, including scents. These generally have a strong sweet smell or imitate the smell of mast or acorns. Hog urine is another attractant used especially for boars. The urine can be collected once a hog has been captured and dispatched. Female urine works the best to attract boars.

A decoy or Judas pig can also be a successful bait. A Judas pig is a pig that is left in the trap to persuade other pigs to enter. For this scenario to work, use a large corral trap with ample food and water. Pigs will attract other pigs, which is why it is important to have a trap that will allow multiple entries. A female in heat may provide the best bet for enticing that big boar. It is very important to feed and water the pig daily and have shade available. Again, the cooler months are better when there is less of a chance for losing the pig due to stress and heat.

Trapped Hogs

So whether you're trapping hogs for consumption, resale, or control, finding a trap full of hogs is always exciting. It is best to check the trap first thing each morning since hogs feed mostly at night. Don't leave traps unattended or you will find a dead hog in your trap. If you aren't able to check the trap daily, don't set it. When checking the traps, it is best to approach from a distance to prevent unnecessary activity around the trap site and to avoid

129

Trapped feral hogs in a corral trap. Now what?

scaring hogs away. Try to keep dog and human activity away from the trap site. If the hog's acute sense of smell notices an unfamiliar scent, the result may be an empty trap.

After all the planning has paid off and the trap is full of hogs, what's next? Even trapping hogs can be dangerous! On numerous occasions, I've had hogs charge at me through the trap. Once, I had my hand on the trap, was too slow when a hog charged, and the porker slashed my hand. Other than a bruised ego, I left with a bloody finger and more respect for hogs. Always keep your hands off the trap when dealing with the trapped animals. Also, you should always use caution when loading and unloading live wild hogs.

If you're going to dispatch an animal inside the trap, use a centerfire pistol if possible and be very careful that the end of the gun barrel is through the panel wire or cage openings. Make sure of the background behind the caged hog and be sure there are no people standing behind it. Also, be careful when aiming the weapon so as to prevent an accidental ricochet. A careless mistake can ruin an exciting trapping experience.

In some cases deer and other wildlife have been trapped inside hog traps. In the event you capture an unwanted guest, approach the trap as slowly and quietly as possible. Secure the trap door fully open and leave immediately. A captured animal can inflict injury to itself out of fright and confusion while trying to escape. After the unwanted animal has left, return to the trap and reset it.

Remember that the key to successful trapping is location, type of bait, and prebaiting. Don't hesitate to try different locations or techniques. Green vegetation dots the landscape during springtime, so trapping may take more effort and ingenuity on your part. The key to a successful hog-trapping operation is patience, experience, knowledge, and perseverance. If you have these qualities, success is waiting for you.

Drop Nets

The drop net is a 60- by 60-inch square net that is supported at each corner and a center pole. The net is attached to the poles with light rope and a blasting cap. An electric line connects all these points in a circuit and then to an electric box with a trigger mechanism. The animals are baited under the net while a hidden observer sits and waits. When the animals are under the net, the observer detonates the charges and the net drops, thus catching everything under it.

This method has been used extensively for trapping white-tailed deer for over forty years. While trapping white-tailed deer during the '70s and '80s, we frequently had to shoot hogs found under the net because they wouldn't allow the deer to come under the net. With the range expansion and problems hogs cause, some people and agencies like this method to trap hogs.

In the Great Smoky Mountains National Park, drop nets have been successfully used in the remote mountainous areas that are accessible only by foot. Personnel feel this technique is advantageous over other heavier traps because they are lighter, easier to transport, and pigs show little hesitation in feeding under the net. That means fewer man hours are spent trapping.

A study in Oklahoma conducted by the Noble Foundation compared trapping success between drop nets and corral traps and found the drop nets were more successful in capturing pigs. This research led to the design of a drop-type corral trap they termed the "BoarBuster." This trap system is a fully suspended, automated corral trap that can be remotely observed and subsequently dropped via smart phone or computer. However, Internet service is required for this system to operate. While this novel approach has proved successful, it may be too expensive, labor intensive, and time consuming for extensive hog removal.

Hog Snaring

While trapping mountain lions in South Texas, a wild hog would frequently wander into our snares. The snare is a flexible wire loop made with a sliding lock to prevent the loop from releasing. We used a foot snare with a tension pad underneath to keep small, nontarget species from being caught. The majority of the hogs we caught were heavy boars. One morning while checking the snares for lions, I found a fairly good-size boar and he was scorching mad. On this particular occasion, my wife Lisa was with me. As you may have gathered from my earlier comments, trapped wild hogs can be perilous and inevitably a snared hog will rush you. Having snared numerous hogs, I was used to their charging. Lisa, however, was not. The boar charged, but came to a sudden stop when he hit the end of the cable. It scared her so bad that it forced her back into the Jeep. That cable was too long and not nearly stout enough to suit Lisa.

The diameter of the cable on these snares should be 3/32- or 1/8-inch with a length of 36 to 48 inches. A heavy swivel attached at the end of the cable will prevent it from kinking and breaking when it tightens around the foot a large hog. The swivel end is attached to a secure object or a drag with a large hook to become entangled when pulled. The loop should be approximately

Snared feral hog.

12 to 18 inches and should be situated in a place where the animal must go through—such as a hole under a fence or a trail between two trees. A longer extension cable or chain may be used to secure the swivel end to the anchor site. The anchor site can be a fence post, tree, or stake.

As the animal goes through the loop, it tightens against the animal and the locking device prevents the cable from loosening or slipping back out. Once captured, the cable tightens the more the animal struggles.

Leg snares use a spring trip mechanism and are placed on the ground. The same size cable is used but a smaller size loop is required since the purpose is to capture the animal by the leg. To prevent smaller animals from being captured, put a foam cushion or sticks set crossways under the trip pan. A larger animal will push the pan through the cushion or sticks, thus triggering the spring.

The easiest and most common type of hog snares are those that go round the hog's neck. Trappers at the U.S. Department of Agriculture Wildlife Services frequently use this type of snare to capture marauding hogs. To prevent the death of nontarget species, a stop should be placed on the snare to prevent it from closing too tightly on the animals' neck. Most animals have smaller neck sizes, thus when the snare is set for an adult hog, smaller animals won't be choked.

If not set correctly, the use of snares can cause damage to fences when larger hogs are caught. When placing a snare in a fence, attach the top of the loop with a clip or small gauge wire to the fence; make a slight twist to the wire to suspend the loop above the ground. The clip keeps the loop open and

Hog snare set under a fence in a travel path. (Photo courtesy of USDA/APHIS)

is easily pulled free when an animal attempts to go through it. The use of snares is a relatively low-cost technique and requires minimal equipment and manpower. You can buy premade snares from many farm and ranch stores, feed stores, or from mail-order suppliers.

Snares are generally placed in known hog thoroughfares such as under or through fences. They also may be placed in trails. Some innovative trappers have even placed them on a telephone pole or tree where hogs have been rubbing. They would anchor the snare to the pole above the rub marks and use light wire to extend the snare outward, leaving an open noose protruding from the pole.

Leg snares and trail sets are much more time consuming to use. We've used them to trap many species of wildlife including mountain lions and bears. When trapping lions in South Texas, we would frequently catch hogs. Because most trails are used by so many different species of wildlife, capturing nontarget species can be a problem. Deer, javelina, coyotes, and raccoons are just a few species that can be inadvertently captured. However, having experience and knowledge of hog habits and travels and setting the right size snare can alleviate some of these captures. This is important because it is virtually impossible to release a nontarget species that's been caught in a snare.

The Javelina ... an American Original

B eing a South Texas native, the javelina has been a part of my life. I was eleven years old and just beginning to hunt when my dad, my brother Allen, and I were invited to hunt deer on a South Texas ranch. Allen was sixteen at the time and had just bought a Remington pump .30-06. The first and only animal he ever killed was a javelina.

Some people love the outdoors and hunting, but Allen went on to pursue other activities and left his time in the field to me. Over the years, I had the opportunity to study and observe many species of wildlife. The species that fascinated me the most and still ranks in the top of my list thirty years later is the javelina.

J. Frank Dobie, the noted chronicler of the Southwest and an avid naturalist, published a story about the javelina in the 1942 issue of *Southwest Review*. This story takes place in the later part of the nineteenth century when a young man named Vandervoort came to South Texas to establish a law practice in the town of Carrizo Springs.

Vandervoort had been there for only a short time when a local man approached him about selling some hogs. Realizing that he would probably need another source of income and wanting the country life, he agreed to look at them. The man explained to Mr. Vandervoort that he had already sold his cattle and was moving away and the hogs were all he had left.

As they rode around the ranch, the man noted to Vandervoort that all the hogs were of the same color and size and that his mark was the stub tail.

An alert javelina. (Photo courtesy of Bob Zaiglin)

After some haggling, Mr. Vandervoort agreed to take them at a set price of $175 for an estimated 1,500 hogs.

It wasn't until many days later when Mr. Vandervoort was riding with a neighboring rancher when they spotted some javelinas. Being proud of his purchase, he explained to the neighbor all about his hogs. It was only then did he realize that he had been swindled: The local had sold him wild javelinas for hogs.

In addition to the stories Mr. Dobie gathered from other folks, he had plenty of personal experiences with javelinas. He had the opportunity to rope javelinas in southwestern Texas and had exhausted himself scaling the Huachuca Mountains in Arizona. He'd also spent quite a bit of time hunting them in Sonora, Mexico. These tales were originally published in the 1942 issue of *Southwest Review* as "Javelina Lore and Hunting," but they can now be found in *Afield with J. Frank Dobie*, edited by Neil Carmony.

The javelina or collared peccary *(Pecari tajacu)* is truly an American original because it is the only piglike creature native to North America. I say piglike because its appearance is much like a wild hog, yet javelinas are a completely separate species. Many people think the javelina is a pig and frequently call it such; however, there are numerous differences that distinguish it from a true pig. (See Table 1, page 153.) Both feral swine and javelinas belong to the mammalian order Artiodactyla, suborder Suiformes, and family Tayassuidae, which includes three species of javelina inhabiting the Western Hemisphere.

Feral hogs and javelinas occupy much of the same range in South Texas. People frequently ask me which is the more dominant animal. I've seen a group of javelinas scare hogs from deer feeders and conversely I've seen hogs run javelinas away. I think it depends on the number of animals and the individual herd composition of each species. One thing is certain: They don't like each other and are seldom together for extended periods of time. Research has provided similar findings regarding their interspatial relationships and interactions.

History in the United States

Based on archeological excavations, the collared peccary is a relative newcomer to the United States, although several extinct species of peccaries once roamed throughout the region. Early explorers were the first to document this strange-looking creature.

Because these animals resembled swine, they called this piglike creature *jabali*, which is Arabic-Spanish for wild boar. According to Mr. Weniger, records indicate that the term "javelina" was used as early as 1765. He claims the word javelina is French as opposed to Spanish in origin and explains why the term was not in general use in the early days of settlement. Some think the word *javelina* may have been derived from the word *javelin* meaning spear or dart, and thus referring to this species' darting speed and agility. Others think the name originated from the word *javel* or *havel*, meaning slovenly (untidy) or "low fellow," which definitely relates to the appearance of the creatures. Wherever the term came from, the name for this creature eventually became *javelina*. It is also known as musk pig, Mexican pig, desert pig, and peccary.

Mary Austin Holley wrote on the zoology of Texas in 1836 and stated: "The pecari or Mexican hog is even yet occasionally met with, on the frontiers, in considerable gangs. They will boldly attack a man, and are considered more dangerous than any other wild animal in Texas. The pecari is of a grayish color and the ordinary size of the domestic hog; its bristles stand erect. It is armed with tusks, several inches in length, which curl back from under jaw, and its aspect altogether is very ferocious."

John C. Duval relates in *Early Times in Texas* how a couple of men within his camp were chased and run up a tree by javelinas before two were shot and the remaining ones dispersed. While this is hard for me to believe, it represents a common cliché and one that I've heard from many people.

Del Weniger investigated the historical reports of the natural history of the javelina and has concluded that the early javelinas were much more fero-cious than they are today. They must have used their gregarious nature to intimidate and dominate their environment through gang mentality. Evi-dently continuous pressure over the last couple hundred years has caused the animal to revert to a more passive and secretive nature. Whether Weniger's conclusions are true is open to speculation and debate among scientists.

Early settlers found that javelina hide made excellent leather, and many were market-hunted for this reason. In many parts of Central and South America, they are still hunted for their hides. William Bollaert, who traveled through Texas in 1843 stated in his journal that the "Mexican hog, or peccary, are found generally in the low hollows of trees and shot; the meat is very good."

Early explorer records detail very few references to the javelina in much of its current range in Texas. However, Del Weniger claims the collared peccary figured much larger in the explorer picture of early Texas than previously reported. He claims it was described over and over from the early Spanish expeditions to the pioneers and surveyors two hundred years later. While the javelina is currently expanding its range into Central Texas, archeological evidence proving past existence in this part of the state is absent. This may be due in part to the increase in woody vegetation, which came about because of range deterioration brought on by early settlers overgrazing the land, or it might be from a lack of natural fires. As the predominantly grassland prairies of Central and South Texas began to be transformed to brushland, it provided a more suitable habitat for the javelina, thus increasing its range in Texas. There is also evidence that the javelina is expanding its range in Arizona and New Mexico for the same reasons.

Captain Flack, writing of his hunting experiences in 1866, reported seeing his first javelina in the palmetto and cane breaks along the San Bernard River of Brazoria County, located in southeast Texas. Flack, and another pioneer named Dodge, also claimed seeing large numbers of javelinas along the Brazos River in 1877.

Vernon Bailey, chief naturalist with the U.S. Biological Survey, conducted the first intensive field studies on the mammals of the Southwest at the turn of the twentieth century and described two subspecies of javelinas in New Mexico: the Texas peccary and the Yaqui peccary.

The Texas peccary was found, reportedly in abundant numbers, in the extreme southeastern part of New Mexico in the sand dunes along the eastern edge of the Pecos Valley. The Yaqui peccary of the Sonora Desert region is found in the southwestern part of New Mexico in several of the mountain ranges, including the Peloncillo, Apache, San Luis, and Guadalupe Mountains. According to Bailey, "They ranged mainly on the Upper Sonoran mountain slopes where dense chaparral and numerous caves in the canyon walls furnish excellent cover and safe retreats and where the food supply is unusually abundant." He further reported that the peccary seems to be equally at home in the upper and lower Sonoran zones.

Vernon Bailey published the first extensive survey of the mammals of Texas in 1905. In it, he described the distribution as ". . . more or less common in southern Texas and along the Rio Grande to above the mouth of the Pecos, thence up the east side of the Pecos valley into the unsettled sand hill region of southeastern New Mexico, and east along the broken edge of the plains to San Angelo and Kerrville, and along the coast to Corpus Christi."

He went on to say, ". . . a few may remain here and there still farther east and north where they once ranged, but they have been pretty thoroughly driven out by the settlement of the country and are now merely clinging to existence in regions of deep rocky canyons or dense thorny cactus and chaparral and in an uninhabited waste of sand dunes." He did not mention the Trans Pecos vicinity of Big Bend and Davis Mountains where they are fairly common today.

In 1939, the U.S. Fish and Wildlife Service estimated the number of peccaries in the United States to be around 50,000, with 35,100 in Texas, 14,300 in Arizona, and 400 in New Mexico. While this number was clearly a conservative estimate, it is obvious that the javelina population increased throughout the latter part of the twentieth century. This increase was due to the protection it received through state laws. These laws elevated its status to a game animal and set seasons and bag limits, thus limiting the harvest. It also prohibited the sale of javelina skins from Texas, while permitting the importation and sale of skins from foreign countries and other states.

Based on these historical records, it appears javelinas occupied a large portion of Texas during the era of exploration where habitat was sufficient, albeit in relatively low numbers in the northern and eastern portions of the state. These fringe or small populations subsequently declined during the time of colonization and settlement. As colonization increased with the European settlers, loss of habitat, overhunting, and commercialization of hides had a disastrous effect on the population. Their hides were tanned and used as leather for a number of items—gloves, bags, purses, shoe tops, and numerous ornamental items—while the bristles were used to make brushes.

I found an interesting story regarding the importance of javelina hides in the book *Memories of Peter Tumlinson Bell*, who lived in Carrizo Springs in South Texas around the turn of the twentieth century. In it, he discussed what became known as the Javelin War:

> There was a very disastrous drouth (sic) in this section of the country in 1886 or '87 and it put most of the cattlemen and sheepmen out of business—it gave South Texas a setback. There are a few people who are old enough to remember and know about it. I do not like to think about that drouth even to this day. Most of the people of this country would have went (sic) hungry it had not been for the javelina hogs.

> There were litterly (sic) thousands of the little hogs in this country at that time and this drouth caused what became known in the history of our county as the Javelin War. Lots of the wealthier ranchers had to participate in the Javelin War because their sheep and cattle had died by the hundreds. Some of them had been worth many thousands of dollars but now was (sic) worth nothing and had to provide for their families. Nearly all of the citizens of this county had to participate in the war of the javelin in order to feed their families.

> One man can be thanked for finding a market for the javelina hides and that was J. L. McCaleb, the owner and operator of J. L. McCaleb Mercantile Company. He also owned and edited a small newspaper there for a spell. A northern firm sent McCaleb some advertisement stating that they would pay cash for javelina hides; $1.00 for the large ones and $.50 for the medium size ones and $.30 for the small ones. McCaleb made a deal with some wholesale men in San Antonio for groceries and he would pay cash and groceries for literally thousands of the javelina hides.

> The Javelin War of '86 or '87 saved the people of Dimmit County from going on relief and it is said to have been about the only one that didn't ask

for help. Now I didn't write about the drouths to let people think that south Texas is subject to drouths, but it will be remembered by all the old timers.

The Javelin Newspaper of Carrizo Springs was named from the javelina of south Texas to commemorate the Javelin War of our county. The paper's sign for many years was a stuffed javelina that had been prepared by a taxidermist. It stood on the front wall of the printing office where the paper was printed each week. The paper changed hands several times and some of them have wanted to change its name but I for one told them to remove my name from their subscription list if they changed the little paper's name. I am happy to say that the paper is still known as the *Javelin*. It is one of the oldest newspapers in south Texas.

Robert Mauermann claimed in a 1943 Texas Game and Fish publication that one dealer near Uvalde handled 15,000 javelina hides during the 1936–1937 season but only 2,500 were from Texas; the majority came from Mexico. Steel traps and hunting with dogs were the primary techniques these early hide hunters used.

Javelina research in Texas began in the mid-1960s to determine the basic life history and to improve the management of the species. Studies also have been conducted in Arizona and New Mexico. These research projects have provided extensive information on the life history of the javelina.

Range and Habitat

The collared peccary is the smallest of the peccaries and has the largest range. It can be found from the southern border states of Texas, New Mexico, and Arizona through Central America and into South America. The white-lipped peccary is larger and found in the warmer, more humid climates—from the Yucatan of Mexico southward into Argentina. The Chacoan peccary is the largest species (80–90 pounds) and is found in the arid regions of northern Argentina, Paraguay, and southern Bolivia. In certain areas of Central and South America the ranges overlap.

Principal Game Birds and Mammals of Texas, which was published by the Texas Game Fish and Oyster Commission in 1945, states that the historical range of the javelina in Texas extended from the upper Texas coast to north and west of Fort Worth, to Red River and westward to Odessa and outlying land, and to the Pecos River. However, by 1945, the range had been reduced to regions south and west of San Antonio, through the Pecos River drainage and the Big Bend region.

The javelina population stabilized throughout the mid-twentieth century to its current range. Land stewardship and an improvement in habitat conditions helped to expand their range and recolonize territories that they historically inhabited. By the 1990s, the South Texas district of Texas Parks and Wildlife Department began documenting a population decline in this historic population stronghold.

Javelina prefer dense brush and thickets for food and cover, using dense timber or brushy thickets for use as bedding cover and protection from the cold. Javelina have adapted to rugged mountain ranges of the western desert as well as the undulating terrain of the South Texas brush country.

South Texas has typically flat to undulating terrain characterized by chaparral brushland that is dominated by mesquite, prickly pear, and various other acacia species. Prickly pear and white-brush provide the necessary food and cover. West Texas is typical Chihuahuan Desert characterized by shallow soils and is dominated by lechuguilla, creosote bush, ocotillo, cactus, and various native desert grasses. In West Texas and Arizona where prickly pear may be lacking, other desert plants such as sotol and lechuguilla provide a food base. Whereas in South Texas they frequently utilize whitebrush thickets, in Arizona they use sacaton grass as cover.

In the Texas Hill country they use thick cedar breaks for cover. Recent reports indicate javelinas are moving into the central and south-central portions of the state that is more of an oak-woodland habitat, and reports from TPWD indicate increasing populations in the Texas Rolling Plains, which is located in the southeast area of the Texas panhandle.

Currently, in New Mexico they are found primarily in the middle and southwestern regions of the state: in Hidalgo, Luna, Grant, Catron, Socorro, Sierra, Dona Ana counties, the Gila National Forest, and White Sands Missile Range. A few may be found in the southeastern parts of the state in the Guadalupe Mountains and in Carlsbad Caverns National Park.

In Arizona, peccaries currently occupy approximately 34 percent of Arizona and have an estimated population of 60,000 individuals. They inhabit all the desert ranges except for a small district west and southwest of Phoenix. In addition, they are found in the adjacent grasslands and chaparral, and in the nearby foothills and mountainsides that are dominated by oak woodland. Population densities in the oak woodlands are much lower and sparse than in the desert ranges.

Throughout the range of the javelina, climate seems to be the main limiting factor on distribution and range expansion. Although javelinas can be found in most types of topography, including deserts and mountainous regions, they are susceptible to cold temperatures and have difficulty negotiating snow. Their susceptibility to cold is evident by their desire to bed together in groups in an effort to keep warm. Many biologists believe that excessively severe cold winters may have a devastating effect on javelinas.

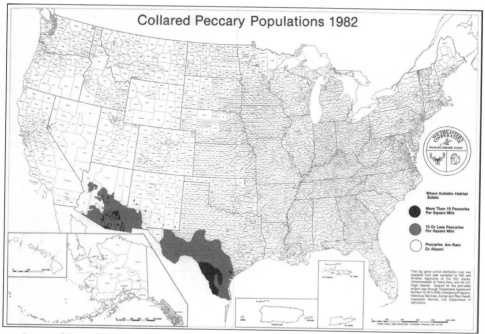

Range of the collared peccary.

Appearance

Javelinas or collared peccaries get their name from the band of white or light-hair collar across their shoulders. They are grizzled in color with a snout and a very short or nonexistent tail. These small ungulates are the least sexually dimorphic of all North American ungulates, meaning it's very difficult to distinguish between the sexes in the field.

Upon observation, the javelina appears to have slender legs with small feet in proportion to its body, especially when compared to the heavier legs of the muscled feral hog. Their ears appear shorter than the hogs. Feral hogs, on the other hand, have a long, straggly tail that is very visible in the field. Javelinas also only have one dewclaw—toelike appendages on the backside of the foot above the heel—on the inside of the hind feet and lack an outside dewclaw, whereas the hog has double dewclaws on each foot. Feral hogs may have up to fourteen teats for nursing young, but javelinas only have eight, of which only four are functional.

Javelina in South Texas. (Photo courtesy of Macy Ledbetter)

A full-grown javelina ranges in size from 32–38 inches in body length and stands 18–23 inches at the shoulder. The average field dressed weight of an adult javelina is about 30 pounds, with the males being slightly larger than the females. A big boar will weigh more than 40–45 pounds.

The javelina has a scent or musk gland located on the middle of its back about seven or eight inches above the tail. In the center is a navel or nipple-looking appendage that secretes a strong, musky fluid that is used for marking the home range and territory as well as serving as a social marker within the herd. It is because of this gland that javelinas have been called musk hogs.

Life History

Javelinas are social creatures that live in family groups that maintain and actively defend their territory. Herd size ranges from 5–25 animals but average about 8–12. The social structure or herd life enables the animals to feed with greater confidence because one of the herd members is always alert to danger and the greater number of individuals provides protection for the group. Within their territory they have resting or bedding grounds that they utilize when traveling to and from feeding areas.

Javelinas are primarily crepuscular or nocturnal animals that seek cover in the warmer times of midday. In the wintertime they may be active throughout the day. Their days usually begin at or slightly before daylight; they feed until midmorning and then they rest. Because they are susceptible to cold temperatures, they will frequently bunch up or huddle together to stay warm. They'll remain inactive until a few hours before dark, whereupon they begin feeding again. Feeding length may increase on colder days or bright moonlit nights. There seems to be a strong inverse relationship between feeding and temperature. As temperature increases, feeding generally decreases.

Pregnant females also will feed longer the closer they come to delivery. Again, during the hotter months, nighttime feeding may increase. While javelinas will generally get in water to cool off as swine do, they will also wallow in mud or dirt. They may live up to ten years of age.

Home Range

A javelina herd is highly territorial of its home range, with the range largely determined by the quality of the habitat and the availability of food. Depending on the individual herds or animals, the javelina may become aggressive and combatant in defending its territory. Its territoriality is marked with scent from the musk gland. When two herds enter into a territorial dispute, aggressive behavior such as tooth clacking, jaw popping, and chasing is evident.

The home range of javelinas in South Texas may vary in size from 200–900 acres while the home range in West Texas may be several thousand acres. There is limited overlapping between home ranges of javelina herds.

Behavior

While the javelina has little physiological ability to adapt to climatic changes, it does, however, have behavioral abilities that enable it to survive a wide variety of climates. They utilize the microclimate of their habitat to compensate for climatic changes. They tend to avoid the hottest locales in the summer while seeking warmer ones in winter. They have limited ability to sweat, and panting assists them in lowering their body temperature. Their best body temperature control is through behavior patterns. For example, seeking warmth and shelter in caves, caverns, and thickets where they may sleep and rest in huddled groups. Some scientists claim their daily movement is influenced by temperature changes as well as the need to feed.

Senses

The javelina has relatively poor eyesight and only a fair sense of hearing, but it possesses an excellent sense of smell. This nearsighted creature has extreme difficulty in identifying objects beyond one hundred yards. These two poorly developed senses often lead to the javelina's demise. Their weak vision and hearing enables the hunter to approach the javelina within fairly close range.

Javelina have an excellent sense of smell. (Photo courtesy of Macy Ledbetter)

As with feral swine, the javelina is missing the tapetum. This is the reflecting layer found in the eyes that causes many animals' eyes to shine at night when struck by direct light. When hunting at night, remember that the javelina's eyes will not reflect light.

Scent marking is very important to the javelina. It uses its scent gland for marking territory as well as social activities. If the herd gets scattered, the scent and their olfactory senses enable them to regroup and maintain herd cohesion.

Teeth

The javelina has 38 teeth including: 4/6 (top/bottom) incisors, 2/2 canines, 6/6 premolars, and 6/6 molars. The young are born with 4 temporary canines and 2 lower incisors. By 18 to 21 months, the final molars have erupted and permanent dentition is complete.

The canine teeth of the javelina are straight; the canine teeth of hogs curve. These sharp canine teeth can be very dangerous. Through the constant action of the jaws, the canines are continually being sharpened. While most predators use the canines for killing prey and tearing meat, the javelina uses its canines primarily for protection and displays in behavioral interaction. The canines of the javelina are the largest of any non-carnivorous species. Unlike the feral hog, whose canine teeth never stop growing, the javelina's canine teeth generally stop growing at four years of age, or two years past full dentition.

Stomach

Because of the canine teeth, there is very little lateral movement of the jaws for grinding; therefore, most chewing is done in a vertical crushing movement. This limited ability to chew and grind may be the reason for the javelina's unusual complex stomach. Although not considered a ruminant like cattle or deer that have compartmentalized stomachs, there are four basic compartments to the javelina's stomach, one of which the primary function is fermentation.

This enlarged simple stomach has a high pH and contains microorganisms that assist in metabolism and enable it to digest fiber more efficiently than the simple-stomach of the domestic or feral swine. It also allows them to assimilate energy more efficiently from its principally herbaceous diet.

Food Habits

While javelinas are omnivorous and will eat plant and animal matter much like their swine relatives, they are primarily herbivores. Their diet consists of succulents such as cacti, sotol, lechuguilla, forbs, fruits, tubers, grass, and mast such as mesquite beans. Although animal matter is a part of the javelina's diet, studies indicate it is of minor importance, and is composed

Javelina skull showing sharp canines.

primarily of insects. Moreover, ingestion of animal matter is probably based on opportunity or incidental swallowing as opposed to vigorously searching for animal matter.

Studies in Texas and Arizona have proven that the prickly pear cactus is an important part of their diet. In Texas, cactus may compose up to 80 percent of a javelina's diet during certain times of the year. Cactus is high in carbohydrates and moisture content, which satisfies a major part of the javelina's water requirements. Although the thorns of the prickly pear does not seem to deter the javelina from eating it, some people claim that the javelina scoots the prickly pear pads along the ground to knock off some of the thorns. Cacti fruits are also important during the summer.

In Arizona, century plants are important in the desert grasslands. Annual forbs provide valuable seasonal supplements to the diet. In the summer and fall, javelinas also cherish hard and soft mast such as acorns, mesquite beans, acacia (spp) mast, and fruits of woody plants.

Arizona studies indicate javelinas spend a considerable amount of time disturbing the soil in shallow rooting for small underground plant parts such as roots, tubers, bulbs, and rhizomes. Their fairly well-defined sense of smell enables them to search for these. Javelinas generally do not root as deeply and destructively as wild hogs. Although they don't damage the habitat like feral hogs, they can assist in the spreading of prickly pear. Javelinas compete very little with other native species for food, but they will "hog" wildlife feeders and eat all the corn. This behavior is what annoys most hunters.

Reproduction

Javelinas may breed and farrow throughout the year; however, the peak breeding season is usually in the late fall and winter with farrowing occurring throughout late spring and summer. A secondary-breeding peak occurs in the spring with birthing occurring in the fall. Although it is possible for a javelina to have two litters per year, it is rather uncommon. However, it does allow them to possibly have a second litter if the first one is lost. Because the North American javelina occupies arid environments, rainfall is extremely important for successful reproduction. Breeding is frequently related to nutrition and habitat quality.

Javelinas are capable of breeding at one year of age. Some may even breed at 10–11 months. Males and females generally reach sexual maturity about the same age. The gestation period for a javelina is around 145 days, with a litter of one to three, but usually two, young being born in late spring. Research in Texas indicates the sex ratio of javelina at birth show a distinct

Table 1: *Major physical differences between javelinas and feral swine.*

DIFFERENCE	JAVELINA	SWINE
Scent Gland	On back above tail	Absent
Tail	Not visible	Long and hairy
Ears	Appear smaller and less visible	Appear longer and generally upright
Hind feet	Fused dewclaw, 3 toes on hind feet	2 dewclaws, 4 toes on hind feet
Hind legs	Ulna and radius fused	Ulna and radius bones separate
Teeth	38	44
	Upper canines grow straight down, lower canines grow straight up, upper and lower generally much shorter than swine	Upper canines curve up, lower canines curve out, upper and lower canines can grow very long
Stomach	Relatively enlarged and complex	Simple monogastric stomach
Gall bladder	Absent	Present

male bias whereas the fetal ratios in an Arizona study were 56 percent females and 44 percent males. The sex ratio will most likely not deviate significantly from a 1:1 ratio.

When born, javelinas have a tannish, light brownish, or yellow color with darker underparts, and when they are about twelve weeks old, the color changes to a darker, grizzled color. After only a few hours, the infant offspring are capable of following their mother. They nurse until about six weeks, but they are capable of eating solid food from about four weeks. At that time (4–6 weeks) they begin to be weaned. At birth, the young already have well-developed temporary canine teeth for defense. And they will use them. I had a friend who had a javelina as a pet, so I know they will definitely charge you!

Due primarily to predation, mortality of young javelina is relatively high, frequently reaching 40 percent. Free-ranging javelinas generally live five to ten years of age although captive animals have exceeded twenty years.

Males do not have a harem as many people believe. They do not pair for life and males may breed several females. When old, the males are often kicked out of the herd to complete their life solitarily. With the exception of a scrotum on mature males, it is very hard to distinguish male javelinas from females. When hunting, a single javelina may be an old male that has been banished.

Diseases

Periodic disease outbreaks can have devastating effects on local javelina populations as was demonstrated in the mid-1980s in South Texas when encephalitis reduced these herds considerably. Diseases such as equine or javelina encephalitis, vesicular stomatitis, rabies, pseudorabies, leptospirosis, and brucellosis also can take its toll on them. Javelina encephalitis has caused devastating losses in Arizona and South Texas. The social or herd structure of javelinas will be a disadvantage if an outbreak of disease occurs. Most javelina occupy the same range as native wildlife and livestock and will be affected by many of the same diseases.

External Parasites

External parasites include fleas, sucking lice, and ticks. Hunters should be prepared for a heavy infestation of fleas once a javelina is harvested. My experience with them leads me to believe they must be the most flea-infested creatures in Texas, if not in the entire United States. Internal parasites may include stomach worms, flukes, tapeworms, protozoan, and blood parasites. There is very little evidence that internal or external parasites pose a significant threat to the javelina population.

Mortality

Although the social structure of javelinas living in herds may be beneficial for food and survival, it is this social structure that makes them more **vulnerable** to excessive harvest by man. Predator control aimed at animals such as coyotes, bobcats, mountain lions, and even feral hogs have caused the javelina population to decline in portions of Texas. Aerial surveys conducted throughout South Texas have showed a dramatic decrease in the javelina population.

Conversely, the wild hog has continued to increase in numbers and distributions. Aside from predator control, many South Texas hunters and ranchers despise this little creature because they eat the corn at feeders that is intended for deer; they also feel the javelina is of little value. With the recent addition of javelina to the Boone and Crockett Club record book, this attitude just may change.

Apart from man, adult javelinas have very few predators other than mountain lions and bears. Because mountain lions and pumas share roughly their entire range, they are the most important natural predator on adult javelinas. Young javelinas have a wider range of predators, including coyotes and bobcats. Researchers in Texas and Arizona claim coyotes are major predators of young javelinas.

I witnessed the aftermath of a black bear attack that killed some javelinas in the Black Gap Wildlife Management Area of West Texas. One morning I recall finding a dead javelina and by looking at the track indentations and drag marks, it was easy to determine what had happened. The javelina herd had been walking down a gravelly drainage when a bear happened upon the herd. The deep impressions in the gravel showed how the chase progressed and the kill site showed plainly in the torn up ground. From the kill site was a drag mark that we followed to the carcass. The javelina skin was turned inside out, which is distinctive of a bear kill. Bear kills on javelina also have been noted in Arizona. Bear attacks on javelinas are probably more opportunistic in nature, and, as such, it is doubtful they pose a significant concern for javelinas.

Other causes of mortality in javelinas include vehicles on highways, nontarget trapping and snaring, and even accidents in the wild. Although

Javelina with young. Note the missing collar on the female. (Photo courtesy of Macy Ledbetter)

extensive tooth wear and other dental problems and infections have been accredited to mortality in feral hogs, it does not appear to be an issue in the collared peccary.

Loss of habitat has also been a problem for the javelina. The clearing of excessive amounts of native brush and prickly pear may be a major limiting factor to javelina populations. Conversely, limited brush manipulation may increase preferred forages, if they are not cleared to excess. How much brush manipulation can be tolerated before reaching a critical point to a javelina population is still relatively unknown. On the other hand, shrub invasion in desert grasslands by overgrazing may improve peccary habitat.

Population Decline

In South Texas, the white-tailed deer is the premium big-game animal, and a trophy buck is literally worth thousands of dollars. Millions of dollars are spent in attempts to produce these trophy animals. Wildlife feeders are an important aspect of quality deer management. Many hunters feel the javelina is a worthless freeloader keeping white-tailed deer from the feeders by eating all the corn.

Illicit and indiscriminate slaughter of javelinas from unscrupulous hunters and land managers has had a devastating effect on local populations. Despite previous thoughts that javelina are not vulnerable to extensive hunting, they are very vulnerable, especially in South Texas where the number of high, game-proof fences continue to increase!

The declining population in South Texas may be due to a multitude of factors that are outside the established realm of mortality factors. These factors include habitat changes, low reproductive potential, perceived low economic value, pressure from feral hogs, and competition with white-tailed deer at feeders. To understand these, we must look at the changes that have taken place throughout the South Texas range of the javelina.

Over the last thirty years, increased numbers of high fences have enabled landowners to control wildlife populations with extreme efficiency, especially such vulnerable creatures as the javelina. These high fences are

157

Beth Zaiglin with pet javelina. (Photo courtesy of Bob Zaiglin)

made of net wire and replace the typical five-strand barbed wire historically used for livestock. Net wire fences put a stop to the free movement of the javelinas throughout their home range; this pressure from landowners and hunters has been devastating.

While many landowners and sportsmen in South Texas consider the javelina to be nothing more than a pest, in Arizona and New Mexico the javelina is considered a valuable game animal and is actively promoted as such. Many nonresidents of Texas, Arizona, and New Mexico consider the javelina as a sought-after, challenging game species. To the New Yorker or Pennsylvanian, the opportunity to harvest a collared peccary may be a once-in-a-lifetime opportunity. However, until the landowners of Texas realize the intrinsic value of the javelina, it will continue to be extirpated.

Some professionals may argue that downturns in local javelina populations are due to drought cycles as well as excessive habitat manipulation. This may be true in certain cases, but in South Texas the long-range, twenty-year trend is down, and I can assure you that we are not in a twenty-year drought. While annual precipitation has a definite effect on javelina reproduction, it generally causes only a temporary downturn and not a long-term one.

Javelina Management

An early record for the management of the javelina can be found in the 1945 Texas Game Fish and Oyster publication *Principal Game Birds and Mammals of Texas*. At that time the javelina was not considered a popular game animal for several reasons: difficulty in hunting it, the inaccessibility of its "haunts," and its "unpalatability."

Many people would have heatedly debated that latter statement especially in areas of the South, southwestern Texas, and Mexico where the javelina

Javelina hunters. (Photo courtesy of Macy Ledbetter)

was regularly utilized as a meat source. Early Texas hunters proclaimed the javelina was tasty if prepared correctly. Even today, you'll find javelina served at wild-game dinners and at hunting camps where a few sportsmen will barbecue the young animals. In cowboy camps, a few old-time Mexican cowboys still savor *barbacoa* from javelina cooked over coals.

Early protection laws proved successful in the javelinas' early recovery, and many private ranches protected the species. As the recovery continued and the population increased and expanded its range, hunting opportunity for javelina also increased, although there was limited access for hunters.

Records from 1945 mention restocking as a possible way to augment the natural process of range expansion, but because the preferred domains had suffered habitat loss, this method was deemed unsuitable. Excessive land clearing, livestock overgrazing, farming, land clearing, and the subsequent loss of cacti as a principal food often stood in the way of early restocking efforts.

In 1945, the records documented little conflict between livestock and javelina. In fact, many ranchers claimed the javelina helped control certain unwanted plant and animal species such as lechuguilla, insects, worms, and reptiles.

Habitat Management

As with most wildlife species, good habitat management is the key. Javelina often prefer thick brush and prickly pear that many ranchers and land managers don't like. Cattle ranchers have made tremendous efforts to develop grasslands for livestock, but these improvements are to the detriment of the javelina. When clearing brush, it is important to maintain interconnecting brush corridors, drainages, and good thick cover with a diverse food base including succulents such as cactus. Many landowners are concerned about the javelina spreading unwanted plants such as mesquite and prickly pear, but research shows this fear to be unfounded. Javelina will not spread unwanted plants any more than cattle or other livestock.

Damage

Unlike the feral hog, the size of the javelina and the potential damage is much less dramatic than that caused by feral hogs. They will grub at the ground in search of succulent forbs or mast, but they generally do not dig deep enough to cause a severe impact. Conversely, this shallow disking may increase forb production and water infiltration.

They will compete with other wildlife for corn or other grains at wildlife feeders, but this problem can be alleviated by putting a 34-inch-tall pen around the feeder. Another concern among landowners is damage caused to net-wire fences by javelinas rooting under it and causing holes under the fence. Staking the holes will curtail further damage.

Although some people believe the javelina competes with livestock for grasses, especially in the desert region, there is very little validity to this. There is some concern about javelinas preying on livestock, specifically lambs and kid goats. While individual javelinas may prey on them in certain circumstances, this behavior is not a common trait.

Population Management

Once the habitat requirements are fulfilled, maintaining a stable population can be accomplished through selective and limited harvest. If you're interested in javelina management, remember that overhunting can be very damaging to the herd. In South and West Texas, aerial surveys are used to monitor wildlife populations, specifically white-tailed deer and mule deer, and I believe that it is important to monitor the javelina population during these surveys as well.

Another way to monitor the population is through herd composition counts or incidental observations. By keeping track of the animals observed, it is possible to make harvest recommendations based on these counts. Try to limit the harvest to no more than 20 percent of an individual herd, concentrating on the males, if possible.

Collecting harvest data is also important and should include the sex, dressed weights, and body condition of the individuals. This allows the manager to monitor the age structure, sex ratio, reproduction, and overall health of the population.

Harvest

In Texas, the annual javelina harvest has remained relatively stable since 1991. Approximately 20,000 javelinas are harvested each year in Texas. While the harvest remains fairly consistent, the population continues to decline, so overhunting or legal harvest does not seem to be a factor in its demise. According to Texas game officials, the decline can be attributed to a number of factors, including habitat loss, drought, feral-hog competition, and illegal harvest. While we can do little to compensate for environmental changes, it is extremely important that we educate landowners and sportsmen on the value of javelina to the native fauna if this little creature is to continue to be a Texan.

Hunting the Javelina

Unfortunately, I can't recall the first javelina I ever killed or how many, but I can remember the time I decided to quit hunting them and just enjoy them. I was studying wildlife management in college and had become a research assistant for a white-tailed deer breeding project on a ranch near Laredo in Webb County, Texas. This position required me to capture, tag, and document breeding chronology of white-tailed fawns. Fawns are born in the summer, and during the birthing season, I spent three months living on this South Texas ranch.

I had a .22 Magnum and enjoyed stalking through the mesquite and prickly pear looking for jackrabbits and javelinas. After successfully hunting several javelinas, I decided to make it more challenging. I had a Colt Python .357 Magnum pistol with me that day, and I decided to see how successfully I could stalk them. I found a herd in the distance and began my stalk . . . slow and steady toward the herd. As I got closer to the herd, the wind was still in my face and the sun was on my back when I noticed the herd was moving toward me. When I was within twenty feet of the herd, I raised my pistol to shoot . . . and then stopped.

I became mesmerized by the herd as they foraged and interacted. I thoroughly enjoyed observing them, and standing there, I decided to lower my gun and back away. To this day, I still get a thrill out of testing my abilities of getting close to a herd of javelinas, but I'll leave the harvest for the first-time hunter.

Hunting javelinas. (Photo courtesy of Wade Ledbetter)

Just like with the wild hog, there are many ways to hunt the javelina. These methods include stand hunting, still hunting, stalking, and driving safari style. In the December 1889 issue of *Harpers' Weekly*, Frederic Remington chronicled an exciting javelina hunt he went on in the Mexican state of Sonora.

After a lengthy train ride through the country, he wrote: "The whole aspect of nature was cruel, with its yellow sparkling sands dotted with cactus, chaparral, and other thorny growths, which cut and scratch if you are not wary." Thereafter, he disembarked at a train depot with an "unpronounceable name." There, he met a local rancher who invited him and a friend to a local ranch to hunt javelinas the following morning.

At daybreak, the *vaqueros* brought horses to Remington and his partner for the hunt. After a while the *vaqueros* broke away from the group to find javelinas. Shortly thereafter, the hunting party heard the sound of brush rustling and horses running, and then out into the open busted a group of javelinas with the *vaqueros* chasing them with lassoes. Remington reported that the vaquero roped the javelina with the lasso "jerking the little pig about like a football." After that, the *vaquero* dismounted, and while walking toward the incapacitated javelina he coiled his rope, drew his pistol, and shot it.

Shortly thereafter, Remington himself had the opportunity to rope a peccary, although he claims it was more tangled and entwined in the rope than professionally caught. Nevertheless, he was able to draw his six-shooter and shoot the peccary.

While roping javelinas was apparently fairly common during the last century in Mexico and South Texas, it is not so presently. We will delve into the specifics of hunting wild hogs and javelinas in the following chapter.

Hunting javelinas can be fun and exciting. It is also an excellent first species for a novice hunter. In some locales where different hunting seasons overlap, an otherwise unsuccessful white-tailed deer hunt may turn into a successful hunting experience.

Javelinas are relatively smelly creatures and frequently can be detected by the human nose. On numerous occasions, I have sniffed out javelinas by locating them by their odor. I always knew when they'd been in the area. They feed noisily, they tend to smack their teeth while rustling through the brush, and they have concerns for being quiet or careful. Hunters can use these characteristics of poor eyesight and noisy habits to easily get into bow, pistol, or muzzle range.

As with most big-game species, the successful pursuit of javelinas begins with the hunter's knowledge of the species' habits. Besides knowing the basic life history of the species, it is important to know their haunts and how to recognize their tracks and signs. Scouting days or weeks prior to the hunt makes for successful javelina hunting and can save a tremendous amount of time and effort on the day of the hunt. While scouting, concentrate on finding watering, feeding, and bedding areas. Because javelina diets change with the availability of food, you'll do well to learn the seasonal diet preferences. There's no use hunting javelinas where they do not occur.

Javelina sign includes hoof marks or tracks, scat, and signs of rooting and foraging. Javelina tracks are cloven-hoofed impressions similar to deer tracks except they're much smaller. Some concavities in the soil are no larger in diameter than a quarter. Because they are herd animals, you will generally find numerous tracks in the same locality. They are different from hogs because the hog track is much larger and the toes are rounded.

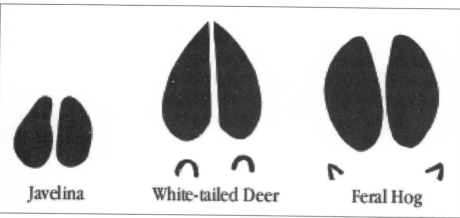

Javelina   White-tailed Deer   Feral Hog

Comparison of javelina, white-tailed deer, and feral hog tracks. (Photo courtesy of TPWD)

A well-placed shot below the ear or in the shoulder will knock the biggest boar to the ground. The type of rifle recommended for the javelina can be much smaller than most big-game species. While a well-placed shot from even the smallest caliber will do the trick, I recommend no smaller than a .222 caliber, .22-250, .220 Swift, .243, or 6mm. I see no need for the larger bores—anything heftier will be a waste of ammo!

Because the javelina generally occupies the warmer, drier climes of the Southwest, many hunters choose light clothing for these areas. However, even here, a blue norther or cold front can drop the temperature 20 degrees or more in a short time. Also, clothing should be chosen based upon the habitat that will be encountered. Good boots, tough pants, and a long-sleeved shirt are mandatory for hunting this creature amidst numerous thorny plants and cacti.

Texas, Arizona, and New Mexico require a hunting license to pursue the javelina. The game laws for the javelina—its seasons, bag limits, and hunting areas—can be found in chapter 11.

Hunting the Wild Hog and Javelina

CHAPTER 10

We'd hear the pack a-bayin'
Up the mountain loud and clear,
But before we rode to 'em
That old sow would disappear.

Or she'd rally 'gainst a boulder
Bristlin' like a porcupine,
Till a dog forgot his caution
Then she'd cut him into twine.

Killin' dogs was just a pastime
To that hog; I'm tellin' you,
With them long, curved, knife-like tushes
She could slice a houn' in two.

She could whip most any critter
On four legs I ever saw,
And she had a perfect record
'cause she never fought a draw.

From *That Spotted Sow and Other Texas Hill Country Ballads*

by Carlos Ashley

It was a cool South Texas morning with a light dew on the ground when Jim released his dogs. The previous evening we had found fresh hog sign around the tank where we were now parked. The dogs were excited and anxious to run. As soon as they hit the ground and completed their morning functions, they bounded into the brush in search of a wild boar.

Soon, a single bark in the distance broke the early morning tranquility. Within a few seconds, the single bark became a chorus of frenzied barking as the other dogs joined into the chase. Filled with anticipation and excitement, we headed toward the sound of the dogs in the distance. As our pace increased to a run, the barks turned into an ear-piercing frenzy of baying hounds.

As we struggled through the mesquite and prickly pear chaparral to reach them, time seemed to stand still. We knew that the dogs could easily

The quarry. (Photo courtesy of Macy Ledbetter)

be seriously hurt or killed if we did not get there soon. As we came around a mesquite tree, Blue, Gator, and Suzie had a 250-pound boar backed into a prickly pear. A quick draw of my .357 pistol and a well-placed, behind-the-ear shot silenced the raging boar and subsequently quieted the excited dogs.

Hunting wild boar is one of the oldest hunting sports in existence, dating back to the Middle Ages in Europe where the hog originated. Noblemen were the first to go on wild boar hunts, and it's still popular in Europe. Now, Americans have discovered the popularity of hunting these creatures—for sport, management, or control.

Hog hunting began in the United States not as a sport but as a way of rounding up free-ranging hogs. In Truett and Lay's book, *Land of Bears and Honey*, they quote Solomon Alexander on life in the last quarter of the nineteenth century:

> At the time the only hogs in the country were razorbacks, some of them only half-wild but more of them as wild as the primitive boars of Europe. A man had to have a good hog dog to do anything with them . . . every settler had a 'hog claim', which he maintained by keeping his hogs ear-marked. When the pigs were marked, the males were generally castrated. There were always plenty of maverick (unmarked) hogs. Few people fed hogs. They could not be driven up and penned.

While I'm sure it was sporting, the primary reason for hunting hogs during this time period was to collect the family hogs or to capture unmarked hogs for market. As fencing and properties began solidifying in America, hog hunting became more of a sport and less of a necessity.

Although the white-tailed deer is the most popular game animal in Texas and probably the United States, very few animals can stir a person's emotion as a wild, free-ranging feral hog. Although most landowners and professional wildlife biologists expound the detriments of feral hogs to native habitat, indigenous species, and agricultural commodities, many sportsmen enjoy hunting and trapping the beast. In Texas, feral hogs have become one of the most numerous huntable large mammals, second only to the white-tailed deer.

Poor Man's Grizzly

Feral hogs provide excellent off-season hunting. They are challenging, extremely intelligent, and wary creatures; they also provide very good table fare. They can be dangerous when wounded, cornered, or when protecting their young. It is the sense of danger that excites many hog hunters. Whereas the cost to hunt dangerous game in Africa or in other countries may cost tens of thousands of dollars, an exciting wild boar hunt may cost only a few hundred. Depending on the hunter and technique used, a boar hunt can be just as exciting as an African big-game hunt.

Whoever coined the phrase "poor man's grizzly" as describing the wild boar knew what he was talking about. Exactly who coined the phrase may be open for debate, but I have heard and read it on numerous occasions. I've also heard the phrase "poor man's buff," this being a comparison to the Cape buffalo. Robert Ruark, that famed journalist from the mid-twentieth century, once said, "An old Cape buffalo looks at you like you owe him money"; Larry Weishuhn, an outdoor writer and a Texan, rephrased it by saying, "An old wild boar looks at you like you owe him money—and he has come to collect."

Feral hogs can provide recreation and economic returns. Because the land in Texas is 97 percent privately owned, landowners may gain economically through offering hunting leases or by providing an additional hunting species. In California, feral hogs are considered game animals, with seasons and bag limits. In Texas and most other states, however, they are considered exotic pests and can be hunted by any means or methods as long as a hunter has a hunting license.

Since 2004, Texas landowners or their agents have been allowed to kill marauding hogs on their property without a hunting license. Feral hogs may even be hunted at night with a spotlight or night vision scope! I would strongly recommend informing the local game warden, though, if you intend to hunt feral hogs like this. There is a zero tolerance policy in Texas toward wild hogs on state-owned land; however, hunting is by drawing or permit only.

Hogs wallowing at midday.

The first organized hog hunt in Texas occurred on the Gus Engeling Wildlife Management Area in Anderson County in February 1978. It was organized on a first-come, first-served basis, and at the time game department officials had no idea what to expect. They were surprised when hundreds of prospective hunters showed up for only fifty spots! Since that time, feral-hog hunting on state-owned wildlife management land has become a much sought-after pursuit.

Hog Hunting Basics

To be successful in hunting feral hogs, it's important to know some basic biology of the feral hog as well as their habits. Most hunting techniques that are used for other game species can be used for the wild hog. It is primarily their feeding habits that determine their location at any given time. Because omnivorous feral hogs will eat nearly anything, the best locations are determined by the time of year and the availability of food.

In general, hogs prefer to occupy low-lying areas such as creeks, rivers, riparian areas, and drainages that have thick vegetation and heavy understory. The time of year may also be a factor in their location. In the hot South Texas summers, you could perchance find hogs around watering areas where the hogs cool themselves. On numerous occasions, I have found them wallowing in the mud during the heat of the day.

Hogs are predominantly nocturnal, preferring to feed primarily during the early morning or late evening hours. On cold and wet days they may move throughout the day. If you're going to hunt feral hogs, find areas where they've been. Look for sign such as wallows in tanks or fresh rooting. Keep an eye peeled for trails at fence crossings, which are fairly easy to locate. If baiting is legal where you intend to hunt, select numerous locations to bait several weeks in advance of your trip.

The opportunistic hog hunter. (Photo courtesy of Macy Ledbetter)

The meat hunter and sport hunter.

The trophy hog hunter. (Photo courtesy of Larry Weishuhn)

The Hog Hunter

There are four basic types of hog hunters: the incidental or opportunist, the meat hunter, the sport hunter, and the trophy-boar hunter. The opportunists are usually hunting another game species such as the white-tailed deer when the hog presents itself. Whether it's a trophy boar or young sow doesn't matter to the opportunist. Chances are the opportunist hog hunter will utilize the meat and cherish the trophy no matter what the size.

The meat hunter on the other hand just wants to put meat in the freezer and doesn't particularly care about the size or shape of the hog or the technique used. They are on a mission to harvest meat and want the easiest and highest percent chance of collecting a feral hog. This may include incorporating several techniques to do so: baiting, using dogs, and even setting traps.

The sport hunter enjoys hunting wild hogs throughout the year. This person is dedicated to pursuing feral hogs for recreation, meat, and the challenge. Most sport hunters enjoy the thrill of the hunt and use these hunts to improve their outdoor skills. I've got numerous friends who started hunting hogs with a rifle only to progress to become avid bow hunters. Subsequently, these people had the opportunity to hunt with dogs and to dispatch them with a pistol or knife. Sport hunters also include the nontraditional-type hunts: dog hunters, helicopter hunters, and high-tech hunters.

While the true trophy is in the thrill of the hunt, a boar with two-inch or longer tusks or tushes is what most trophy hunters are after. These razor-sharp teeth can be dangerous. Most likely, the trophy hunter will utilize the services of a guide, which may also include dogs and horses.

Trophy hunters will exhibit more patience than other types of hog hunters and will not be tempted when a group of boars are spotted, but will rather use restraint in anticipation of the larger boar that may be lurking in the shadows. Big boars are usually solitary and may be the last hog to arrive. They frequently are to be found lagging behind a sounder or family group of sows and young hogs, especially if there is a sow in estrus.

Whatever type of hog hunter you are, biological knowledge about the animal can increase the success of your outing. Once you have a basic knowledge of the habits of wild hogs, you can locate prospective dwelling places by looking for sign. To successfully hunt the wild hog requires prescouting, scouting, planning, strategy, and implementation.

Field Judging

Field judging your quarry can mean estimating the weight of the hog for meat hunters or evaluating the length of the tusk for trophy hunters. Keep in mind that the mature wild hog will stand about 30 to 32 inches tall. If you are a meat hunter, you may prefer to harvest a smaller hog, which should be more tasty and tender when cooked. If you are around a wildlife feeder, you may want to put a mark on the legs of the feeder or a tree nearby to aid in estimating the height of the hog when it arrives.

Note the hog's physical characteristics such as snout length, teats, or the scrotum. This will help you decide whether it's an old boar or sow or a young hog. The same can be true of a smaller pig. I've known people who have harvested a small pig only to find out that it was too small—a quart-size animal with very little meat and barely worth processing. Granted, young hogs are tasty, but a thirty- to forty-pounder is premium. Ultimately, if you're a meat hunter, you're going to harvest whatever gives you the opportunity.

The trophy hunter, on the other hand, is searching for a big, mature tusker. A large boar with a big head and long curling lower tusks is the name of the game. Attempting to judge the length of the tusk can be a challenge in itself. A good binocular or a spotting scope is critical in the evaluation.

As I mentioned before, any hog with lower tusks of two inches or longer is considered a trophy. Look at both tusks to determine if one side may be broken. It's also important to get a good look at the teeth. In general, any hog whose teeth are visible to the hunter when looking through a riflescope will prove to be within the trophy category. The more white of the teeth that is visible, the longer the tusks will probably be.

Hog rootings.

Keep in mind also that the teeth may be stained or the lips may be covering them, so make sure you get a thorough look. This is especially true if you're not with an experienced guide. Most hog hunting guides should be able to assist you in judging a hog's teeth. One thing's for sure: If you have a sure-enough big tusker in your sights, you will know it.

Prescouting

Prescouting for feral hogs includes reading and educating yourself about the creature you plan to hunt. The next step involves locating areas where hogs have homesteaded or are known to roam. For inexperienced or first-time hog hunters, this may mean reading classified ads in hunting magazines, newspapers, or on other outlets. You may want to contact your local game department, biologist, game warden, or county agent. Don't be duped into selecting the first person you talk to without first getting references. Remember to follow-up any potential leads with references from clients, landowners, or previous hunters.

Scouting

Once you've found a place to hunt, you can save a lot of time and effort by scouting the hog's turf. Scouting entails learning about the locale where you plan to hunt: the topography, geography, and actual evidence that feral hog live in the area. It doesn't matter if it's government-owned land or a private ranch; scouting basics stay the same. Look for terrain that will most likely host wild hogs, then find where they water, feed, and loaf. If you don't already know, learn what feral hog sign looks like and where to locate it. In the following sections I'll show you what to look for and how to make your hunt successful.

Hog Sign

Feral-hog signs are fairly easy to distinguish and include hoof tracks, rooting, wallows, rubs, scat, hair, trails and crossings, and even the damage they've left behind. Often, an individual can make their determination from a combination of the above-mentioned signs.

Tracks

Hog tracks are fairly easy to distinguish from other cloven-hoofed ungulates (deer and javelina). Hog hoofs are wider and rounded or blunt at the ends whereas the separation in deer hoofs fits closer together with more pointed toes. A quick reference is the rounded end, splayed appearance, with width wider than the length. Javelina tracks are generally smaller, shorter, and pointed. Because javelinas are herd oriented, extensive numbers of tracks may be found where they have roamed, which further distinguishes them from hogs. Deer tracks are pointed at the end with a more heart-shaped appearance. As with deer, dewclaws may be seen in soft soil, sand, or mud and are not absolute identifiers of sex or age.

Rooting

Although hog rootings may be easy to distinguish, sometimes people confuse them with those made by armadillo, javelina, or other creatures of the woods. A "hog root" can be described as soil the hog has tilled or turned over with its snout while searching for underlying insects, fresh vegetation, roots, or tubers. The tilled ground can consist of only a few square inches or can cover several acres. People who dislike feral hogs cite

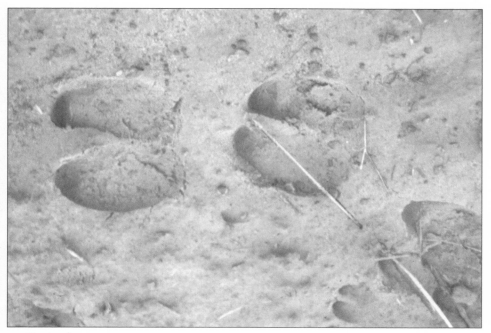

Hog tracks.

Hog wallows.

the rooting activity as their main complaint—grievances well founded when you consider the hogs have been known to root up farm crops, ranch land, and even golf courses! While the depth of the rooting doesn't necessarily differentiate a hog root from that of another creature, the extensiveness is usually a telltell sign.

Feral-hog rooting activity is usually quite extensive. The depth can, however, be a definite giveaway. In South Texas, I've seen hog excavations up to three feet deep. The depth is due to several factors: soil type, soil density, ground moisture, and vegetation. Armadillos do not generally dig but tend to scrape the surface material. While javelinas are not vigorous rooters, they will occasionally lightly till the soil looking for fresh vegetation, acorns, or some roots. Their rooting appears as a shallower, singular line, as opposed to purposeful, deep concentrated excavations of wild hogs.

Wallows

Hog wallows are indentions, imprints, or depressions in wet, muddy places where the hogs have lain down or rolled around in. Hogs use mud to cool themselves and to protect themselves from insects and the sun. There is an upsurge of wallows during the warmer months when heat and insects increase. Wallows are usually found along the bank of a stock tank, riverbed, streambed, lake, or any riparian area where there is freestanding water. Generally, you can see the basic outline of the hog in the soft mud, often even the hairlines.

It's fairly easy for the novice to determine the age of the wallow and tell how fresh the wallow is. Older wallows may be dry or crusted over. If the wallow is dry, caked, and cracked, it's probably several days old, whereas fresh wallows will still be wet. I've visited wallows where the hogs have left moments before and was able to see water drops trailing off into the woods. Wallows will also fill with water, increasing its lifespan and subsequently its use. Hogs will frequently urinate and defecate in the wallows and hoof tracks will be found in and around them.

Rubs

Hog rubs are where the hog has rubbed its back against something to scratch itself, wipe the mud off, or coat itself for insect protection. Rubs can be found on fence posts, trees, or telephone poles. Frequently they'll rub on creosote telephone poles or fence posts to coat themselves with the oil based creosote as an insect repellent. Sometimes you may be able to determine the size of the hog by the height of the rub. Keep in mind though that when a hog rubs, it often stands on its toes, so its height may be somewhat exaggerated.

Hog rub.

Trails and Crossings

Looking for fence crossings is another sign that may prove helpful in finding that wild hog. They are fairly easy to distinguish because there is generally a good-size hole in the fence and hair can be found on the top wire where the hog's back rubbed against it. Hog hair can be distinguished from deer hair or javelina hair by its color, texture, length, and sometimes its split ends. Most of the time you also will find hog tracks or rubs in the same area.

Trails may be slightly more difficult to locate but once again, knowing the basic biology and habits of the hog may help. Feral hogs frequently use the same travel routes or trails when traveling from bedding and resting places to feeding grounds, so finding these trails and crossings can be helpful in locating hogs. It is more likely that you will find hogs on trails near water or thick brush / understory rather than on other game trails.

Loafing or Bedding Areas

I think you could remain on the side of political correctness if you called a hog lazy. During hot weather hogs show little ambition to move while the sun is high overhead. They seek secluded, thickly wooded areas and dense cover in which to rest. These bedding or resting areas may be found near watering or feeding areas. The hogs usually won't go far from food, especially if there's a good source. In South Texas, I've found these areas in whitebrush thickets and the areas around stock tanks. These may be rooted, wallowed out, or dugout areas often having a distinctive, strong swine odor similar to a domestic hog farm.

Sows also use these areas to have their offspring. In these farrowing areas, the beds are lined with grass or some other type of material. Find a fresh loafing or bedding ground, and you may have found a good place to hunt.

Scat

Hog droppings, dung, or scat is easily distinguished from that of other woodland creatures. While hog dung is easy to identify, it is hard to describe. Let's start the description with what it doesn't look like. It is not pelleted like the white-tailed deer or elongated as the coyote or lion. It somewhat resembles a small calf's droppings in that it is relatively thick and round or somewhat large and tubular, and it frequently lands in rippled piles. It may even have the appearance of a pile made by a large dog. Looking at the scat may also indicate what the hog has been eating and where the hog may be feeding and spending its time. Lastly, the freshness of the scat determines if the animal is still in the vicinity and gives valuable insight to the hunter or trapper.

Hog Damage

Another indicator of the presence of feral hogs is the damage they've left behind. Besides the rooting and wallowing, there are other types of damage that can be attributed to wild hogs. Trampling is another notable sign, which is caused when hogs are searching for or traveling to and from food sources.

Hog scat. (Photo courtesy of Don Zaidle)

This telltell sign is especially noteworthy in farm fields with crops or freshly cultivated agricultural land.

Fences may show signs of hog damage where large holes are created from hogs traveling through them or under them. Other damage such as destroyed wildlife feeders, livestock feed bins, torn up hay bales, and destroyed watering troughs are further examples of hog damage.

Hunting Techniques

Most of the standard hunting techniques used for other species can be used to hunt feral hogs successfully. The best times to hunt wild hogs are in the morning and evening. For morning hunts, it is important to arrive at your destination thirty minutes to an hour before daylight. This allows the woods to quiet and your scent to dissipate. This is especially important during warmer weather because hogs are much more mobile early. On colder days they may be active throughout the day.

Stand Hunting

In Texas, hunting from stands is the most common method used, often coincidental with white-tailed deer hunting. In Texas, the term stand hunting generally means a manmade deer blind; however, it also can mean brush blinds, tree stands, or observation points. When I use the term observation points, it could be on the side of a hill, the edge of a field, or on roads.

Stand hunting also may be good during the off-season, provided you maintain your feeder throughout the year. Other productive sites can be found around fields with row crops, vegetables, or hay. Glassing from the side of a hill or field where hog activity has been seen or where hogs are known to travel also can be productive.

Using bait, you can enhance promising areas to promote success, and the most auspicious areas will be near water or thick brush. Corn is usually the best bait, especially in a spin-cast feeder, but you can use other types of feed or food scraps.

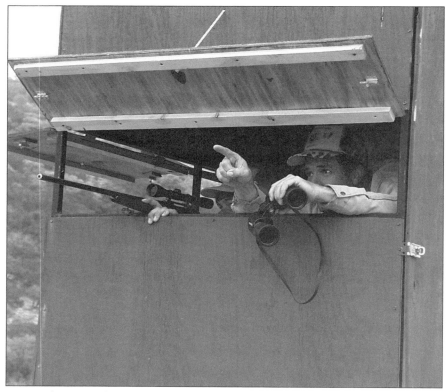

Hunting from a stand. (Photo courtesy of Macy Ledbetter)

Tree stands also can be very productive if they're located near trails and crossings that prescouting has deemed promising. When a boar or wild hog is seen and is not within shooting range and probably won't be, the still hunt or stalk can begin. With a good binocular or spotting scope, a hunter can see the tushes of a trophy boar from far away.

Still-Hunting

Still hunting and stalking generally go hand in hand and require patience and perseverance. The object of still-hunting is to move as slowly and as quietly as humanly possible. This technique involves moving very slowly into the wind, stopping frequently to look and listen in an effort to locate the hog before he locates you. The stops should be long enough to allow nature to resume its pace . . . then wait a bit longer before proceeding. Once you find the hogs, stalk to get within range.

After arriving at your hunting grounds, be sure to park downwind and far enough away that game don't hear you arrive. Exit the vehicle quietly and don't slam the door. If your automobile is equipped with a security system that honks the horn when you lock the door with the remote controller, lock the vehicle manually.

I've had excellent luck walking up tail waters or drainages leading toward stock tanks, especially on warm days, and I have crept close to hogs that I've found wallowing in the mud. Sneaking over tank dams or around thick corners also can be fruitful. Feral hogs have relatively poor eyesight compared with most wild animals but have very acute senses of hearing and smell. They also seem to have a sixth sense because even if you do have a successful stalk, they will still bolt into thickets just as you get within lethal range. Your chances will improve by wearing camouflage and using some sort of cover scent.

Stalking

Stalking wild hogs and javelina is one of the most challenging ways to bring meat to the table. Stalking entails locating the animals and then attempting to get within lethal range before the animal spots you. This technique can be especially productive when hunting javelinas. Due to the javelina's poor eyesight, a hunter working upwind can easily get within rifle range.

You begin your stalk by first finding the hog. Glass the landscape through a binocular, check for hoof tracks crossing the road, or watch for other fresh sign. Once you spot the hog, it is a matter of stealth and technique. It is best to approach the hog from downwind, and try to keep a barrier such as a tree between you and the hog. As you move toward him, slowly check the hog's position. Concealment is priority one while approaching the quarry.

It is also important to move very slowly while frequently stopping. Each time the hog resumes feeding or some other activity, you can continue.

Stalking with the sun on the back is another advantage to use. This technique involves incorporating much of the same style as still-hunting except the location of the quarry is known. Sneaking up on feeders, fields, tanks, or other known hog haunts can be very successful. As with still-hunting, wearing camouflage and possibly using a cover scent will improve your success.

Safari Style

Safari-style hunting is fairly common in South Texas and is often incidental during other hunting seasons. It involves driving around, often in a high-racked vehicle (a stand mounted above the vehicle), where the hunters have good visibility. This is opposed to being inside the vehicle where the hunter must get out of the vehicle, locate the animal, and try for a shot. The safari hunter is already out of the vehicle, has his gun close at hand, and he is prepared for any opportunity that can arise quickly. Most hogs will not stay around if they see an approaching vehicle, so a quick shot is usually required.

If possible, the driver should try to drive with the sun on his back, heading west in the early morning and east as the sun goes down. Also, it is important to approach into the wind. Not only does the wind conceal the smell, but it rustles the tree leaves, which often masks the engine and wheel noise of the approaching vehicle. While driving, head for known hog activity locales such as feeders, bait stations, livestock feeding areas, stock tanks, ponds, farms, and cultivated fields. During hot summer days, watering holes may prove productive. Once you arrive, use the stalking technique or if you have hog dogs, release them.

Hog Drives

Hog drives in the United States have been around in various forms for more than two centuries. Drives originated because farmers and ranchers didn't have fences to contain the hogs. Many of the ranchers in the late 1800s in south-central Texas raised domestic hogs and would allow them to range freely in the native countryside where they could forage on whatever they could find. All the hogs were marked with the rancher's particular brand and the males were castrated.

Once a year the ranchers would attempt to capture their hogs and bring them home and put them in a pen. It might take several weeks or months to gather all their hogs, even with the excellent well-trained hounds they used. When all the ranchers had all their hogs penned, they would start their drive to the nearest livestock market or rail yard, usually somewhere that was over a hundred miles away. In those days, a hog drive was similar to a cattle drive in that it used horses and dogs to push a thousand or more hogs down the trail. I bet that was a sight! And many that escaped into the

Preparing for a hog hunt with dogs.

woods became wilder and more feral, thus aiding the establishment of hogs in Texas. "Get a-long little hoggies, get a-long"!

Hunting drives also date back to the old days when a hunter would enter a thick stand of brush or a canyon, making a lot of noise in the hopes of driving the quarry from their lair. Natives, as well as white hunters in Africa or India used this technique to drive lions or tigers to a stationed hunter. In North America, Native Americans used this practice, as do some white-tailed deer hunters today. It is still popular in several European countries where hog populations are established or increasing.

This method involves several individuals and a shooter. The hunter is placed at a location where the hogs are likely to cross. His partners enter the brush, canyon, or area where hogs most likely are and begin moving toward the shooter. In an effort to push the hog out of the thicket, the partners move slowly. The shooter must have a clean and open line of fire, preferably an opening with a clear view. When the hogs leave their hideout, most likely the window of opportunity will be very limited, so the more space the shooter has, the better his chances. Many times, dogs are used to help flush the hogs out, thus incorporating dog hunting with the hog drive.

Dog Hunting

The following is an article of mine from *Texas Trophy Hunter Magazine,* reprinted with permission:

> The first time I hunted hogs with dogs was around 1984 in Gonzales County. And what a first time it was. Terry had the dogs and the horses, and most importantly access to a large ranch to hunt on. And yes, I said horses.
>
> There are many techniques used when hunting hogs with dogs but nothing beats the awesome thrill of trailing a group of hounds on horseback. Flashlights strapped over your shoulder, the beautiful starry skies above your head, and the only sounds interrupting the quiet night are crickets, frogs, and the plodding of the horses' hoofs. The dogs trotting out in front on the trail sniffing and searching for a wild hog to chase and when they

find one, the silence is broken by excited yaps and barks. So, hold on to your saddle because the heart-throbbing chase is on.

However, there would be no horses to carry us this hot, dry and windy late March afternoon when we met at the ranch gate. Hardly conducive conditions when hunting hogs with dogs when cooler, calmer, damper type conditions are preferred. Weather conditions are important factors for a successful hunt since the dog's sense of smell is a vital aspect.

Fortunately we were hunting with an experienced hog hunter in Danny Roberts of Uvalde, who has excellent dogs. Along with Danny was his protégé Jason Rowan; ranch manager Dwight Belicek and his son, Trenton, Jeff Sheedy, a hog-dog hunter in his own right; and a pack of nine dogs. Generally hog men don't use this many dogs, but several were young dogs in training and the best way to train young dogs is with a well-trained older experienced dog.

I enjoy hunting hogs, and have lots of opportunities, but seemingly never enough time, so when I had the chance to write a story about dogs and hogs, I eagerly made the time. After a short introduction, gear check, and strategy planning meeting we headed toward the nearest stock tank. Being so warm and since it was still daylight, the hogs probably hadn't started moving yet, so we hoped to possibly catch one or two laid up in a nearby thicket.

Wild hogs, feral hogs, or wild boar, whatever you call them, are predominantly nocturnal unless the weather is cold, overcast, rainy, or generally nasty—then they may move throughout the day. En route to the tank, we passed an irrigated oat patch with a corn feeder along the edge, so we let some dogs out just in case a hog was in the vicinity.

Two experienced bay dogs or strikers were released. They trotted fifty to a hundred yards in front of the truck while making wide circles into the brush, nose to the ground, or they would stop and stick their noses in the air, hoping to catch a whiff of a hog either on the ground or in the air. The smell of a hog won't stay long on the ground on hot, dry, dusty days. On windy days, a whipping wind can confuse the dogs and make it difficult for them to locate the origin of the odiferous hog. The dogs detected nothing near the field, so we loaded them and continued on toward the tank.

Stopping before reaching the stock tank, we released the dogs again and let them run. The first strike was sounded below the tank dam by one of the

191

Former World Champion all Around Cowboy Phil Lyne (far right) preparing to hunt hogs from horseback. (Photo courtesy of Larry Weishuhn)

dogs, and soon the second dog had joined in. We'd found some hogs! The sound of barking or yelping dogs when chasing a hog is music to the hunter's ear. So we parked near the tank dam, listened and waited, hoping the dogs were on a fresh trail before we headed toward them. Unfortunately, the trail was old or the hogs had outsmarted the dogs, so we loaded the dogs and headed off. Another tank, another oat field, and a couple more corn feeders produced nothing. As the sun sank in the west, I had a feeling it was going to be a long night.

Dogs have been used for sustenance hunting for thousands of years. Hunting with dogs began in the Middle East, and as civilized man expanded his range into Europe, so did the use of dogs. According to some literature, hog hunting or an earlier form called "pig-sticking" can even be seen on Egyptian hieroglyphics and engravings found on Roman and Greek tombs.

The actual sport of hog hunting as we know it can be traced to the Europeans as they began colonizing India and Southeast Asia in the early to mid-1800s. In India it became an aristocratic sport for officers of the British Raj. This type of hog hunting involved horses and dogs and the use of long spears to dispatch the animal. Riders would chase the hog on horseback and when within range thrust the spear into the running hog. Pig-sticking became so popular in India that organized hunt or tent clubs with annual competitions and trophies or cups became the vogue.

Maj. Robert W. Foran in his 1933 book *Kill or be Killed* claims that many people, himself included, considered pig-sticking a real he-man sport and the premier sport of India during that period. He said, "Wherever there are sporting pigs to be found, fair ground over which to gallop fast, and good horses to carry you, this great sport will always find ardent devotees."

Trained dogs baying a wild hog. (Photo courtesy of USDA/APHIS)

As in my first hog hunting experience in Gonzales County, hunting from horseback is popular especially in South Texas; however, the art of spearing the animal from the back of a horse is seldom attempted. Instead, when the hog is bayed the hunter dismounts and kills the pig with his weapon of choice, oftentimes a long hunting knife.

Gilbert Gonzales, a hog hunter from Pearsall, prefers to hunt from a horse and uses a short barrel .30-30 caliber or .44 Magnum rifles. He claims that once the hog is bayed, you arrive at the hog sooner, thus preventing injury to the dog. He also claims that the angle is better for shooting and you're less likely to step on a rattlesnake.

I understand his concern about snakes since we killed four rattlesnakes the night of our hunt. Dog men such as Danny and Jason prefer to use a long-bladed knife for fear of a stray bullet hitting one of the dogs.

Using a well-trained pack of hog dogs and with an experienced hunter, the thrill of hunting a hog with dogs is unmatched. Often, dogs can be the key to success when hunting wild hogs. If the hogs are not moving, a well-trained hound with its keen nose, hunting instinct, and training will almost guarantee a shot at a wild hog. Dogs are generally used in the early morning hours when there is fresh scent on the ground. The dogs are taken to areas where hogs are known to range, or where earlier scouting trips have indicated fresh hog activity.

The dogs are then released to run around in search of fresh scent. If fresh scent is detected, a loud bark signals the other dogs to respond, and the chase begins. The excited barking sound of the pack of hounds on the trail means they're hot on the trail of a porker. By this time, the guide and you are also in hot pursuit of the running dogs, running through the thick brush and understory so that the dogs don't get too far away and out of hearing.

The use of horses can be very useful when trying to keep up with the running dogs. For individuals who've never hunted hogs on horseback, it in itself can be a rewarding experience. When the dogs stop running and their barking changes into a frenzied excited baying, you know they have the animal cornered.

At this point, you must get there as quickly as possible to prevent the hog with their razor-sharp tusks from hurting or killing the dogs. Many good hog dogs have been killed or even seriously injured by a wild hog. Most good dog men carry their own surgical kits and veterinary supplies with them to patch up any serious injuries. Keep in mind, these dogs are extremely valuable to the owners and the loss of any good hog dog can be emotionally as well as economically devastating.

There are two basic types of dogs used to hunt wild hogs: the chase/bay dogs and the catch dog. The bay dogs chase the hog until it is cornered, all the while barking wildly and nipping at the hog. The catch dog actually goes into the fight and latches onto the hog, holding it until help or the hunter arrives.

Efficient hog dogs always work as a team: each one attacking or nipping when the hog turns to face another dog, thus keeping it constantly off-guard and lively. If it turns, the dogs move in and bite, causing the hog to turn and face the attacker. Many people hunt hogs with dogs for the sport and to watch the action of a well-trained dog at work; some do not even kill

Catch dog wearing protective gear. (Photo courtesy of Macy Ledbetter)

A successful hog hunt with dogs. (Photo courtesy of John Miller)

the hog after the chase. Many hunters in South Texas catch the hogs and castrate the males only to release and to chase them another time.

Many breeds of dogs are used for hog hunting but the most common include black-mouthed curs, Lacys, leopards, Plotts, black and tans, redbones, as well as crosses of these and other dog breeds. The Catahoula was named the Louisiana state dog in 1979 and supposedly named for a dog originating in or around Catahoula Parish. This short-hair, multicolor breed is believed to have descended from a mix of Spanish and American Indian dogs. Catahoulas were widely used for herding cattle and swine and continue as a working breed today, either on domestic cattle or wild hogs. The Lacy breed was supposedly bred in the hill country northwest of San Antonio in the late 1800s and used to round up range hogs to drive them to market. The ancestry of the Plott hound supposedly goes back to boar hounds used in Europe in the last century.

Some of the best hog dogs I've seen are mixed breeds or even mutts. I've known several hunters who would go to the animal shelter to find dogs they believed had potential. Although I'm not a hog-dog trainer, one of the methods used to train young pups is to let them run with a pack of trained hounds. Teasing is another method that involves capturing a young wild pig, putting it into a stock trailer or small pen with a potential hog puppy, and then letting the two tangle for short periods of time.

Catch dogs are usually cross-bred with some strong-jawed species such as a pit bull. Pure pit bulls are seldom used because stamina is required for

Hunting javelinas can be especially dangerous to dogs. (Photo courtesy of Bob Zaiglin)

long chases and prolonged fights. Once a hog is bayed, the catch dog goes to catch and then hold the hog by the ear. Using a dog-protective vest around the chest can prevent serious lacerations from the hog slashing at the dog with its tusks.

Once the hog is bayed or caught, there are many ways to dispatch the animal: pistols, bow and arrow, rifles, black powder, and even a long-bladed knife. Hunters should use extreme caution when attempting to dispatch a wild hog with a knife. A big wild hog can be very strong and to say the hog becomes even more dangerous when stuck is an extreme understatement. It is mandatory that the hunter be backed up with a pistol or rifle because the hog will come at you and you will be very tempted to drop the knife or spear and run. The lost art of "pig sticking" is discussed later.

As with hog hunters, dogs also can be used to trail javelinas. Although it may increase the success of the hunt, javelinas can be especially dangerous to dogs. A javelina can run for a long distance but will generally seek protection in thick brush, a ground depression, a cave, or some other protected area before making its stand. Rest assured, the javelina will generally win the battle.

A javelina can rip a dog to shreds, and if the dog survives, it will require many stitches. Once the javelina is bayed, the hunter must arrive quickly to dispatch it—all the while being careful not to shoot the baying dogs. The hunter should be able to complete the hunt in an expeditious manner. I don't recommend trying to "stick" a javelina. They are lightning quick, have shorter legs and overall body length than a hog, razor-sharp pointed canines, and a belligerent personality. An attack by a javelina can lead to severe pain and emotional scars for life.

Helicopter Hunting

The following is an article of mine from *Texas Trophy Hunter Magazine,* reprinted with permission:

The clouds had not quite burned off as we finished our helicopter survey for deer last February. As the machine landed on the Purple Heart Ranch south of Hondo, I got out and Josh Kinser got in. Josh, an avid hunter, is the director of field activities for Military Warriors Support Foundation, a nonprofit organization dedicated to our wounded warriors. A purple heart recipient and combat veteran of Iraq and Afghanistan, Josh was not looking for Taliban or insurgents today, but feral hogs or the hogiban! Maybe they can be classified as insurgents, considering they're not native to Texas and are causing havoc throughout the state . . . and we weren't in a Blackhawk, but a four-seat Robinson R44 helicopter, piloted by Dusty Holt of Holt Helicopters.

Today, his mission was to seek out and destroy the enemy or kill all the feral hogs that Dusty could put him on. Behind Josh observing and spotting, was another combat veteran, J.D. Williams, a triple amputee and

A hunter's view of the prey from a helicopter. (Photo courtesy of Macy Ledbetter)

passionate hunter who had spent many hours in the air but never after hogs. J.D.'s story is much like many of our American heroes: a young sniper who joined the military to fight for our freedom and defend the homeland only to be blown up by an IED (Improvised Explosive Device).

I first met J.D. at the Purple Heart Ranch the previous hunting season when Josh asked if I would guide him for the weekend. We hunted several times together in a brush-covered ground blind where he was able to harvest a nice ten-point buck. As we sat in a box blind late one rainy evening, a large group of hogs came out near the feeder. They were nervous and soon scattered but not before I could see that one of them was a big tusker. Although hunting for deer, J.D. asked if he could take a hog.

"Of course," I told him. "We can try for the big boar if he comes back out."

Shortly thereafter, the hogs came back to the feeder, less the trophy boar. With the gun resting on the blind's window base, he took careful aim . . . and that's when I told him to hold off. I said that if he wanted to take more than one, he needed to get ready and I would work the bolt. And that's what we did!

After the first shot, I reached over the gun and worked the bolt; I did the same after the second shot and then a third. By that time the hogs were gone. Three shots and three hogs! J.D., a Montana native who has hunted all over the country, thought killing three hogs at one time was one of the most exhilarating hunts he had ever been on. I was proud to have been the one to guide him.

The Purple Heart ranch is dedicated to heroes like Josh and J.D., offering them a place to hunt and relax as they cope with a tragedy and try to get on with life. Like so many South Texas ranches, the Purple Heart has more than its share of hogs. So the opportunity for veterans to hunt hogs from a helicopter was the ultimate challenge. After a couple hours we had twelve dead hogs on the ground, and the excitement that showed on their faces when they landed at base camp was thrilling for me to watch.

Over the course of the next few weeks I had the chance to let more warriors hunt hogs on other ranches from the helicopter. Since 1 September 2011, many other hunters have been able to hunt hogs from the helicopter throughout Texas, and not just incidental to wildlife surveys.

A new law passed in 2010 by the 82nd Texas legislature and subsequent new rules adopted by the Texas Parks and Wildlife Commission allow landowners and sportsmen to pay or accept fees to participate in aerial hunting operations for hogs and predators. This law was written to be a management tool and not intended to be or construed to be a sporting bill. The use of helicopters to control feral hogs is one of the most effective methods available in South, West, and Central Texas where tree canopy cover is thin and low growing, or inaccessible for other methods. An experienced aerial gunner can easily harvest over one hundred hogs in a day! Now a novice can participate and experience the thrill of hunting hogs from the air, a byproduct of the bill. Has HB-716, designed to help manage the state's expanding hog population and nicknamed the "pork chopper bill," had any success since its inception?

Dusty Holt of Uvalde, who I frequently fly with, is optimistic and feels the new law has actually helped in controlling hog numbers. While it won't eradicate a population, he feels the added pressure of additional aerial gunning has generated a slight reduction. Specifically mentioning farmers, he claims that many landowners will allow hunting for hogs if they don't have to pay for it.

Perhaps his point is correct. Last year I was on an aerial hunting expedition, and we ended up hunting over 8,000 acres instead of the original 1,500 acres, which may not have happened if the new bill wasn't available. A quick Internet search found several companies specializing in helicopter hog hunts, and most helicopter companies that specialize in game surveys and wildlife work are available for hog hunting or varmint hunting as well.

Mark Mapston, district supervisor of USDA Wildlife Services, disagrees. He believes the pork chopper bill has had little or no effect on the overall hog population in Texas. While USDA comparable harvest numbers from 2011 to 2012 are still being tabulated, increased hog harvest for that agency is due primarily to extra monies that were allocated for hog control. In fact, a Texas Department of Agriculture grant of $420,000 was allotted for hog control in 2012. Holt and Mapston both agree, however, that aerial hunting or gunning is an effective technique in controlling a feral hog population temporarily in specific areas. Is aerial gunning combined with other control efforts, including hunting and trapping, effective in reducing the overall population in Texas or is it just compensatory?

In compensatory mortality, a biological term, hunting and trapping may serve to replace the natural mortality operating on a population; compensatory mortality helps to keep the population density in balance with what the environment can support. For example, do fire ants affect the bobwhite quail population or will 80 percent of the quails die regardless of the circumstances? In other words, natural mortality will occur at a specific rate and death losses from other sources will compensate for other causes. In the example given, fire ants do cause mortality in bobwhite quail populations, but without fire ants they would likely die from other causes such as predation, weather, or diseases. I believe the same can be said with feral hog populations in Texas. The pork chopper bill and aerial gunning are tools in the arsenal of control options; however, it is only a temporary stopgap measure.

Spotlighting

Because hogs are primarily nocturnal especially in the spring and summer, hunting at night may increase your chances. Hunting at night is continuous action, fairly fast-paced, and enjoyable—depending on the state game laws. When I say fast-paced, continuous action, I don't necessarily mean success at hog hunting. You are constantly moving and you get to see wildlife of all descriptions.

In Texas, it is legal to hunt hogs at night. You have to have a valid hunting license and I would strongly recommend contacting the local game warden ahead of time. Besides establishing a good relationship, it prevents unnecessary confrontations. Nothing upsets a warden more than being called out in the middle of the night just to find it's a hog hunter out spotlighting. Also, you should refrain from hunting hogs at night during another legal season, such as deer season. If you have any questions, read the latest game regulations or contact the local warden or conservation officer.

As I said, hogs' eyes don't reflect like most wildlife, such as a deer or raccoon, so most of the time you're looking for the body of the animal. Without the reflective eyes, hogs can be difficult to see in thick cover and shadows, especially if they've rolled in a waterhole and have caked their pelage with mud. As they sneak around in darkness, they trick the hunters' eyes. Was that a hog . . . or ghost? While the use of a red filter on the spotlight may not be necessary, it is recommended because it keeps the night more serene and natural. Using bright spotlights may make the hog easier to see, but it also lightens the entire area, which might scare the hogs away.

My two favorite spotlighting techniques involve driving nonstop while shining every possible nook and cranny where hogs may be congregating. The other technique involves leaving the light off while stealthily maneuvering to the chosen location. This location may include prebaited areas, fields, or open areas for calling.

Upon reaching your destination, get situated with gun at ready, turn on the light, and scan the area for the distinctive shapes or movements of hogs.

Hogs eating corn. (Photo courtesy of USDA/APHIS)

If no hogs are seen, turn the light off and wait silently before trying again. You can overlook hogs on the first attempt. You can utilize this off-and-on technique throughout the night in the same locale or move to another location and try again.

Drifting

Drifting or floating for hogs is a technique that I have only read about. If your hunting area has a navigable waterway such as a creek or small stream, you may want to consider using a canoe, kayak, johnboat, or float tube to catch hogs as they wallow along the bank. One article I read tells the story of a hunter who regularly floats in a creek that goes through a ranch and has consistently been able to get within range of a wild hog as he floats downstream. He claims if you paddle quietly, the hogs often remain largely undisturbed, possibly because they think the hunter's just another log floating down the creek. Imagine the hog's surprise when the log explodes into gunfire! Make sure the creek or stream is not considered a state waterway where hunting may be illegal.

Calling

The art of calling wild hogs is still in its infancy. Wild hogs can be very vocal in the brush as they feed. Despite their wariness and intelligence, they're fairly noisy in their feeding routine. I've heard hogs in the woods as they fed and I was able to take a stand and wait. There are commercially available mouth calls that imitate the sound of hogs grunting and feeding; there is also a call that makes the sound of a large boar. The sound of squealing piglets can be imitated by blowing harder. Two commercially available electronic hog calls include the "piglet in distress" and "hog-feeding frenzy." Although I've had minimal success using them, I read one article where a hog came up within two minutes. Another outdoor writer and avid hog hunter claims to have called up several dozen hogs using a mouth call.

Being around wild and domestic hogs for over twenty-five years, I have seen them react to such sounds. The piglet in distress will probably bring in a sow as opposed to a boar. If they haven't been disturbed, hogs may come to a call out of curiosity . . . just don't overdo it and scare them away! Hogs often vocalize reflexively when they find food. If food is discovered, the hog's greed, hunger, or competitive nature brings other porkers running. When another hog hears the energized feeding passion of one hog, it means dinner has been served. Use the feeding-frenzy call around baited areas for optimal results.

One of the best calls is the sound of a deer feeder going off, especially in winter. There are now factory-made devices that imitate the spinning sound of a corn feeder going off . . . and it works! The ranch must have feeders and the hogs must be acclimated to the sound, however. Be judicious with using this call: You'll train the hogs to avoid the sound if it's overused in conjunction with the noise of firing guns. As with all calling, hogs must be in the area for them to be effective. Some states have regulations regarding the use of electronic calls, so know the laws before using an electronic call.

Baiting

The most common baits are grains such as corn or milo. The grain can be used plain and dry, sweetened, soaked in water and soured, or soaked in diesel. That's no misprint you read. As you may have gathered, hogs will eat nearly anything edible, no matter what it smells like. Many animals and birds, especially deer, shun the diesel soaked corn, but not the gluttonous wild porkers. Bait can be scattered on the ground, buried, or placed in a hog feeder. Using a shovel or post hole digger, dig a hole six to twelve inches and fill it with an odiferous bait.

Besides the commercial spin-cast wildlife feeder, a rolling hog feeder can be made with a barrel, small drum, five-gallon can, or large-diameter PVC pipe. Drill small one-half-inch to five-eighths-inch holes in rows up and down the feeder, but not too many. Attach a large swivel on one end of the feeder and secure it to a stake with a length of cable or chain and another swivel. As the hog roots at the barrel, it rolls across the ground and feed dribbles out of the holes, tantalizing the animal. As the hog is enthusiastically rooting around the barrel, you can be planning your shot.

Creosote poles or oiling stumps can also be used to attract hogs. In South Texas most transmission poles that transverse ranchland will have the obvious signs of mud rubbed around the bases—and obvious sign of hogs in the vicinity. Many hunters suggest using old railroad ties and old transmission poles cut to about five-foot lengths set in the ground, or free-standing stumps with oil-soaked burlap bags attached as an attractant for wild hogs. They love to rub against them for the smell and to scratch. It may even assist in reducing insect infestation. For added assurance, bury spoiled corn around the hog pole.

Commercial hog attractants such as natural or manufactured liquids or dry, sweet-based feeds are available at most sporting retailers or by mail

Holding the hog by the back leg preparing for the coup de grâce.

order. Diverse scents such as sow-in-heat can be put on sponges, in vented containers hanging on a tree limb, or directly on the ground. Whatever you decide, baiting increases your odds of success tremendously, especially when hunting with a bow or handgun. Most commercial hunting operations in Texas, especially bowhunting outfitters, maintain baited areas for their customers.

For javelina, the best bait is whole corn. None can resist the tempting flavor of fresh corn and once found they will return time and time again. As a matter of fact, it's the javelina's craving for corn that has caused the demise of many in South Texas. Javelinas compete with the more popular and profitable white-tailed deer; consequently, they are considered a nuisance at wildlife feeders. Like any nuisance, they then become vulnerable to illegal killing or overharvesting. (See chapter 8 for more information on baiting and trapping.)

Pig-Sticking

It was hot for May, even by South Texas standards. It was around 5 PM and the temperature was hovering over 90 degrees when John came by to ask if I wanted to try for some hogs. John, a wildlife technician and avid hog hunter, has some of the best hog dogs in South Texas. *Why not*, I thought, *anything to break the monotony of the long hours we'd been putting in attempting to trap mountain lions for a research project.*

We'd been working in the riverbottom of the Nueces between Cotulla and Freer in the heart of the South Texas brush country since March. Every morning was the same: check the traps and look for lion sign. Only when we had a lion captured was the monotony broken. Another way to break the doldrums of inactivity was to go hog hunting. We were in the perfect spot for that as South Texas is host and haven for one of the largest populations in America.

On warm, late afternoons, the best place to look for hogs is around watering areas like a stock tank. So when we left the camp, that's where we headed. As we got close to the tank, approaching downwind, we let the dogs trot in front of the truck to look for and smell out the beasts. As we approached the third tank, one of the dogs let out a quick yelp before launching into a prolonged barking serenade. The other hounds quickly followed suit as they caught up to Red, the lead dog, who was hot on the trail.

We knew immediately that the dogs had found some hogs and the chase was on. Even before the truck had come to a complete halt, John and I bailed out because we knew that if we lost sight and sound of the running, barking dogs we may never see them again. Grabbing his .44 Magnum carbine, we bolted after the dogs. Mesquite, prickly pear, and blackbrush slowed us at times, but we alternately sprinted and fell back to a jog.

Time was of essence. If the hog stopped and challenged the dogs, it could mean death to the dogs if we weren't there to help. Although the distance seemed to cover the county, the chase only lasted for about a mile before the barking sounds of the dogs turned into an excited frenzy.

The hog was bayed and fighting the dogs, slashing at them with its razor-sharp tusks. When we arrived, we saw that the hog was a sow of about a hundred pounds, but still very dangerous. While the dogs had the hog bayed, John was able to grab the pig's back legs. With the dogs barking frantically

The Delhi Tent Club pig stickers, India, 1892.

and the pig squealing hysterically, John lifted its back legs off the ground while placing his foot on its neck. I killed the pig with a well-placed thrust of an eight-inch hunting knife through the heart. I realize nonhunters and even some experienced hunters may find this offensive or even repulsive, but I've included this lost technique because of its historical significance in hog hunting. Hunting hogs with a knife or spear is called "pig sticking," and while it is seldom done in the same manner as early explorers or British officers of the Raj did it, it still is an exciting and dangerous way to dispatch hogs. First-time hunters should not attempt this because it can be risky.

Pig-sticking originated in the wilds of Europe and India when nobility would go hunting on horseback in search of wild boar. When a wild boar was found, it was chased into open country and thrust with a spear. The British even imported the sport of pig-sticking into Africa, substituting warthogs for wild boars.

Sir Samuel White Baker devoted a chapter to the wild boar in his book *Wild Beasts & Their Ways*, which was first published in 1890. Baker, who hunted throughout Europe, Asia, Africa, and America in the mid-1800s, enjoyed hunting wild boar with dogs and killing them with a knife. He reminiscences:

> The large and heavy hunting knife was an admirable weapon for this style of hunting, as both point and edge could always be depended upon. . . . The skin of a boar is tough and requires an acute point; otherwise, the blade would fail to penetrate at the critical moment when the vital place should be exposed.
>
> The scrimmage when a boar is seized, and the larger dogs crowd upon him, must be seen to be understood. It is a difficult matter during such confusion to discover a clear spot where the knife can be driven behind the shoulder without injuring one of the hounds; some hold on like bull-dogs, others lose their hold, and again spring madly upon the boar's back, seizing thoughtlessly the first portion of the animal that meets their teeth.
>
> Nothing requires more cool dexterity than to come in exactly at the right moment, to assist the pack and to prevent serious casualties, which would assuredly happen if the struggle were indefinitely prolonged. A masterly attack on the part of the hunter, with a clever thrust exactly behind the shoulder, completes the victory in less than half a minute.

Maj. Robert W. Foran in his book *Kill or be Killed* recounts a story of an Indian army colonel who strongly objected to the term "pig sticking," feeling it was highly objectionable. He felt it should be called "hog hunting." This colonel claimed it signified a barbaric innovation and served to illustrate the degeneracy of the modern times, this being the turn of the twentieth century. I am sure the opinion of a Victorian gentleman more than a hundred years ago mirrors similar thoughts of many people today as we enter into the high-tech world of the twenty-first century.

Major Foran went on to claim that many people, himself included, considered pig-sticking a real he-man sport and the premier sport of India during that period. He said, "Wherever there are sporting pigs to be found, fair ground over which to gallop fast, and good horses to carry you, this great sport will always find ardent devotees."

Although hunting from horseback is a method used to hunt hogs in the United States, the art of spearing the animal from the back of a horse is seldom attempted. Instead, hog dogs chase the hogs with horsemen following until the hog is bayed. The hunters then dismount and "stick" the pig with a long hunting knife. I once saw someone use a spear, and I have to say that whether hunting from a horse with a spear or dispatching the hog with a long knife, "pig sticking" is not for the faint of heart. It is certainly not for the inexperienced hog hunter.

Guns and Loads

I don't claim to be an expert on rifles or ballistics, but I have hunted a tremendous number of hogs and javelinas. While hogs can be hunted with a variety of weaponry, a centerfire rifle is the overall choice for most sportsmen. I have seen hogs killed with calibers ranging from .222 to .375 H&H Magnum and nearly every caliber in between. I recommend a minimum caliber of at least a .243 or 6mm. Although smaller calibers will do the trick, a heavier caliber provides more shock and penetration, which helps prevent wounding. A poorly placed shot results in a wounded and dangerous wild hog, and this is especially true if the wounded hog is cornered in a thicket.

The .22-250, .243, .308 Winchester, 30-06, .270, and the .280 are all good calibers; however, I believe the .30-06 or .270 are probably the best all-round calibers for hunting hogs. They have the power to penetrate even the thickest shield on a wild boar. After hunting many years and downing many hogs with my .270, my personal favorite is the .260 Remington.

This caliber has proven stopping power, and it is light and handy when trampling through the brush. Larger calibers get heavy after lugging them around in the field for a few hours. As mentioned in an earlier chapter, for hunting the lighter javelina, a smaller caliber such as a .222 caliber, .22-250, .220 Swift, .243, or 6mm will suffice.

There are many types of rifle actions: pump action, single shot, semiautomatic, lever action, and the ever-popular bolt action. Any of the aforementioned actions will work on feral hogs, so the choice of actions is a matter of personal preference. The main drawback to a single shot, however, is that it doesn't offer you a second chance. The AR-assault-style sporting rifle is gaining a lot of popularity amongst hog hunters for several reasons: They are now available in several calibers with magazines that can hold ten to twenty or more rounds, they fire rapidly, and they are easy to purchase. With a brass catcher, they are especially popular for hunting hogs from helicopters. For hunting with dogs or in thick brush, an open-sighted lever action .30-30 is an excellent choice. In situations such as this, a quick shot is frequently required.

Whatever caliber or rifle you choose, the key to a successful hunt is shot placement. Nearly any caliber rifle can kill a tough old boar with proper shot placement, but a poorly aimed shot from even the largest of calibers can wound one. A strategically placed bullet behind the ear of any size hog will bring it crashing down. The next target is the heart shot placed behind the shoulder.

Nearly any of the heavier factory loads are sufficient. You want a bullet that will produce penetration and expansion. I would definitely stay away from the smaller varmint-type loads that manufacturers offer.

Scopes and Binoculars

A scoped rifle comes in handy when hunting hogs. Because hogs are hunted in so many different locations and are so unpredictable, I prefer a 3X9 variable scope. You can adjust the magnification down to the lowest setting for close shots and crank it up to the highest setting for long shots. These work especially well when standing, still hunting, or stalking wild boars. In areas where visibility is limited, I prefer a smaller fixed-power scope such as a 4 or 6 power. In close quarters such as thick brush, a scope may prove ineffective. In these scenarios, a quick shot may be needed and finding the target within the scope is difficult.

In my opinion, a good binocular is essential. Because hogs are so wary and intelligent, searching the terrain from afar will increase success. Good-quality optics are invaluable when attempting to field judge the size of your hog or its trophy category. If you spot the hog before it spots you, you can plan your strategy accordingly.

Handguns

Handgun hunting is one of the fastest growing shooting sports, and throughout most of its range the wild hog offers excellent opportunities. Pursuing wild hogs or javelinas with a pistol can present challenging and exuberant moments. To make a clean shot, you must get within a confident distance—that is, be close enough to hit the mark. Factor in the intelligence of a wild boar, and that can be a very difficult thing to do. To me, the most exciting part of the hunt is maneuvering within range of such a wily and potentially dangerous creature. If you are lucky enough to get within range, you'd better have enough gun or you will just upset the beast! Also, remember that many of the "hunting handguns" these days are single shot, so make the first one count.

Although smaller calibers such as the rimfire .22 long rifle can do the trick, don't use it! The minimum caliber to use in handgun hunting should be a centerfire caliber .357 Magnum, but even that is considered light for a big boar. The .44 Magnum or even the .41 Magnum can be very effective. I enjoy hunting hogs with an open-sighted .44 revolver with a 6-inch barrel

Outdoor writer Larry Weishuhn with a nice boar he killed with a pistol. (Photo courtesy of Larry Weishuhn)

because it's more versatile. You can wear it in a holster, use it with dogs, dispatch trapped hogs, or carry it in the truck for other purposes. It's just handy to have and to use. For some reason, I prefer having an extra shot or two immediately available. To increase success, shots for wild hogs should be less than 50 yards.

There are many single-shot specialty pistols available in higher calibers for hunting, and these are generally scoped. A good solid rest is mandatory regardless of the type of handgun you use. Larry Weishuhn, noted outdoor writer and hunter, prefers single-shot handguns such as the Thompson Center Contender in .44 Remington Magnum, .30-30 Winchester, .375 Winchester, or .45-70 Government with a 2.5–7 power variable scope. He further recommends a bullet that penetrates as opposed to one that expands like most factory loads.

Proper shot placement is imperative. (Photo courtesy of Larry Weishuhn)

Many handgun hunters use the semiautomatic in .45 ACP or 10mm. They shoot fast and the magazine can hold more cartridges than a revolver. Although a capable cartridge, I believe the 9mm is probably too light for hunting, but it works well up close when dispatching trapped or bayed hogs. A red-dot, laser-point scope can be beneficial in these situations, and a good quality, low-power pistol scope on revolvers and single shots can increase success substantially.

Shot Placement

Shot placement is the key to any successful hunt. For rifle shots, I prefer placing the bullet through the heart or shoulder. I suggest a neck or head shot when hunting with a handgun or when hunting at close range. Remember, the thick shield that surrounds the big boars shoulder area acts like armor. In the long run, your accurate shot placement and handgun proficiency may keep you out of a jam.

Few sports can be as exhilarating as going after wild boars with a handgun, but it can also be very dangerous. A poorly placed shot can turn an enjoyable hunt into a nightmare when trailing a hog that's been wounded. An angry hog waiting in the thicket for someone to come in after it will cut, slash, and bite without remorse.

Before hunting wild boars with a pistol, practice from different ranges and different angles. Train yourself in making quick, safe shots (not like Wyatt Earp). Learn to safely place a deadly shot in a short time. This may prove to be a valuable skill. Besides practicing, understand your limitations. If you can only shoot accurately at 50 yards, don't attempt a 75-yard shot. Wounding a boar with large, razor-sharp tusks not only places yourself but also your hunting buddies, your guide, his dogs, and the horses potentially in harm's way.

Topnotch hog handgunners possess more than a few skills. They love to practice their shooting, fire hundreds of cartridges per month, and can hit their intended target dead center. Foolish is the hunter who buys a pistol, shoots a dozen rounds at a tin can, and thinks he can—with any

A successful bow hunter.

degree of accuracy under hurried conditions—stop a charging boar in a thorny thicket.

First-class hunters have patience and self-control. Frequently you may have to wait for the boar to get within range. Know your limitations! I've let hogs walk by without firing a shot, only to have them return an hour later offering another chance. Had I taken a shot, the hog would have been in an adjacent county an hour later.

Archery

Bowhunting is another fast-growing outdoor sport and hog hunts are especially desirable. Bow-and-arrow hunters can practice their skills in the back yard and can hunt hogs year-round, especially during the off-season for other species. Bowhunting for hogs can be a tough challenge for first-time bow hunters, and it can be very disheartening if the hunter is unprepared.

If you're going to hunt hogs with a bow, practice is essential. Practice from different angles and distances, and if you're planning to hunt from a tree or bow blind, practice your shooting from comparable heights. A poorly placed shot can result in missed shots, a wounded animal, and even lost hogs. Remember that a wounded hog is a dangerous hog. The draw weight of the bow is critical and should be calibrated to the ability of the hunter. The heavier the bow's draw weight, the increased likelihood the hunter has of harvesting a hog, especially with thick-shielded boars. I recommend a minimum draw weight of fifty to sixty pounds.

In bowhunting, penetration is important because blood loss is the key to harvest. A sharp three- or four-blade broadhead with a solid design is crucial for penetrating the wild hog's shield or shoulder. Cutting nose broadheads have better penetration and are recommended over the cone or pyramid type. I also recommend getting within twenty-five yards and not attempting to stick a hog at forty to fifty yards. Due to the toughness of a hog and frequently the lack of a blood trail, a tracker should be considered.

Bowhunting also requires greater hunting skills, stealth, and outdoor savvy because you must get so close to the animal. Using the wind, sun, camouflage, cover scents, and bait will enhance your success. Shot placement should be broadside into the heart or lungs. A slight quartering-away angle is also good, but don't forget about the tough shield that covers the shoulder. Hunting from a tree stand or bow blind over bait or a trail crossing can be fruitful.

A quality binocular and rangefinder are essential for the bow hunter. The rangefinder tells you know the exact distance for a well-placed shot and more humane kill. Finally, there are a tremendous amount of high-tech archery products on the market today that can truly enhance your capabilities.

Muzzleloaders

The use of muzzleloading rifles is also gaining popularity. As with handguns and archery, many hunters are discovering the enjoyment of using a black-powder rifle for hunting wild swine. When properly loaded with the right bullet and powder, the muzzleloading rifle has more than enough foot-pounds of energy and power to penetrate even the toughest boar. I suggest using a .50 or .54 caliber, loaded with the highest powder charge recommended by the manufacturers.

Bullet placement is crucial in muzzleloading weapons because the bullet is solid and does not expand, unlike most hunting bullets. Because muzzleloading bullets are easily deflected, make sure you have a clear shot. As with archery and handgun hunting, be patient and know your limitations.

After the Shot — Tracking and Trailing

You have now successfully harvested your wild boar. The shot was clean and the hog fell where it was standing. If the shot did not go according to plan, be prepared for a post-hunt challenge. Tracking an upset, sharp-tusk, wounded hog that is looking for someone on which to take out his frustrations is not a pleasant scenwario and can be harrowingly frightful. Wounded hogs have injured many hunters.

To begin with, always know your quarry. As with any animal that is hunted, mark the location of the animal with a landmark. Wait for at least fifteen minutes before going to the animal. You must remain away from it to allow time for its expiration. If the hog has run off, cautiously approach the vicinity carrying your gun at ready and with the safety on. Keep your eyes peeled for blood, hoof tracks, broken brush, or tree limbs.

Note the color of the blood. Bright red blood usually means an artery or heart shot, whereas a pinkish color or bubbly texture often means a lung shot, both of which will be fatal. Finding no blood or blood mixed with stomach contents means the shot was poor . . . and it signals an increased probability that you lost the animal. There are times, however, that a hog will not leave an easily followed trail. This is due to its thick shield, skin, and ability for a hog's blood to coagulate.

After the hunt, a memorable photograph. (Photo courtesy of Dusty Holt)

Increasing the risk to its pursuer, a wounded hog will seek the thickest brush it can find. Because a hog is capable of traveling a long way when hurt, be prepared for a hike. Hope that by the time you reach the hog, it will have expired. Just to be sure, have your gun ready and throw something like a rock or stick at the animal. To prevent the above discussion, I cannot stress the importance of a quick, clean, humane, well-placed shot. The hog is a very tough creature that requires practice, patience, and extreme prejudice.

Jeff Copeland, an avid and very experienced bow hunter, recommends several things when following a blood trail: First and foremost is never walk on the trail where the animal traveled—always stay to the side. Never allow more than two people to assist because the more people there are, the more likely it is to destroy some of the sign.

Also, don't just look at the ground because often the blood may be up higher on brush, weeds, or high grass. Finally, take your time and never push a wounded animal. This is excellent advice for all hunters, not just bow hunters.

Photographing the Hunt

The hunt is complete, the adrenaline has subsided, and you're reveling in your success. It's now time to document the occasion. Before preparing the carcass for the taxidermists, make sure you take plenty of good, high-quality photos to show friends and for posterity. With any luck or foresight, you already began taking pictures during the hunt, especially if it was an exhilarating hunt with dogs or from a helicopter.

Since the digital age of photography and the invention of the smart phones such as the IPhone and IPad, the hunt has never been easier to document. The old days of photographing through the eye of a 35mm camera are over. I've personally failed to capture great photos numerous times because I thought I had film in the camera only to discover later that the camera was empty. Film was costly and you had to wait to see if the pictures were quality. With the small digital cameras and phones visible, the image is instantaneous . . . and cheap! So take as many as you can.

I would strongly suggest that you respect the animal and limit the amount of blood and guts in the picture. The antihunters and animal-rights activists would cherish any opportunity to use such pictures as propaganda for their cause. Clean any bloody areas and set the animal in a photographic position. For quality pictures, in addition to the animal itself, take into account lighting and the background. Consider using your imagination during the photo session, such as a picture of you walking toward the animal or a ground view silhouetting the head. Good-quality photos can make the memories last, and who knows, they may even be used for that hunting article you always wanted to write.

Clothing

The type of clothing you choose is dependent on the type of hunting you're going to do, the season, and the terrain. Because most hog hunting can be done throughout the year, clothing should be dependent on the season. I would recommend that good hunting boots and cotton long-sleeved shirts and pants be mandatory no matter what the season. In cooler weather, wearing layers of clothes is important so that you can remove outer garments as the day warms. I'm not going into a lot of detail on clothing except to say that you need to use common sense and discuss these things with the landowner, guide, or outfitter. If you're still-hunting, stalking, or open-stand hunting, wearing outer camouflage clothing may prove beneficial.

I strongly recommend you wear snake boots or snake leggings when hunting javelina or feral hogs, especially in the spring and fall when rattlesnakes are most active. Not only will you have protection against fangs and tusks, in some places such as the brush country in South Texas, everything seems to stick, sting, bite, or poke you.

Scents

Feral hogs have an acute sense of smell—just look at how deep some of them root in their search for food. Because of this keen sense, some hunters like to use masking scents. I have never used them and have had very good luck. Perhaps if I had used them, maybe I would have had even better luck; I can't say. Be careful of the scent you use because some scents may alarm the hog more than your natural smell. Of course, using wind direction and screening cover to your advantage is mandatory.

Miscellaneous Gear

There are many other items that may be helpful when hunting wild hogs and javelinas. A day or fanny pack may be useful for extra ammunition, a knife, bone saw, whetstone compass, GPS unit, first-aid kit, toilet paper, rain suit, water bottle, and snacks. The majority of items are personal preferences and dependent on the location and type of hunt you're planning.

Where to Go

If you're interested in hunting or trapping wild hogs in Texas, they can be found in virtually every ecological region and most habitat types. From the piney woods of East Texas, throughout Central and South Texas, and into portions of North and West Texas, they can be found in nearly every Texas county. They can also be found throughout the southeastern United States. I read a recent article that claimed Alabama hosts approximately 30,000 hog hunters. In California, there are hogs in 53 of the 58 counties. Oklahoma claims hog live in 55 of 77 counties. According to Reginald Barrett of the University of California at Berkeley, it would take an estimated 70 percent annual herd reduction through hunting, trapping, natural mortality, and other removal to suppress a herd growth.

Most states have wildlife management areas with hunting opportunities available through public drawings. In Texas, hogs can be hunted on all wildlife management areas and even some state parks where they're found. In 2003–2004, the Public Hunting book listed nine state-owned areas including Gene Howe WMA, Mad Island, Peach Point, and the Matador WMA. Javelina hunts are also available on five listed areas including the Chaparral WMA, James Daughtrey WMA, and the Black Gap WMA. Feral hogs are also allowed during javelina and most deer hunts in unlimited numbers. On federal land, hog hunting may also be allowed. In Texas, hunting is allowed on wildlife refuges and forestlands; however, check with the proper federal authorities to find out the availability, dates, and requirements.

With their current wide distribution and high population, a little research and a few phone calls should have you in the field in a very short time. Start your search for a place to hunt with hunting magazines, newspaper classified ads, and hunting-lease directories. Many outfitters now have websites available or links to general hunting sites. Telephone calls to guides, outfitters, hunting buddies, local wildlife officials, game wardens, county agents, and the local chamber of commerce should prove helpful and informative.

Once you begin searching, you'll find opportunities for hunts of every description available throughout the United States, and for all types of hunts. From guided, all-inclusive hunts to do-it-yourself types, and from guaranteed kills to no guarantees. One thing is for sure and that's there are plenty of hogs and many people who want you to come and get 'em.

Guides and Outfitters

If you do not want a do-it-yourself hunt, there are many guides and outfitters available to choose from. The outfitters may be the landowners themselves or their agent. A few outfitters work from a distance and act merely as a booking agent between the customer and another outfitter. The outfitter usually furnishes the hunting land, guides, food, and lodging. The outfitter may also be the guide.

The guide, however, accompanies the hunter and acts as spotter, scout, and advisor. He'll spend the majority of his time at the hunter's side, taking him to where hogs roam and strategically placing him in positions to get a shot. Most of the hog-hunting guides are experienced and knowledgeable of the animal and the terrain to be hunted. They can improve the odds of success for the hunter, especially a neophyte.

When choosing a guide of outfitter, you must first decide the state and region you want to hunt. Then using the various venues previously mentioned, find the outfitters or guides operating in the area where you want to hunt. Don't base your choice of guides or outfitters solely from the yellow pages in a phone book or from a website on the Internet. Once you have decided on a few choices, it is important to contact the outfitter or guide and request his brochures, price lists, and references. Contact the references and investigate through other channels. NEVER BOOK A HUNT IF THE OUTFITTER IS RELUCTANT TO GIVE HIS REFERENCES.

After completing your preliminary investigation, the next step is to ask the outfitter or guide specific questions: For example, you could ask if there have been any changes in kill fees or if there are costs not shown in the literature you received. Other questions might include how many other hunters you'll be hunting with, the number of hunters per guide, the cleaning and dressing fees, cold storage fees, and any other extra costs. Get a general itinerary of each day's hunt and the hunting strategies of the guide, and don't forget to ask about hunter success rates. Confirm the dates and hours of your arrival and departure. Inquire about lodging, meals, gear required, transportation for yourself, taxidermy services, and find out how you will get your meat back home.

Final words of wisdom for hog hunters:

- Never underestimate the hog's intelligence.
- Learn the biology, behavior, and patterns of the wild hog.
- Practice your technique constantly, and then practice again.
- Be patient!

The Taste of Wild Pork

CHAPTER 11

People often ask me if wild hog is worth eating. I can attest that the feral hog is one of the best-tasting animals ever to inhabit the brush. While I'm working on this chapter, sliced hog loin, spiced and simmering with onions and potatoes in olive oil, is simmering in the kitchen. In a few minutes, I'll take a break and I'll have a nice meal with a glass of Merlot.

Wild-boar meat has become a profitable market for many people in South Texas. Many gold-star restaurants are now serving wild boar on their menu for extremely high prices. Europeans have been eating boar meat for centuries and are also importing wild hog from Texas packing plants. It is interesting to note that buyers are looking for hogs that weigh over two hundred pounds!

The small, sleepy South Texas town of Cotulla has an annual Wild Hog Cook-Off that attracts thousands of visitors each year to enjoy wild hog meat and have fun. Teams compete for the cherished honor of cooking the best wild pork in the world. This county fair also has a ranch rodeo, carnival, food booths, and entertainment, all a tribute to wild swine. Surely these thousand people can't all be wrong! So between upper class Americans and average Americans, as well as Europeans, wild hog for a meal must have some merit.

As a domestic show pig producer and an avid fan of *properly prepared* wild game, I find the wild hog beyond comparison. Even the old boar can be tasty. I mention properly prepared because as with most wild game, preparation

Perfect size for eating! (Photo courtesy of Alton Paris)

of the kill and handling of the carcass is important to the final taste. The animal's age, sex, harvest technique, postharvest handling including the dressing, and even the outside temperature affect the quality of the meat. In my opinion, the best size hog for eating is one that weighs between fifty and a hundred pounds, although larger hogs can be tasty if prepared correctly.

The proper care for the kill is the most important part of preparing any wild game animal. Once the animal has been harvested, it is important to field dress the hog as soon as possible. If you wait, the body's fluids will negatively impact the flavor of the meat. I've noticed the season of the year also has an impact on the meat.

Field Dressing

I recommend using disposable rubber gloves during the cleaning process to avoid direct contact with reproductive organs and blood. The chances of contracting a disease from feral swine are very slim; however, it is best to be cautious. Pork can spoil quickly, so it is important to get the animal cleaned and chilled as quickly as possible. Clean the pig immediately upon killing it, especially in the warmer weather. Field dressing wild hogs is similar to dressing any game.

Many people prefer to clean the hog while it is hanging upside down with a gambrel between its legs. I prefer laying the hog on its back and cutting into the pelvic area between the legs. Whichever way you choose, cut deep enough to reach the pelvic bone but take care not to cut the entrails, which are visible directly above the pelvic bone. Turn the knife upside down and insert it horizontally into the cavity so that the blade is just touching the inside of the belly. Cut upward toward the sternum or breastbone, but make sure the point of the knife does not penetrate the stomach. Some people form a "V" with their index and middle fingers of the opposite hand as a knife guide, which helps raise the skin and keep the blade away from the entrails.

At this point, cut through the sternum to the neck (you may have to use a bone saw). This cut will open the cavity and expose the vital organs; reach in at the neck and cut the esophagus. If you do not want to cut through the sternum, cut the diaphragm and reach up under the sternum and cut the esophagus. Using the esophagus as a handle, pull the entrails out until you reach the pelvic bone, cutting the diaphragm as the entrails are being pulled out.

At this point, cut from the pelvic bone to the anus with a saw (or loping shears) and complete the process by cutting the remaining skin at the anus. If you do not have a tool to cut the pelvic bone, circularly cut skin around the anus and pull the entire entrails out above the pelvis. The gloves should be buried with the viscera. Wash your hands with soap and warm water. If possible, allow the meat to hang and chill in a cooler for a few days before butchering.

To skin the animal, begin by circularly cutting all the legs above the feet or at the knees. At this point I would recommend hanging the carcass upside down with a gambrel to hold the back legs apart. Next cut the skin toward the belly or the cleaned cavity. You may also insert the knife blade outward and cut toward the belly. From the back leg start peeling the skin, pulling it downward over the hams. Complete the skinning process by peeling the skin down until you reach the neck. On larger boars, as you wrestle and cut past the bulky, cumbersome shield you may encounter difficulties that require more skill and patience to finish the job. Cut the head with the remaining skin and you're through.

Javelina can be cleaned in the same manner. Be careful, however, when cutting around the musk gland on the back. Since the scent gland is located within the skin, make sure you peel the skin where the gland is found away from the meat instead of using a knife when skinning the animal. Accidentally puncturing this gland could release the oil and taint the meat. And since the musky secretion may be on the hair and bristles surrounding the gland, try to avoid touching this area. Your hands or knife could transfer the musky odor onto meat. I would strongly recommend letting the carcass hang or soak in ice water for a short period to help draw any wild taste out.

Javelina meat should be prepared with a little more care. They can be prepared with the same recipes as wild hogs, but I would recommend trimming the meat of any fat, gristle, and nonappealing bits and pieces. Also, soak the meat in a mixture of vinegar and water (just a couple tablespoons in two cups of water is plenty—too much vinegar will leave the meat tasting like vinegar) or milk for two to four hours before cooking. This will help draw out the "wild taste" and improve the flavor. Slow cook the meat but be vigilant to prevent it from drying out; keep it moist by liberally dabbing it with sauce or marinade. Prepared properly, javelina roast or loins can be delicious.

Butchering

If commercially butchered, I'd recommend having it processed using the same cuts as store-bought pork: ribs, pork chops, roasts, and sausage (pan and link). To me, boneless roasts are excellent cuts. Having the shoulders sliced makes excellent country-style ribs.

From field to the grill.

There are numerous ways to butcher hogs, depending on what you want to do with the meat and the processing tools available. For field butchering, cutting out the backstraps and loins whole is a good starting point. Next, remove the hams and shoulders whole, followed by the ribs. Finally, trim any excess meat off the carcass for use as sausage or ground meat. You may even trim the meat off the shoulders or hams if you want more ground meat or sausage. It's very important to double seal or wrap the meat in freezer paper or airtight bags to prevent the meat from getting freezer burn.

The main difference between feral hog and domestic pork is the amount of fat in the meat. Feral hog meat and domestic pork can be prepared in the same variety of recipes. It is important to cook pork thoroughly, but since feral pork is leaner than domestic pork, slow cooking the meat is best. By slow cooking a roast in the oven or crockpot, the meat will fall off the bone.

For smaller cuts such as ribs, pork chops, or loins, barbecuing is popular and extremely tasty. Remember to baste the meat frequently during barbecuing or wrap it in foil after the outside has been seared. This gives a great grilled flavor while locking the moisture and flavor inside. Any cookbook has recipes for pork and will suffice for wild pork, as long as you remember to prepare the meat with the proper spices and advanced care. I've enclosed a few simple recipes that should help you get started.

Recipes

Marinades, Sauces, and Seasoning

Whether you are cooking javelina, wild hog, or any type of wild game, a good marinade is mandatory for a flavorful meal. Marinades can tenderize and enhance the flavor of wild game and it is best to let the meat stand in the refrigerator for at least twenty-four hours or more. There are many excellent commercially made marinades available at the local grocery store. Also, a simple marinade of Italian dressing, French dressing, tomato juice, or milk works very well. This is the simplest marinade that you can make at home:

    1 pound butter
    ½ onion
    1 lemon (juice and rind)
    Seasoning salt
    Pepper
    Garlic powder

Melt the butter and cut the lemon and onion into large pieces. Add these ingredients to the butter along with the salt, pepper, and garlic powder. Let this mixture simmer for 15–20 minutes. Liberally sop this simple marinade on the meat while it is slowly cooking. Adding Worcestershire sauce, red wine, or barbecue sauce can make a more complex and delicious marinade; it is also the basis of a barbecue sauce. Some people even put beer in the marinade!

I prefer a simple recipe of seasoning salt, lemon pepper, and Worcestershire sauce for seasoning meat. Once you trim the meat of fat, gristle, and anything else that's undesirable, dribble Worcestershire sauce on it. Put the meat in the refrigerator until you are ready to cook it. Right before cooking, rub the seasoning concoction over all sides of the meat. (Please note: Adding salt and pepper to the marinade will start the cooking process. Use the marinade by itself and put the salt and pepper on just before you start to cook the meat.)

Appetizers

Many people use the ribs of the hog as appetizers because they are tasty and cook relatively fast. Another appetizer that is absolutely delicious and I've actually made complete meals of them are called *wraps*.

Use whatever cut of meat you want (a loin is an excellent choice) and prepare it for cooking.

Slice a 3- or 4-inch piece about ½ inch thick and season it. Beat it with a tenderizer and then lay it out flat.

Put a slice of cheddar cheese and slice of mild jalapeno pepper on the meat and wrap it up.

Complete the wrap with a piece of bacon and secure with a toothpick.

Put this on your barbecue pit and it will drive your friends crazy!

Roasts and Hams

Roasts and hams can be baked, barbecued, and smoked; they can also be cooked in crockpots. To bake a roast or ham, first trim off any nonappealing aspects (fat, gristle, blood-shot meat, etc.). Next, place the roast in a deep baking pan and season thoroughly with seasoning salt, Worcestershire sauce, and lemon pepper. Add a few ounces of water and line the pan with potatoes, onions, and carrots. You may want to cover the top of the roast with bacon strips to allow the bacon flavor to slowly absorb into the roast.

Cover the roast and slow cook at 275–300 degrees for 3–4 hours or until tender, marinating the roast frequently. Remember, the slower it cooks, the more tender and flavorful it becomes, but don't let it dry out.

To slow smoke or barbecue the ham or roast, prepare it as previously described and then liberally season it with your favorite seasoning salts and spices. I prefer to let it cook uncovered in the smoker or on the pit for about one hour to give it a good outer brown covering. Then cover it with bacon, onions, and lime, and then wrap it in foil to continue to slow cook. The size of the ham or roast will determine the length it should stay on the pit, usually 3 to 4 hours.

If barbecuing, use your favorite barbecue sauce initially during browning and while cooking. It may dry out if you cook it directly on the pit without foil; however, an indirect fire from the end of the pit or the firebox allows the meat to slow cook without losing a lot of the moisture. This type of cooking is similar to barbecuing a beef brisket.

One of the easiest and tastiest ways to cook a roast or ham is in a crockpot. Cook it the same way you would cook a commercially packaged roast, except that you'll need slightly more preparation. Again, it is important to trim any excess fat and gristle off before seasoning. Then simply put it in the crockpot with a cup or two of water, onions, potatoes, and whatever else you desire, and turn it on low. Cook it 8 to 12 hours and you will have a delicious meal with tasty gravy.

Carnitas

To make carnitas, begin by baking the roast or ham as instructed above. Cook for about 2–3 hours or until the meat separates easily from the bone and then remove it from the oven and scrape the meat away, discarding the bone and leftover fat. Turn the oven up to about 375 degrees and then place the boneless meat into the pan and cover with the leftover juices. Bake the meat uncovered in the oven for 30–45 minutes or until the meat is brown and most of the liquid has evaporated. After the meat has cooled lightly, shred the meat and place on a large platter. Carnitas can be served with Spanish rice, pinto beans, flour tortillas, and picante sauce for a flavorful meal popular south of the border.

Pork Chops

There are many ways to cook wild pork chops: barbecued, pan fried, or chicken fried. Make sure you trim the excess fat and gristle from the chops prior to cooking. For barbecuing, I suggest first seasoning the meat before putting it on a hot fire to sear one side; then turn it over, pour on the barbecue sauce, and let the other side sear. Turn it over and sauce the other side, and shortly the chops will be ready. You want to cook the chops fully without overcooking them or they'll turn out tougher than leather and taste like it as well. All you want to do is lock in the flavor.

For fried pork chops, I like to soak the meat in water or milk for an hour or so before cooking. Season the meat with salt and pepper or your favorite seasoning salt. Dip the chops in batter made from one cup of milk and one egg (increase accordingly to amount you're going to fry) and then roll them in flour. Some people season the flour and even dip the meat in flour, then the batter, then the flour again (double dipping). Once thoroughly coated, drop the chops into ½ inch of hot grease and cook until red juices are coming out the top and the flour has turned color, then turn over to complete the cooking. Once it's turned over, you will usually complete it in less than five minutes. Use the leftover grease to make delicious cream gravy by adding flour and milk.

Loins

The loins or backstraps are the prime cuts of the wild hog and are delicious. You can cook them whole, sliced as steaks, or butterflied. Whole loins can be baked, barbecued, roasted, pan fried, or chicken fried. Or, as I mentioned at the beginning of this chapter, it is hard to beat sliced loin with onions, bell peppers, and potatoes slow cooked in olive oil.

To start, trim all excess nonappealing aspects and then soak them in water or a marinade overnight. Most of the cooking types can be done as a roast or ham. To pan fry or chicken fry, simply cut the loin in steaks and fry them the way you would a piece of beef or domestic pork. For specific recipe instructions, look at the way I fry pork chops. Remember that a wild hog and a domestic hog are the same and recipes used for any commercial pork dish can be used for a wild pig. The key is in the preparation!

Country-Style Ribs

Country-style ribs are the pork shoulders sliced or cut in horizontal sections to give them a riblike appearance. Country-style ribs are not only an excellent cut for barbecuing but also a good use for the shoulders. Once you've trimmed all the nonappealing aspects from the meat, season or marinate it and then throw it on the pit. Use your favorite barbecue sauce and barbecue them the way you prefer.

Ribs

One of the most sought-after parts of the hog are the ribs, especially if it's young and fat. Properly cooked, the ribs can be the choice cuts. Wild hog baby-back ribs are outstanding! They can be cooked in the oven or barbecued. When cooking them in the oven, place them in a shallow pan, bone side down. Sprinkle them with seasoned salt and lemon pepper, add chopped onions, and cover. Cook the ribs at 275 degrees for 2 hours or until tender, basting with your favorite marinade frequently during cooking.

For delicious barbecue ribs, season the meat as above and place them on a hot grill. Sear them quickly on the meat side and turn them over. At this point you can put barbecue sauce on them and wrap them in foil (recommended)

Delicious, mouthwatering barbecue ribs. (Photo courtesy of Alton Paris)

to continue cooking. This keeps in the moisture and flavor. Alternatively, put them in the corner of the barbecue pit with the meaty side up to slow cook. Continual flipping of the ribs will cause them to lose moisture, so be careful because you don't want them to dry out.

Ground Meat and Burgers

If you don't want to make sausage from the trimmings of the hog you've just harvested, an alternative is ground meat. Ground wild hog mixed with 10 percent beef tallow makes an excellent burger. You can also use the meat for spaghetti, casseroles, enchiladas, or meat loaf. Experiment with your ground meat by looking in your favorite recipe book. You might surprise yourself and your family with what you can do with "boar burgers."

Sausage

Without a doubt, wild hog makes the best pork sausage you can find. I have breakfast sausage and link sausage in my freezer year-round. Sausage is made from coarse, ground meat of wild pork and sometimes mixed with venison. Once coarsely ground, the meat is mixed with seasoning usually comprised of salt, pepper, sage, garlic, and a host of other secret spices. There are also many commercial prepackaged sausage seasonings available. After mixing the coarse ground meat and seasoning, run the meat back through the grinder at a finer setting. Then you can package the meat as breakfast sausage.

If you're making link sausage, grab the catgut and prepare the sausage stuffer. If you are going to make it yourself then you probably already know how to do so; if not, have your neighborhood butcher or meat processor take care of it for you.

Carne Guisada and Stew

Carne guisada is the South Texas term for cut up meat in gravy. It is an excellent use of trimmed meat and pieces that are too small for steaks. After preparing the meat, cut it up in 1" pieces and put in a frying pan with hot grease covering the bottom. Pan fry this meat until it's done, turn the fire down and add flour and water to make the gravy. You may want to roll the meat in flour before putting it in the skillet. If this is the case, adding water when the meat is complete will make the gravy. Taste and season the gravy, then cover the skillet and continue slow cooking for about 30 minutes. Serve over rice or pasta, or just roll it up in a tortilla with a dash of picante sauce.

Stew can be made in a crockpot or big pot. After preparing the meat and cutting it up into 1" to 2" chunks, season it, then boil it until it's tender in 1 to 2 cups of water. Add carrots, potatoes, onions, and any other vegetables you want with a small amount of cooking oil and stew seasoning (commercial or salt, pepper, garlic, chili powder, etc.) and cook for 30 minutes or until the vegetables become tender. Reduce heat and let simmer for 30 minutes or until you're ready to eat. In the crockpot, I've let it cook 4–6 hours.

Shish Kabob

Wild hog meat makes an excellent shish kabob. After trimming the meat, cut it into 1" to 2" cubes (I like to tenderize it first), and season with your favorite ingredients. Cut onions, bell peppers, potatoes, carrots, or any type of vegetable you prefer into 1" to 2" pieces. Alternately, put pieces of meat and vegetables on the skewer. Once the shish kabobs are made, you can barbecue them or bake them. I prefer to barbecue them over a low- to medium-heat fire, basting them with my favorite sop, turning them frequently. When done, you have a complete meal ready to enjoy, with very little mess to clean up.

Smoking

Smoked hams and sausage are excellent. If you're having your sausage made professionally, make sure that they smoke it for you. Also, have the processor smoke a ham while he's at it! Sausage is much better when it has been smoked. If you're going to smoke it yourself, there are many ways to do it.

If you have an outdoor smoker, build a small fire at one end of the pit with your favorite hardwood: Mesquite is a good choice, but hickory, pecan, or oak will suffice. Once the fire has burned to a good hot bed of coals, add a few more pieces of wet or green hardwood. Place the sausage or ham at the opposite end of the coals and close the smoker. Keep the temperature between 130 and 150 degrees. If you do not have a smoker, you can improvise by using any closed device (sheds, barrels, etc.) that has an air intake at the bottom and a damper on top. Smoke for 4 to 6 hours depending on how much smoke flavor you want. You may have to experiment a few times to perfect the technique.

A State-by-State Overview of Laws and Regulations

E ach state has its own laws and regulations governing the hunting of wild hogs; however, most view the hog as a pest and have little regard for it. The following information is a general overview of hunting, comments, and opinions regarding the wild swine and javelina in the various states in which they occur, taken from their respective websites. I have only included the primary states that harbor wild swine and/or javelina even though other states may have reported them. It is important to note that any specific information regarding seasons, bag limits, and hunting opportunities mentioned are subject to change.

While reviewing the various agencies concerning feral swine, many regulation changes have taken place over the last ten years from more restrictive hunting laws to very liberal regulations involving their take. At the end of each state is its wildlife agency and contact information for specific laws, regulations, and hunting information. An excellent site to direct you to respective agencies is www.huntinfo.org.

ALABAMA

In Alabama, a 2009 study estimated there was $74 million in crop and forest damage by feral swine each year. In 2012, wild pigs were reported in all 67 counties, up from 52 in 2001; they currently occupy approximately 38 percent of the land. Alabama classifies the feral swine as a game animal.

There is no season or bag limit on private land; on public land, feral swine may be hunted in conjunction with scheduled hunts with a weapon legal for that hunt. There are 35 WMAs that have huntable hog populations. On many WMAs there are specific hunts for hogs. A hunting license is required to hunt on public land. It is illegal to transport live wild hogs from one property to another.

Alabama Department of Conservation and Natural Resources
64 N. Union St.
Montgomery, AL 36130
334.242.3465
www.outdooralabama.com

ARIZONA

In Arizona, javelina were not legally designated as big game until 1929, when a season from 1 November through 31 January was authorized and a bag limit of one javelina per year was imposed. Hunter interest gradually increased, particularly among nonresidents, and the javelina became an important game animal in Arizona after World War II. By 1950, hunters were purchasing nearly 10,000 javelina tags and taking more than 1,000 animals a year. In 1959, an archery javelina season was initiated, and by 1971 more than 30,000 hunters were harvesting more than 6,000 javelinas per year. This pressure was deemed excessive in some game-management units, and permit-only firearm hunting was instituted in 1972.

To further curtail hunting pressure and to better distribute hunters, permit-only HAM (handgun, archery, and muzzleloader) hunts were initiated in 1974, and archery hunting was limited to permit-only hunting in 1992. In 1999, 12,580 firearm permits, 7,760 HAM (handgun, archery, muzzleloader) permits, and 9,220 archery permits were authorized, which resulted in a harvest of 6,363 javelinas.

Javelina hunt-permit tags for limited permit javelina hunts may be obtained only through application and drawing procedures prescribed in current

240

regulations. The archery-only spring javelina season generally runs throughout the month of January in certain hunt areas. The general season runs mid- to late February, while the HAM javelina season may run concurrently with the general season. There is also a "youth only" season that also runs in early February. Any firearm or bow and arrow as described in current regulations are lawful methods to take javelina. The javelina bag limit in Arizona is two javelinas per calendar year with no more than one per open area.

In recent years, feral pigs have been sighted near Mud Mountain and Black Rock Mountain in Game Unit 13B. Hunters are encouraged to harvest them, and no license is required.

Arizona Game and Fish Department
5000 Carefree Highway
Phoenix, AZ 85056-5000
602.942.3000
www.azgfd.com

ARKANSAS

Long before it was known for football, the razorbacks of Arkansas were found in various locations throughout the state. Today, they are present in every county in Arkansas. According to the Arkansas Game and Fish website, feral hogs cause numerous problems, and this includes habitat destruction. Many sensitive habitats are small and fragile, such as the unique acid seeps in portions of the Ouachita Mountains and the cedar glades in the Ozarks. These places are attractive to feral hogs, and they cause major, sometimes irreparable, damage.

Despite the problems hogs cause for wildlife, habitats, and people, they also provide recreational hunting opportunities. The Arkansas Game and Fish Commission receive many inquiries each year about feral ("wild") hog hunting. Since 30 July 1999, hogs may be taken during open hunting seasons if they are roaming freely upon public land and the weapon used is legal for the season. Feral hogs may also be taken on private land at any time, as long as the hunter has legal access and the landowner's permission. Hunters with a revoked hunting license may not hunt feral hogs.

A hog that has escaped from its pen is not considered a feral hog until five days have lapsed. If the owner gives notice to adjacent landowners, the hog isn't feral for ten more days. It is illegal for individuals to release hogs on any land in Arkansas for future hunting opportunities. Hog hunting is quite popular in the state and is, in fact, the major reason hogs were released into the wild.

Arkansas Game and Fish Commission
2 Natural Resources Drive
Little Rock, AR 72205
501.223.6300
800.364.4263
www.agfc.com

CALIFORNIA

In California wild hogs were classified as game animals in 1957. Originally there were no seasons or bag limits. They are currently found in 56 of 58 counties. The latest information on hunting wild pigs taken from the state's website says the general season is open all year and there is no daily bag or possession limit. On average between 3,000 and 4,000 wild pigs are reported harvested in California each year, although higher annual harvests have been estimated. In 2012, revenue from wild pig tags exceeded one million dollars.

Any person twelve years of age or older who possesses a valid hunting license may procure a wild pig license tag as specified in Section 4654 of the fish and game code. Any person hunting wild pigs must carry his license tag. Immediately upon harvest, he must fill out both parts of the tag, clearly mark the date of the kill, and attach the tag to the carcass. The report card portion must be immediately returned to the department. At the request of this state, go directly to their website for current regulations.

The law also authorizes the California Department of Fish and Wildlife to issue depredation permits if the hogs are causing severe damage. This allows the landowner to eliminate offending animals through methods that include nighttime spotlighting and trapping for humane dispatch. Wild hogs can only be trapped by authorization of the California Department of Fish and Wildlife. Other than the depredation permit, the landowner or agent may be authorized for "immediate take" when hogs are damaging or threatening immediate damage to land or property.

California Department of Fish and Wildlife
1416 9th Street
Sacramento, CA 95814
916.445.0411
www.wildlife.ca.gov

FLORIDA

Florida has the second largest population of feral hogs in the United States. Wild pigs are legally classified as wildlife and are found in all 67 Florida counties. Hunting opportunities are available on private ranches, hunting preserves, and public land. On private land, wild hogs can be hunted or trapped with landowner permission using any legal weapon. There is no closed season, bag limit, or size limit for wild hogs, and no hunting license required on private land. You may hunt hogs at night without a night permit.

On Wildlife Management Areas (WMA), wild hogs may be harvested during most hunting seasons, except for that of spring turkey, with required management permits. On some WMAs, daily bag limits and minimum size may apply. All legal weapons include rifles, archery, muzzleloaders, crossbows, and handguns. You may not hunt at night on WMAs.

Florida Fish and Wildlife Conservation Commission
620 South Meridian Street
Tallahassee, FL 32399-1600
850.488.3831
www.myfwc.com

GEORGIA

In Georgia feral hogs can be found on both public and private land. On public land, hog hunting is usually restricted to deer season; however, some hunting is allowed during special hog hunts or during small game dates. On private land, there is no closed season or bag limit on feral hogs. Hunting over bait or at night with a light is permitted. A resident hunting license is required to hunt feral hogs for all resident hunters sixteen years old or older, except when hunting on land owned by them or their immediate family (blood or dependent relationship) residing in the same household. Nonresidents must meet nonresident license requirements.

The taking of feral hogs on Wildlife Management Areas (WMAs) and National Forest land is allowed with archery weapons during state archery deer hunts, with deer firearms during firearms deer hunts, and with small-game weapons during small-game hunts unless otherwise specified. Hogs may not be hunted with the aid of dogs during deer season. There is no limit unless specified in the WMA listings. Hunting and WMA licenses are required.

Hunters and any person accompanying them must wear at least 500 square inches of hunter orange as an outer garment above the waist during managed hog hunts. Hunting at night is prohibited on WMA land. All hunting license requirements must be met. Feral-hog control permits may be issued to landowners and their authorized agents to alleviate damage with allowance to hunt from vehicles.

General information regarding stocking, handling, and processing feral hogs in Georgia can also be found on its website. Relocation of feral hogs is illegal unless they have tested negative for brucellosis and pseudorabies within thirty days prior to being moved. It is illegal to stock hogs on any land that is not fenced to prevent escape. Also, any facility that processes (cuts, wraps, smokes, etc.) hogs for a fee must be licensed as a red meat establishment by the department of Agriculture. The licensing requirement does not apply to anyone processing a feral hog for their own use.

The total estimated agricultural damage and losses in Georgia exceeded 84 million dollars in 2011.

Georgia Department of Natural Resources
Wildlife Resources Division
2070 U.S. Highway 278 S.E.
Social Circle, GA 30025
770.918.6404
www.georgiawildlife.com

LOUISIANA

In Louisiana, feral hogs are considered "Outlaw Quadrupeds" by the Louisiana Department of Wildlife and Fisheries. They are found in all sixty-four parishes, and they may be harvested year-round on private land by almost any means and methods, including hunting, trapping, snaring, and with the aid of dogs. Feral hogs may be harvested at night from the last day of February to the last day of August on private property with the written permission of the landowner or his agent. Artificial lights, infrared or laser sighting devices, or night-vision devices may also be used with legal firearms; however, you must notify the parish sheriff's office twenty-four hours in advance of any such hunt. The use of sound suppressors on the firearms is permissible from March through August on private property with a valid permit issued by the Bureau of Alcohol, Tobacco, Firearms, and Explosives.

A basic resident or nonresident hunting license is required of all persons to hunt, take, possess, or cause to be transported any wild bird or quadruped. Also, hunters may take hogs during any legal hunting season on most WMAs using only guns or archery that are legal for the concurrent specified seasons in progress. Some WMAs may allow hunting with dogs and trapping. Based on a mail survey during the 2012–2013 hunting season, deer hunters in Louisiana harvested approximately 161,000 feral hogs. This number excludes hogs harvested by professional trappers, government personnel, and landowners.

Louisiana Department of Wildlife and Fisheries
P.O. Box 98000
2000 Quail Drive
Baton Rouge, LA 70898
Hours 8 AM–4:30 PM M–F
800.256.2749 | 225.765.2800
www.wlf.louisiana.gov

MISSISSIPPI

In Mississippi, feral (wild) hogs are very prolific and readily adapt to a variety of habitat types. They have adapted so well in certain areas of the state that they are causing considerable damage to agricultural crops and tree farms. Hogs are categorized as nuisance animals that may be trapped or killed by any means or methods on private land.

Hunters must have a valid hunting or trapping permit to hunt or trap wild hogs. Baiting is allowed; however, certain restrictions exist during regular hunting seasons. On public land, the agency responsible for the land has jurisdiction and it's the hunter's responsibility to contact the agency before hunting a nuisance animal. Dogs cannot be used to hunt hogs during spring turkey season. It is illegal to trap and transport wild hogs without obtaining a live wild hog transposition permit and following the regulations that it demands.

Mississippi Department of Wildlife, Fisheries and Parks
1505 Eastover Drive
Jackson, MS 39211-6374
601.432.2400
www.mdwfp.com

NEW MEXICO

The javelina is classified as a game animal in New Mexico and hunters must possess a valid resident or nonresident javelina license with a valid tag. All licenses are issued by drawing. There are no over-the-counter licenses available for javelina. All hunters and trappers who use United States Forest Service or Bureau of Land Management land must have a habitat management stamp and habitat management and access validation permit. Legal sporting arms include centerfire rifles or handguns, muzzleloading rifles or handguns, shotguns that are no smaller than a 28-gauge and that fire a single slug, bows and arrows, and crossbows. The bag limit is one javelina per year; javelina meat does not have to be removed from the field.

Javelina youth hunts are also available in certain areas on certain dates. Applicants must be under eighteen on the opening day of the hunt, provide proof of hunter-education certification to apply, and carry their certificate when hunting with a firearm. New Mexico is divided into hunting units and applications are drawn on this basis.

Wild hogs in New Mexico are an unprotected species with no seasons or bag limits; however, general hunting rules apply: These include no hunting with artificial light, gaining permission to hunt on private land, and following other general hunting rules. Residents and nonresidents may hunt feral hogs year-round without a license. It is illegal to import, hold, release, sell feral hogs, or operate a commercial wild hog hunt.

New Mexico Department of Game and Fish
1 Wildlife Way
Santa Fe, NM 87507
888.248.6866
www.wildlife.state.nm.us

NORTH CAROLINA

In 1979 the North Carolina legislature gave the boar the status of game animal; however, in 2011 it was changed to a nongame animal due to its range expansion and destructive nature. Currently, there are no seasons or bag limits, but a valid hunting license is required. They may be hunted year-round during normal shooting hours and at night with a special permit. The first open season was held in the Cherokee National Forest in 1936 and in the Nantahala National Forest in 1937. A free feral swine trapping permit is required to trap a hog in North Carolina.

The North Carolina Wildlife Resources Commission
1751 Varsity Drive
Raleigh NC 27606
919.707.0010
www.ncwildlife.org

OKLAHOMA

The Oklahoma Department of Wildlife Conservation does not require a hunting license on private land except during the firearms big-game seasons. There are no seasons or bag limits. Hunters must comply with all other regulations pertaining to those seasons such as wearing blaze-orange clothing. On public land, specifically Wildlife Management Areas, a hunting license and a filled or unfilled deer license must be in possession during the regular firearms deer seasons appropriate. On some WMAs, when other seasons are open that allow dogs, it is legal to hunt hogs with dogs. No feral hogs may be removed alive from a WMA. It is illegal to hunt hogs at night except for those landowners who qualify for a depredation permit from their local game warden.

Oklahoma Department of Wildlife Conservation
1801 N. Lincoln
Oklahoma City, OK 73105
405.521.3851
www.wildlifedepartment.com

SOUTH CAROLINA

Feral hogs occur in every county in South Carolina. A hunting license is required to hunt feral hogs. There are no closed seasons or weapons restrictions for hunting feral hogs on private land. The use of electronic calls for feral-hog hunting is permitted statewide on private and WMA land. Dog hunting for feral hogs is allowed year-round on private land statewide. Hogs may be hunted at night using baits, electronic calls, artificial lights, and night-vision optics with bow and arrow and an iron-sighted pistol that does not exceed 9 inches. A centerfire rifle or shotgun cannot be used without a permit, except from the last day of February to 1 July, upon notification to SCDNR.

Feral-hog hunting on WMAs is permitted during any open season for game unless otherwise restricted. Check individual WMAs. On WMA land, weapons used to hunt hogs are limited to the weapon(s) that are allowed for the current open season on the WMA. Feral hogs may not be hunted at night on any WMA land. No hogs may be taken live from any WMA in the state. It is illegal to remove hogs from the wild without a permit to transport them.

South Carolina Department of Natural Resources
1000 Assembly Street
Columbia, SC 29201
803.734.3886
www.dnr.sc.us

TENNESSEE

Feral swine are found in nearly 80 of the 95 counties in Tennessee. Formerly considered big game, in 2011 Tennessee Wildlife Resources Agency reclassified them as a destructive species to be controlled by means other than sport hunting. On private land, there are no seasons or bag limits, and they can be trapped and baited when there are no open big-game seasons.

With a permit, landowners may hunt at night with a spotlight. There is no bag limit, either sex is allowed, and the use of dogs is prohibited. On publicly owned land, the season is open during scheduled big-game hunts unless otherwise specified. There is no bag limit, either sex is allowed to be taken, and the use of dogs is allowed during any proclaimed bear-dog hunts. Wild-hog control hunts on WMAs allow the use of dogs.

Tennessee Wildlife Resources Agency Central Office
Ellington Agricultural Center
PO Box 40747
Nashville, TN 37204
615.781.6610
www.tn.gov/twra

TEXAS

In Texas, feral hogs are considered livestock and are not regulated by Texas Parks and Wildlife Department (TPWD). They are considered a nongame, exotic mammal with no seasons or bag limits; however, a hunting license is required to hunt them. Landowners may hunt them on their own property without having a hunting license. Because they are not indigenous to Texas, TPWD has a zero tolerance policy concerning feral hogs on state-owned land. Although not considered a game animal, they are very popular among hunters and represent the second most numerous huntable large mammals in Texas.

The Texas Animal Health Commission prohibits the trapping and release of wild hogs from one location to another without first having been quarantined to determine whether they are disease free. You may trap them for meat or you can send them to terminal markets providing they're not released into the wild.

The javelina is classified as a game animal in Texas and hunters are allowed to take two per year. According to the most recent Texas hunting and fishing guide, approximately fifty counties have a year-round season. An additional forty-three counties have a fall and winter season that runs from 1 October through 28 February. There are an estimated twenty thousand javelinas harvested each year in Texas.

Feral hogs are considered a nongame, exotic mammal in Texas. (Photo courtesy of USDA/APHIS)

Texas Parks and Wildlife Department
4200 Smith School Road
Austin, TX 78744
1.800.792.1112
www.tpwd.state.tx.us

As previously noted, feral swine are rapidly expanding their range northward. For example, in 2008 feral swine were first discovered breeding in New York; these were in four distinct populations that caused an estimated damage exceeding one million dollars.

Although density numbers and exact distribution are unknown, reports in western Canada indicate the spatial distribution of wild pigs is increasing rapidly. With approximately 1.5 million domestic pigs on 930 farms in Saskatchewan, there is strong concern about the possibility of interactions among feral swine, especially as it relates to potential disease transmission.

Final Thoughts

CHAPTER 13

Late one evenin' just at sundown
I was ridin' home right slow,
When I passed a lonesome waterhole
And saw . . . it was a sow.

Ole Spot was trailin' down the hill
And right behind her trotted
Ten baby pigs not ten days old,
And ever' one was spotted.

I stopped and stared; she studied me;
My eyes filled like a fountain;
And there I gave Ole Spot a deed—
A deed to Cedar Mountain.

She's still on Cedar Mountain,
Though I seldom see 'er now;
You can bet that's one dominion
Where the Queen's a spotted sow.

From *That Spotted Sow and Other Texas Hill Country Ballads*

by Carlos Ashley

Through these pages I have attempted to enlighten you on the most up-to-date biological information on wild hogs and javelinas. I hope you've been entertained as well as educated. I know I've overlooked or inadvertently left information out. Furthermore, I realize some of the information submitted in this publication may be unsettling, especially regarding control measures. It is important for the reader to understand and comprehend all aspects of this topic fully in order to make educated decisions.

If you are a hunter or sportsmen, I hope you can take some of this information with you to the field. As Major Wardroup commented ". . . in after years as you sit, perchance. In some less happy spot smoking your pipe before the fire, the old scenes shall rise again before you." For all hunters, I would urge good hunting ethics to be part of your experience as you pursue

The author with a nice boar.

these creatures. The hunting world is losing its members and as urban sprawl continues and wild game habitat falls to the bulldozer and tall buildings, this loss will continue. As a landowner, hunter, or sportsman, be respectful of your quarry regardless of your opinions or biases and always respect the habitat and environment these hogs inhabit.

What does the future hold for feral hogs in Texas or the United States? Reiterating what Frederick Olmsted stated near Crockett in 1854, "We were annoyed by hogs beyond all description." He went on to say, "These animals proved, indeed throughout Texas, a disgusting annoyance, though after procuring an excellent dog a day or two after we were rid of the worst of them."

I'm sure there were other explorers and settlers in the southeastern United States sitting around their campfires cussing or discussing this creature during that period, just as we do today. Whether a benefit or detriment, an asset or liability, the wild hog has been in the southeastern United States for over four hundred years and has become an integral part of its fauna.

So in closing, I would like to use the words of Major A. E. Wardroup in his book *Modern Pig-Sticking*: "And now, friend, it is time that I bid you 'Good-bye.' I trust that you will pardon the various imperfections of this book and realize that the shadowy ego of the writer is but a means for trying to tell you of this great (Indian) sport; a medium such as a painter might use when trying to paint his picture, all in vain though it may be."

Appendix I
Facts, Fantasies, Myths

Are Feral Hogs, Russian Boars, and Javelinas Native to America?

Feral hogs (*Sus scrofa*) are also called European hogs, Eurasian or Russian boars, razorbacks, piney woods rooters, and a host of less descriptive names. They are an Old World species and belong to the family Suidae, the same family as our domestic swine breeds. This includes domestic hogs gone wild, true European wild hogs, and varying degrees of hybrid crosses between the two. In South Texas, they are frequently confused with our native javelina or collared peccary *(Tayassu (Pecari) tajacu)*, but there is no direct relationship. Although the swine family is not native to the Americas, the javelina is a native of North America.

What's the Difference between a Feral Hog and Russian Boar?

Taxonomically, there is no difference between domestic swine, feral hogs, and Russian boars. Researchers have attempted to distinguish between wild swine and Russian boars through physical, morphological, genetic, and behavioral traits, but to no avail. Although not absolute, there are many distinguishing physical features.

How Do You Tell the Difference between a Feral Hog and a Russian Boar?

Although there is no genetic difference between a feral hog and a Russian boar, they have distinguishing physical characteristics. The feral hog appears similar to the domestic hog but is generally smaller, more muscular, and possesses a rangier and, therefore, wilder appearance. Relative to domestic hogs, the Russian boar has a longer and leaner body; sloped appearance; longer snout; straighter tail; long coarse hairs that are darker in color and more grizzled; and smaller hams.

Some may have the appearance of domestic swine traits; these include coloration, more ham, and shorter snouts. It is important to note that the more generations in the wild a hog can claim, the more it will revert to a European appearance. A feral hog with ancestry that has been free-ranging for generations may be extremely difficult to differentiate from a true "Russian boar."

Are Russian Boars and Feral Hogs Related?

Maybe! Russian boars, feral hogs, and domestic swine can readily interbreed because they are the same species. The location of the hogs and the history of their release in the stamping grounds will determine whether the animal you harvested has any European blood. As I just said, many generations in the wild can produce a more European-looking hog, and these are frequently called a Russian boar by sportsmen.

Are Feral Hogs and Javelinas Related?

No! While feral hogs and javelinas may appear similar to some people and while they often share the same range, they are not related. They are both mammals belonging to the taxonomic order Artiodactyla (even-toed ungulates), but javelinas belong to the family Tayassuidae and hogs belong to the family Suidae.

What Is the Difference between a Feral Hog and Javelina?

There are many differences between the two. The most obvious is the feral hog's long, straight tail compared to the very short or nonexistent tail of the javelina. The feral hog may exceed two hundred pounds whereas the javelina seldom exceeds fifty pounds. Feral hogs come in many colors, shapes, and sizes while javelinas are grizzled gray with a white band or collar around the shoulder. Javelinas also have only one dewclaw on the hind feet whereas the hog has two. Though you will find a musk or scent gland on the backs of javelinas, you won't find one on a feral hog. See Table 1 in Chapter 9 for a list of differences.

Are Feral Hogs Dangerous?

All wild animals have the potential of being dangerous, especially when wounded or cornered. In a natural state, feral hogs would prefer to run and escape danger, so they are not considered dangerous. Extreme caution should be maintained when tracking any wounded animal, trapping animals, or encountering females with young. The razor-sharp teeth on a feral hog combined with its lightning speed can cause serious injury.

Do Feral Hogs Eat Deer Fawns, Rattlesnakes, Turkey Eggs, Lambs, and Kid Goats?

Feral hogs are opportunistic eaters and will literally eat anything that is in its path, and that includes snakes. Generally only a small percentage of their diet consists of meat or animal parts. They are not keen predators, nor do they hunt down and chase snakes. If they stumble across a snake and can catch it, they will eat it. It has been documented that they eat kid goats and lambs; however, it is not always clear whether they have scavenged their meal or had actually killed it.

Can Feral Hogs Breed Three Times a Year?

This is probably one of the most talked about myths concerning feral hogs. Theoretically and chronologically it could occur, but it is nearly impossible in a practical sense. Although a hog has a gestation of approximately 115 days, only 1 in 3 will have a second litter and none will have three litters.

Nutrition is a major factor in the production of double litters. Also under good nutritional conditions, they are capable of breeding at 6–9 months of age, so one sow can be a grandmother by the end of its first year. So whether a female can have 1, 2, or 3 litters a year, is rather moot: This species is so extremely prolific that the population expands exponentially.

Do Pure Russian Boars Have Split Hair Tips and Are the Piglets Always Striped?

This myth has been around for many generations. In actuality, biologists have confirmed that any hog can have split-hair tips and the young can have stripes. At one point it was believed the only way to tell the difference was the number of chromosomes. It was claimed that domestic pigs had one or two fewer chromosomes. To date, there is no definitive way to distinguish the difference between Eurasian wild hogs, feral hogs, or hybrids. But does it really matter?

How Big Do Feral Hogs Get?

Despite stories of 400- to 500-pound wild hogs, the average boar will usually weigh between 150 and 175 pounds. A sow is generally between 125 and 150 pounds. Occasionally, a wild hog can reach upward of 400–plus pounds, but they are rare. There is no doubt that trying to load a 200-pound dead hog into the back of a pickup feels much more like you are lifting 400 pounds.

Usually, a hog of that magnitude is not too far removed from domestication. I recently saw a picture of a hog that supposedly weighed over 1,100 pounds. After personally observing literally thousands of wild hogs, I am very skeptical of such claims. To begin with, very few domestic hogs can even reach that size. I also had a friend who trapped a wild hog one time and intentionally kept him on full feed just to see how large he could get. Once that hog reached 1,000 pounds it could barely even walk.

What Is the Shield of a Feral Hog?

Feral hogs are equipped with a shoulder hide that is made of a tough scar tissue. This "shield" is formed through continuous fighting, and it hardens as the animal ages and survives more fights. When hogs fight, they usually face each other, and they use their tusks as weapons to hook each other in upward slices.

Do Feral Hogs Carry Diseases?

Feral hogs may carry pseudorabies, swine brucellosis, hog cholera, tuberculosis, bubonic plague, tularemia, and anthrax. In general, diseases from wild hogs do not pose a significant threat to humans; however, these diseases can be transmitted to livestock and other wildlife. It is important to vaccinate all livestock, especially in areas where large feral-hog populations are concentrated. It is also recommended to use disposable rubber or latex gloves when field-dressing wild hogs.

External parasites include dog ticks, fleas, and hog lice. Internal parasites include kidney worms, stomach worms, roundworms, and whipworms. Liver flukes and trichinosis are also found in hogs.

How Long Do Hogs Live?

Generally, feral hogs rarely live more than six to eight years in the wild. They seem to be fairly susceptible to teeth and gum diseases. While conducting research in South Texas, only a handful of hogs out of more than three hundred were older than six years (seventy-two months). I know a man who trapped a wild boar and kept him in a pen until it died when it was nine years old.

What about Feral Hog Mortality?

Other than man, feral hogs have very few natural predators after they reach about three months of age. When they are piglets, they are susceptible to coyotes, bobcats, mountain lions, bears, and even other hogs. Sows are fairly good mothers and will attempt to protect their litters. As with domestic hogs, however, sows sometimes kill young accidentally by rolling on them while nursing.

One time while trapping mountain lions, we came across about six dead pigs scattered across about one-half acre. Upon investigation, it was obvious that a mountain lion had been honing its hunting skill on these little shoats. The next day we caught a forty-pound juvenile male lion over the dead hogs.

Can You Fence to Keep Feral Hogs Out?

Feral hogs are extremely tough creatures and unless the fence is made of concrete, it is hard to hog-proof a fence. They are the most tenacious creatures around, especially when it involves food or mating. There have been many domestic sows that have been bred from a determined feral boar. I've even heard stories of electric fences that were built to keep hogs out. It seems the hog would start running toward the electric fence squealing before it ever hit, knowing the fence would send a shock through it.

There are certain types of fences that can keep hogs out but they are generally cost prohibitive. Topography and soil type play a role in the effectiveness of a fence. The best type of fence to keep hogs out would be heavy gauge net wire buried underground about six to twelve feet with railroad ties tied to the base. Hog panels provide fine exclusion fences around small perimeters. Bear in mind that if a hog can get his snout in the net wire, he has the potential of enlarging the hole, tearing the fence, and busting through.

What Are Common Feral-Hog Signs?

Feral-hog signs are fairly easy to distinguish. Their hoof impressions are usually wider, blunter, and rounder than a white-tailed deer or javelina. You'll generally find wallows—areas where the hog has rolled around in the mud to cool off—around the watering holes. Rooting in an effort to find roots and tubers is another sign a hog is nearby.

In South Texas, I've seen holes up to three feet deep! You'll find rubs on trees, creosoted electric poles, fence posts, and boulders where the animal has rubbed or scratched his side. They're easily recognized because hogs will leave mud all over them. Their hair often catches on fences or crawl areas and is fairly easy to distinguish from deer, javelina, and most other wild creatures.

Feral-hog scat, distinguished by its size and shape, resembles small calf droppings as opposed to deer pellets or tubular excrement from coyotes. Often, you can identify the roaming grounds of feral hogs through a combination of the signs.

Can I Successfully Eradicate a Feral-Hog Population through Hunting or Trapping?

In a free-ranging herd, I think it would be impossible to permanently and completely eradicate a wild-hog population. You may have some temporary relief but they will come back. The best a person can hope for, generally, is control through continued hunting and trapping. Even so, you may have a glimmer of hope to eradicate hogs from a hog-proofed or isolated pasture providing there is no way for hogs to immigrate into the area. Otherwise, be prepared for a labor intensive and expensive job that may never end.

Can You Hunt Javelina and Feral Swine?

Yes. In the three states where javelina are found they are classified as game animals with seasons and bag limits and all laws relating to such. Feral hogs, on the other hand, are not generally classified as game animals (although in some states they are); therefore, they may not fall under the regulatory control of state game agencies. Regardless of the classification, feral hogs are hunted in most states on public as well as private land.

Are Feral Hogs Safe and/or Good to Eat?

Yes, meat from the feral hog is extremely tasty and much leaner than domestic pork. Meat from older boars is frequently tougher and rank-tasting, but proper preparation can make even the toughest old boar tasty. As with all pork, the meat should be properly cared for, well cooked, and prepared just like market hogs. Generally, the slower the meat is cooked, the more tender and tasty it becomes.

Is a Big Boar Fit to Eat?

While a large boar may not be as tender and tasty as a younger hog, they are definitely edible. A lot of what makes the boar taste bad is the time of year it is killed, the food it has been eating, the way it was processed after the kill, and ultimately, the way it is prepared for the meal. If a hunter takes a boar after it has been chasing a sow in the late summer or fall, the carcass may need more careful preparation than one killed during the spring when he's been fattening on spring vegetation.

It is important to dress the hog immediately upon harvest, wash it out, and hang it. If the weather is warm, like it is in South Texas, it may be important to hang it in a cooler. I prefer to let it hang for twenty-four to forty-eight hours before butchering. For tastiest results on a large hog, cover the pan and cook the meat slowly in an oven or on the barbecue pit.

Do Javelinas Have a Negative Impact on Agriculture or Domestic Swine Producers?

Javelinas rarely cause appreciable agricultural damage due to their range, feeding habits, and behavior, nor do they impact commercial swine operations. Javelinas are less susceptible to common swine diseases such as swine brucellosis and are not considered to be carriers. In certain situations, javelinas may cause limited damage to farm crops; they have been documented to occasionally kill a young lamb or kid goat.

Are Javelinas Dangerous?

As with wild hogs and other wild animals, javelinas can be dangerous. Their razor-sharp canines can make serious cuts if challenged. They generally are not aggressive, preferring to avoid humans and normally retreating when possible.

While on a public javelina hunt in a wildlife management area in South Texas, one excited hunter arrived one evening and reported that the javelina he shot had come after him. Upon further investigation, I deduced that the javelina was cut off from cover and was just trying to escape. The hunter had placed himself in the way.

I'm sure his story will remain about how the javelina charged him and he had to kill it to save himself. This is an example of how the javelina gets its reputation for fierceness. The javelina has poor eyesight and this aggression is mostly due to its inability to distinguish things.

As I mentioned, the javelina can be dangerous, especially when cornered and scared. When scared, javelinas will frequently pop their teeth, creating a bone-against-bone sound. This sound is a warning sound to any potential dangers and can be frightening to an unsuspecting hunter.

Do Javelina Boars Mate for Life?

They do not pair for life nor do they have a harem as many people believe. Javelinas are polygamous and males may breed with several females.

Appendix II
Results of Study into the Food Habits and Seasonal Food Components in the Diets of Feral Hogs

Our study was conducted within seven counties in the western side of the Rio Grande plains that are located in the South Texas ecological region. The climate is typically characterized by short winters and moderate temperatures. Rainfall averages 20–24 inches, east to west respectively, within the study perimeter, with the majority of rainfall occurring in the spring and fall. Droughts are frequent and habitat recovery therefore is slow. The topography of the region is flat to gently rolling, interspersed with many creeks and drainages with numerous livestock watering ponds distributed randomly. Vegetation is predominantly low-level diverse chaparral brush dominated by mesquite *(Prosopis glandulosa)*, prickly pear *(Opuntia spp.)*, and acacias *(Acacia spp)*.

A total of 197 feral hogs were collected during nine seasons from September 1989 through November 1991. We randomly collected a minimum of 25 feral hogs during each season: September–November (Fall); December–February (Winter); March–May (Spring); June–August (Summer). The stomach contents were analyzed and separated into the following classes: grasses, forbs, roots and tubers, woody browse, cactus pads, cactus fruit, corn (shelled), hard mast, soft mast, vertebrates, invertebrates, and debris or unknown plant or animal matter.

Overall, vegetation comprised approximately 93 percent of the annual diet by volume while 6.6 percent was animal matter. The average percent volume for the various food classes was 22.4 percent grasses, 17.3 percent roots and tubers, 14.4 percent corn, 14.0 percent forbs, 10.4 percent cactus fruits, 9.0 percent hard mast, 4.9 percent cactus pads, 4.2 percent vertebrates, 2.4 percent invertebrates, 0.6 percent soft mast, and <0.1 percent woody browse. Approximately 0.3 percent was debris or unknown plant or animal matter. Woody plant seeds and nuts represented hard mast, whereas soft mast consisted of the fruits and berries of plants. Annually, grass, forbs, and roots/tubers occurred highest in percent frequency. Corn, cactus fruit, and hard mast showed seasonal variation due primarily to availability.

Spring and summer diets were dominated by vegetative matter with 80–95 percent, respectively, composed of grasses, forbs, roots/tubers, or cactus pads. Grass was greater in the drier spring (below average) of 1991, whereas forbs were proportionally higher in the diet during the wetter spring (above average) of 1990. The highest occurrence of invertebrates in diet was during the wet spring of 1990. Summer diets shifted from predominantly spring herbage (grass and forbs) to available prickly pear fruit and hard mast. Hard mast was predominantly mesquite and guajillo [a chili] and comprised approximately 23 percent of the summer diet.

Approximately 50 percent of the fall diets were dominated by under-ground plant parts and corn, with herbaceous vegetation and cactus parts constituting approximately 32 percent. In winter, grasses and corn comprised approximately 60 percent of the average diet. Heavy consumption of corn in the fall and winter diets can be attributed to heavy baiting and supplemental feeding of wildlife by landowners and sportsmen. Corn is readily available whereas natural winter mast such as acorns is limited and may serve as a replacement. A mild climate and long growing season in South Texas often enables a considerable amount of winter growth of vegetation.

Animal matter comprised only 6.6 percent of the annual diet by volume varied by season. Caterpillar larva was the major invertebrate food we identified. While we recognized certain mammals, birds, and reptiles, we could not tell whether these were scavenged or preyed upon. In northern Alabama, one study found turkey embryos in three hog stomachs and masticated muscle tissue in one stomach. Photos from game cameras revealed feral swine scavenging on hog carcasses, which led the authors to speculate that the meat was scavenged, an act that I believe occurs more frequently than predation.

The results of our surveys showed that the diet of feral hogs in the Rio Grande plains of South Texas was composed chiefly of plant materials, and were similar to those conducted in the coastal plains of South Texas, Davis Mountains in West Texas, northern Alabama, California, Florida, the Great Smoky Mountains of Tennessee, and South Carolina, where vegetation also comprised a major part of hog diets. In general, feral hogs selected forbs from among herbaceous forages when available. Oaks are not abundant in western South Texas, so acorns are replaced by various acacia beans (e.g., guajillo, blackbrush), mesquite, and corn.

Animal matter constituted only a small percent of the feral hog's diet in South Texas. This compares with the majority of other studies conducted

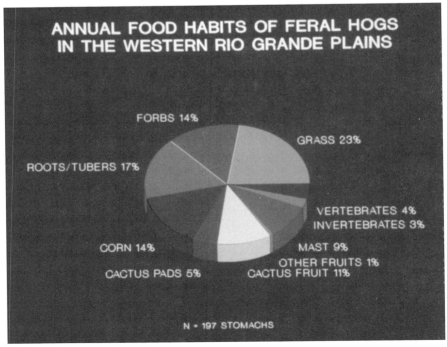

Diets of feral hogs in South Texas.

throughout the United States on the limited consumption of animal matter, although a few studies have reported significant amounts. In the Great Smoky Mountains of Tennessee, animal matter comprised less than 0.5 percent of the total annual food consumed. In South Carolina, animal matter included centipedes, earthworms, grubs, crabs, and mussels, whereas in Tennessee, primary animal matter included earthworms; centipedes; millipedes; and beetle, moth, butterfly, and fly larvae (maggots).

Diet variability in this study is attributed to annual precipitation, length of growing season, diversified plant communities, and the large study area. Our study showed that habitat diversity in the Rio Grande Plains allows feral hogs to utilize all habitats found within this region and that hogs shift their diets seasonally, based on food availability.

Although annual precipitation is important in forage production, we found no apparent correlation between temperature variations and feral-hog diets, although climate may affect availability of certain plants at certain times of year. High ambient summer temperatures usually do not affect the availability of forage, but they may decrease the nutritive values of available forage as well as have an effect on food consumption. Because of plant diversity in South Texas and plant adaptability to climatic extremes, some foliage or fruit is generally produced in every month of the year except during extreme freezes.

The results of this study indicated there was very little direct predation of feral hogs on native wildlife. There is dietary overlap and competition for preferred foods of many game species, which other researchers across the United States have also concluded. By comparing known foods of other wildlife species, the results of this study were analyzed to determine the potential impact feral-hog foraging might have on game and nongame animals.

Appendix III
Hog Terminology

Barrow — a male hog that has been castrated before reaching breeding age and the development of secondary sex characteristics.

Bar or barr — a slang term used to identify a barrow or castrated wild hog.

Bayed — when pursuing hounds stop a hog and it turns to fight the dogs.

Baying — the act of hounds pursuing and ultimately causing the wild hog to stop and face the dogs.

Blades — see Tusks.

Boar — a male hog with full sexual capabilities. Frequently this term is used to classify all wild hogs regardless of sex.

Busted — the term used by dog hunters when a bayed hog quits or escapes the bay and continues its dash to freedom.

Catch dog — a dog that is used to hold onto a wild hog once it has been bayed.

Cut — castration, or the removal of male reproductive organs.

Cut hog — see Barrow, Bar, or Cut.

Cutters — see Tusks.

Dewclaws — the back two toes of an ungulate or hoofed animal. In wild hogs they will usually touch the ground when the hog walks.

Domestic swine *(Sus scrofa domesticus)* — male and female individuals from populations of domesticated forms of swine existing under some form of conscious artificial selection by man other than that exerted by hunting and trapping (Mayer and Brisbin, 1991).

Eurasian wild boar *(Sus scrofa ssp.)* — male and female individuals from populations of wild—living swine native to Europe, Asia, or North Africa that have no history of domestication in their ancestry. This includes all subspecies of swine except domestic swine, *Sus scrofa domesticus,* (Mayer and Brisbin 1991).

Farrow — when a sow gives birth to piglets.

Feral swine or feral hogs *(Sus scrofa)* — individuals from populations of wild—living swine with a domestic ancestry that includes recently escaped or released animals and animals from populations that have been wild for more than one generation (Mayer and Brisbin, 1991).

Gilt — a young female swine that has not yet bred and is generally less than one year of age.

Grinders — slang term for molars or the upper canines. It may also be used to describe the upper and lower canines.

Grizzled — a grayish color usually made with dark hairs having white tips. The grayish color of a wild hog or Eurasian boar.

Hybrids or wild boar X feral hog hybrids *(Sus scrofa)* — individuals from populations of swine with some combination of both feral hogs and Eurasian wild boar in their ancestry. Animals that are mostly Eurasian wild boar in their ancestry or that have a questionable presence of feral hog in their ancestry are referred to as wild boar (Mayer and Brisbin, 1991).

Mane — the long hairs found along the top of the neck and along the middle of the hog's back. Frequently when scared, angry, or cornered, the hairs will stand up—hence the name razorback.

Pig — A young swine. Javelinas are occasionally referred to as pigs, although this is technically incorrect.

Pig-sticking — the act of hunting with a knife or spear usually following a chase with trained hounds.

Run some hogs — terminology referring to the act of chasing after or hunting wild hogs with hounds.

Russian boars *(Sus scrofa ssp.)* — see Eurasian wild boar.

Shoat or shote — a young hog that has not reached sexual maturity; can be a boar or gilt.

Shield — the tough cartilaginous hide covering the shoulder of the wild hog. This shield may be one to two inches thick and is generally found on boars. It is formed through continuous rubbing and fighting with other boars.

Sow — a female swine that has produced offspring or is pregnant; often used for females over one year of age.

Split hairs — the split tips of the hair of a wild hog or Eurasian boar. Generally the domestic hog does not have split-end tips.

"Stick 'em" — terminology used for the act of stabbing a hog in the heart to dispatch it.

Trailing — the act of following the trail of a wild or wounded hog.

Tushes — see Tusks.

Tusks — the elongated upper and lower canine teeth of a hog or javelina. Tusks continuously grow and they sharpen themselves on each other as the mouth moves. The tusks on wild hogs will curve whereas the tusks of javelinas are straight.

Witters — a term sometimes used for the upper canines.

Appendix IV
References and Selected Reading

Anonymous. *Principal Game Birds and Mammals of Texas*, their distribution and management. Austin: Von Boeckmann-Jones Co., 1945.

Ashley, C. *That Spotted Sow and Other Hill Country Ballads*. Austin: Shoal Creek Publishers, Inc., 1975.

Atkinson, M. J. *The Texas Indians*. San Antonio: The Naylor Company, 1953.

Bailey, V. "Mammals of New Mexico." *North American Fauna*. [United States Department of the Interior, Fish and Wildlife Service], 53 (1932): 1–412.

Baker, S. W. *Wild Beasts and Their Ways*. London: Macmillan, 1890.

Barrett, R. H. "The Feral Hog on the Dye Creek Ranch, California." *Hilgardia*, Vol. 46 (1978): 283–355.

Cabanau, L. *Wild Boar in Europe*. Cologne: Konemann Verlagsgesellschaft, 2001.

Castañeda, C. E. *Our Catholic Heritage in Texas*. Volumes I–VI. Austin: Von Boeckmann-Jones Company, 1936.

Chapman, J. A. and G. A. Feldhamer. *Wild Mammals of North America: Biology, Management and Economics*. Baltimore: John Hopkins University Press, 1982.

Coats, M. E. Jr., Philip S. Gipson, et alia. *Proceedings of the First National Feral Swine Conference*. Fort Worth: Texas Animal Health Commission, 1999.

Davidson, W. R. and V. F. Nettles. *Field Manual of Wildlife Diseases in the Southeastern United States*. [Department of Parasitology, University of Georgia] Athens: Southeastern Cooperative Wildlife Disease Study, 1988.

De Cordova, J. *Texas: Her Resources and Her Public Men*. Philadelphia: J. B. Lippincott & Co., 1858.

Fisher, R. A. Sr. *The Guide to Javelina*. San Antonio: The Naylor Company, 1957.

Fox, R. F. *An Evaluation of Control Techniques for the European Wild Hog* (Sus scrofa) *in the Great Smoky Mountains National Park of Tennessee*. Unpublished thesis, University of Tennessee, Knoxville, 1972.

Gipson, P. S., B. Hlavachick, and T. Berger. "Range Expansion by Wild Hogs across the Central United States." *Wildlife Society Bulletin*, 26(2) (1998): 279–286.

Gooch, B. *Hunting Boar, Hogs, and Javelina.* Tabor City, North Carolina: Atlantic Publishing Co., 1989.

Hanselka, C. W. and J. F. Cadenhead, eds. *Feral Swine: A Compendium for Resource Managers.* College Station: Texas Agricultural Extension Service, 1993.

Hanson, R. P. and L. Karstad. "Feral Swine in the Southeastern United States." *The Journal of Wildlife Management* 23 (1959): 64–74.

Holley, M. A. *Texas. Observations, Historical, Geographical and Descriptive.* Baltimore: Armstrong & Plaskitt, 1833.

Hyde, N. *Love, Live to Hunt the Hog.* Private printing, 2004.

Jackson, A. "Texotics." *Texas Game and Fish*, 23 (1964): 7–11.

Killian, G., L. Miller, J. Rhyan, T. Dees, D. Perry, and H. Doten. [K. A. Fagerstone and G. W. Witmer, eds.] *Proceedings of the 10ᵗʰ Wildlife Damage Conference, 2003.*

Kramer, G. *The Complete Guide to Hunting Wild Boar in California.* Long Beach: Safari Press Inc., 2003.

Laycock, G. *The Alien Animals: The Story of Imported Wildlife.* Garden City: The Natural History Press, 1966.

Mapston, M. E. *Texas Feral Hogs.* San Antonio: Texas Wildlife Damage Management Service, 2004.

Mayer J. J. and I. L. Brisbin Jr. *Wild Pigs in the United States: Their History, Morphology, and Current Status.* Athens: University of Georgia Press, 1991.

Newcomb, W. W. Jr. *The Indians of Texas: From Prehistoric to Modern Times.* Austin: University of Texas Press, 1961.

Olmsted, F. L. *A Journey through Texas: A Saddle-Trip on the Southwest Frontier.* Austin: Von Boeckmann-Jones Press, 1962.

Robb, B. *Hunting Wild Boar in California.* Lakeland, Florida: Larsen's Outdoor Publishing, 1989.

Schmidly, D. J. *Texas Natural History: A Century of Change.* Lubbock: Texas Tech University Press, 2002.

Schmidt, J. L. and D. L. Gilbert, eds. *Big Game of North America, Ecology and Management.* Harrisburg: Stackpole Books, 1980.

Schmitz, K. L., ed. Proceedings: National Feral Swine Symposium, Orlando, 1997. Sponsored by USDA (APHIS), Florida Department of Agriculture, Consumer Services.

Smithwick, N. *The Evolution of a State or Recollections of Old Texas Days.* Austin: Steck-Vaughn Company, 1968.

Sowls, L. K. *Javelinas and Other Peccaries: Their Biology, Management, and Use.* College Station: Texas A&M University Press, 1997.

Taylor, R. and D. R. Synatzske. *The Javelina in Texas.* Texas Parks and Wildlife Department (2008), PWD BK W7000–1669.

Taylor, R. *The Feral Hog in Texas.* Texas Parks and Wildlife Department. Federal Aid Report Series No. 28, 1991.

Taylor, R. B. and E. C. Hellgren. "Diet of feral hogs in the western South Texas plains" in *The Southwestern Naturalist* Journal, 42 (1997):33–39.

Taylor, R. B., E. C. Hellgren, T. M. Gabor, and L. M. Ilse. *Reproduction of Feral Pigs in Southern Texas.* Journal of Mammalogy, 79(4) (1998): 1325–1331.

Tinker, B. *Mexican Wilderness & Wildlife.* Austin: University of Texas Press, 1978.

Towne, C. W. and E. N. Wentworth. *Pigs from Cave to Cornbelt.* Norman: University of Oklahoma Press, 1950.

Triplett, T. *The Complete Book of Wild Boar Hunting.* Guilford: The Lyons Press, 2004.

Truett, J. C. and D. W. Lay. *Land of Bears and Honey.* Austin: University of Texas Press, 1984.

Waithman, J. *Guide to Hunting Wild Pigs in California.* Sacramento: California Department of Fish and Game, Wildlife Programs Branch, 2001.

Weniger, D. *The Explorers' Texas: The Animals They Found.* Vol. 2. Austin: Eakin Press, 1997.

West, B. C., A. L. Cooper, and J. B. Armstrong. *Managing Wild Pigs: A Technical Guide.* *Human-Wildlife Interactions* Report Monograph 1 (2009): 1–55.

Wood, G. W., ed. *Research and Management of Wild Hog Population.* Georgetown, South Carolina: The Belle W. Baruch Institute of Coastal Ecology and Forest Science at Clemson University, 1977.

Wild Hog Websites

There are many wild hog or wild boar sites that can be found on the Internet. Simply type in wild boar, wild hog, wild pigs, or feral hogs in the search engine and hundreds of hits come up. The majority of hits are hunting sites or outfitters offering hunts for wild hogs; however, even these offer valuable biological information. Other sites have general biological information, wild boar meat, recipes, festivals, and stories. Over the last few years, most state wildlife agencies also have information on feral hogs on their respective websites.

About the Author

Texas born in 1958, Richard B. (Rick) Taylor is a Certified Wildlife Biologist with over thirty years' experience in natural resource management. A range and wildlife graduate of Texas A&I University, he worked as a senior staff biologist for Texas Parks and Wildlife Department for twenty-seven years.

During his tenure, he provided wildlife and habitat management assistance to private landowners on over 1.5 million acres of Texas rangeland. His technical guidance has won landowners the prestigious Lone Star Land Stewardship Award for the Edwards Plateau Ecological region in 2004, the South Texas Ecological region in 2006, and the Aldo Leopold Statewide Land Stewardship Award for 2012. He has assisted in numerous wildlife research projects including white-tailed deer, feral hogs, mountain lions, bears, game birds, and various nongame species.

He is the author and/or co-author of numerous technical and nontechnical publications including "Common Woody Plants and Cacti of South Texas," "A Field Guide to Common South Texas Shrubs," Brush Management for White-tailed Deer," "The Feral Hog in Texas," and "The Javelina in Texas." His articles have appeared in *Texas Trophy Hunter, Texas Parks and Wildlife,* and *Texas Wildlife* magazines, to name a few. As the former Principal Investigator for bears in Texas, he is currently writing a book on Texas bears.

Rick is an adjunct wildlife instructor and serves on the advisory board for the wildlife department at Southwest Texas Junior College in Uvalde. He is also a licensed real estate Broker specializing in farms and ranches.

Rick and his wife, Lisa, reside in Uvalde, TX.